CRITICAL ISSUES
IN
PUBLIC RELATIONS

Critical Issues
in
Public Relations

By
Hill and Knowlton Executives

With a Foreword
By
Max Ways
Member of the Board of Editors, *Fortune*

Prentice Hall, Inc.
Englewood Cliffs, N.J.

Prentice-Hall International, Inc., *London*
Prentice-Hall of Australia, Pty. Ltd., *Sydney*
Prentice-Hall of Canada, Ltd., *Toronto*
Prentice-Hall of India Private, Ltd., *New Delhi*
Prentice-Hall of Japan, Inc., *Tokyo*

Library of Congress Cataloging in Publication Data

Hill and Knowlton, Inc.
    Critical Issues in Public Relations.

    Includes index.
    1. Public relations—United States—Addresses,
essays, lectures. 2. Industry—Social aspects—
United States—Addresses, essays, lectures.
I. Title.
HM 263.H535   1975   659.2′0973   75-19323
ISBN 0-13-193888-6

Printed in the United States of America

PROLOGUE

 W hen I was a boy, I was told that every Hoosier grew up to be a poet like James Whitcomb Riley, a novelist like General Lew Wallace, Meredith Nicholson or Booth Tarkington, a humorist like George Ade or Kin Hubbard, a statesman like Tom Marshall or Albert J. Beveridge or just a plain politician like Tom Taggart.

Thus assured that my future would be a success in any of these paths, I had a hard time deciding which one to follow, but finally at 15 I settled on being a novelist. Having made the choice, I set to work at once and in a few months had a bushel-basket filled with scores of thrilling pages of the great American novel. I felt pretty good about this until a hired hand commandeered the bushel-basket and tossed the great American novel into the barnyard half filled with pigs. He must have thought it was corn, and if he did, he was right.

When that bubble burst, I became more imbued than ever with the idea of seeing the world. This was inspired by the reflection of the street lights of Indianapolis glowing in the sky over the city every night. As a boy, I would stand by the hour looking longingly at those lights 20 miles away and dreaming of the day when I would get to the big city to see and experience its wonders.

Eventually, I settled down to the earthy job of a newspaper reporter, my first job being on the Shelbyville, Indiana, *Republican* at $6.00 a week. Then, one day in 1927, I hung up my shingle in the new fascinating field of what was to be public relations. Then it was called simply Corporation Publicity.

For the past 48 years this has given me a ringside view of the passing show of the most incredible period in all history—a period of wars, revolutions and bewildering change. I have been shaking in my boots most of the time, but I have never had a dull moment.

Just as an example of our glorious record in this memorable epoch, we have achieved the killing and maiming of more people in our wars than in all of the wars in all of the centuries before. We have piled up a government debt in this country exceeding, I believe, the cumulative debts of all the governments in the world put together in all of those past centuries.

Moreover, we have invented rockets which will send men to the moon or speed bombs thousands of miles on-target to kill millions of men, women and children. Meanwhile, our society has been modernized, motorized, jetized, televised and computerized.

All this change has had the effect of catapulting our society from the Age of Innocence into the Age of Materialism and Affluence. Many feel that we are mired down in an excess of materialism and that this is a major cause of the unrest among large segments of our population.

Today in America there is in motion a widespread search for the "What and Why" of things. Nothing escapes questioning. Nothing is sacrosanct, whether it be Religion, Big Business or the Establishment in any of its manifestations. On the other hand, some are asking whether the high values we are attaching to profits and the GNP are not too high, while on the other hand some are asking whether we can afford tomorrow—whether we can afford all the billions upon billions needed to maintain the quality of life upon this earth.

There is no doubt about the benefits to society from constructive criticism leading to the correction of real abuses or practices in business or anywhere else that are not in the public interest. Government regulations that are useful and legislation that is for the good of all the people can never be faulted.

Unfortunately, the pendulum often swings too far. Sound criticism sometimes explodes into hysteria. People are just as likely to be harmed as helped when hysterical pressures force hasty and ill-advised regulations and legislation.

Business, which directly or indirectly provides the work and income for most of us, is the subject of much criticism just now. But to say that all business is bad is just as absurd as to say that it is all lily-pure.

To the extent that criticism spurs business to re-examine its policies, its products and its operations, it is helpful. And it is even more importantly helpful if these examinations result in steps to correct whatever may be found that is not in the public interest.

In other words, if business wants to avoid penalizing legislation, it needs to set its house in order. But first of all, it needs to close the credibility gap. Obviously businessmen, like everyone else, want to "put the best foot forward." But when this is attempted by double-talk and concealment of pertinent facts which the public has a right to know, the only result is to widen the credibility gap.

The great need is for a new concept of corporate communications based on the belief that a better educated, more sophisticated public is sick and tired of being fed pabulum. Candor and straightforward talk to people is the only way to achieve credibility, and that applies not only to business but also to government, education and anything else of public concern.

The businessman who wants to win public favor will take the people into his confidence in matters concerning their health and well-being, explain clearly and frankly what his problems are and what he is doing to solve them. Fortunately, a few forward-looking companies are already pointing the way in that direction, and important movements are afoot to explain to the American public the meaning and functions, in their interest, of private enterprise.

The greatest achievement I have seen in my lifetime is the growing recognition that you can't demolish or kill an idea with a gun or a bomb—that public opinion is the final all-controlling force in human society. But public opinion that is misinformed, misled or lied to can be a destructive force. Business needs to show, by policies and acts in the public interest and by speaking out clearly and convincingly to people, that it is worthy of their support and confidence. In my opinion, the survival of private enterprise will depend on how well this job is done.

The hope of the future, as I see it, lies in the fact that in our society we have free speech and free choice in the marketplace and at the polls. People can demonstrate, petition and holler to their heart's content. If we have gone, as many believe, too far toward materialism in America—or if we should go too far in any direction—, then education and second thoughts, it is to be hoped, will eventually return us more nearly to a balanced position. And that will be good for us all.

John W. Hill

CONTENTS

Government Relations

Media Relations

Public Interest Issues

International Public Relations

Reprise: The Critical Issue

FOREWORD

Who Needs
Public Relations
?

By Max Ways

Member, Board of Editors, FORTUNE

Everybody seems to be aware of an activity called "public relations" which during the Twentieth Century has experienced a rapid elevation of importance. Its rise, however, cannot be said to have been buoyed up by a tide of popular approval. On the contrary, the term "public relations" has a bad taste in the public mouth. While trying to improve the reputations of their clients, the practitioners of public relations let their own profession's reputation decline. Their function was to explain the activities of the organizations they represented; yet the essential nature of their own activity and the reasons for its expansion have remained widely misunderstood. The public relations profession today is subject to the bitter imperative, "Physician, heal thyself!"

Whether the public likes it or not, the public relations function will probably continue to expand during the next fifty years. The reasons for expansion, past and future, lie very deep in the character of modern society, in fundamental trends that are most unlikely to be reversed or retarded. It cannot be healthy to go on placing more and more emphasis and dependence on a function society neither understands nor respects.

Practitioners of public relations differ one from another in the scope of their activity. Once confined to feeding information to the media, now many have branched out into advising clients on such a wide range of problems that a description of their work would sound like that of a management consultant firm. Nevertheless, the core function around which their activities cluster is the effort to transfer information and viewpoints from one context to another—usually a larger—one.

This essay tries to explain the rise of public relations as an appropriate—indeed, an inevitable—concomitant of the way society is moving. I had better make it clear at the outset that I approve, generally, of these basic trends and that, therefore, I regard the rise of the public relations function as a necessary and valid development. From this conclusion, it does not follow that I am prepared to embark on a defense of the public relations business as it has been, is now or will be practiced. I assume that this activity, like all other forms of actual behavior, is not as bad as it could be and not as good as it ought to be. Between those wide limits, I have a further impression, which I could not support by hard evidence, that the practice of public relations has been recently improving—both in its skills and on a scale of morality. I doubt, however, that the rate of such improvement is sufficient to offset the ever-increasing burden of responsibility which modern life throws upon the public relations function.

I have a parallel set of opinions about my own profession, journalism. There's not a doubt in my mind that journalism, decade by decade, becomes "better"; more accurate in detail, more careful in generalization, more lively in presentation, more honest, more fair. But whether, despite all this, journalism in the last fifty years has gained or lost ground relative to the public's increasing need for better journalism is another—and much more painful—question.

The journalist's traditional attitude toward the public relations man has been one of skepticism, often mixed with hostility and contempt. Skepticism toward any and all sources of information must remain as part of the armor of all responsible men—and especially of responsible journalists. But in my case, at least, hostility and contempt are no longer directed at public relations men as a group. For many years I have recognized that the flow of public information could not be sustained in volume or quality without the public relations profession. I have come to see the element of advocacy or special pleading implicit in most public relations work as an inevitable and, indeed, a wholesome aspect of a pluralist and decentralized society.

I am still infuriated by specific instances of evasion, distortion and outright deceit on the part of particular practitioners of public relations. But I also recognize that we journalists often infuriate serious public relations men when we go whoring after a glittering phrase or a dramatic conflict, thereby neglecting some important, though dull, facts that might be more pertinent to the discharge of our duties to our readers. But neither set of defects will be diminished unless we start with the recognition that two vastly expanded activities, public relations and journalism, have functions to perform that are essential to the health and vigor of modern society.

Public Relations' Negative Image

Quite alarming (and not to public relations men alone) was the popular tendency, egged on by certain journalists, to attribute the whole Watergate mess to "the public relations mentality." Widespread acceptance of this diagnosis was the more remarkable because there was so little to substantiate it. None of the main actors involved in Watergate had ever been professionally engaged in public relations. (One, H. R. Haldeman, had been in a quite distinct business: advertising.) Most of those responsible for Watergate (including Nixon, Mitchell, Liddy, Erlichman, Colson and Dean) were lawyers, a very old profession not noted for an orientation toward public relations. (I have never heard—and I'm glad I haven't—Watergate interpreted as a product of the "legal mind.") Moreover, the White House schemers from the first week of Watergate through the week of Nixon's resignation, handled the public relations aspect of their problem with conspicuous incompetence and insensitivity. Whatever may have been responsible for that mess, Watergate cannot reasonably be blamed on "the public relations mentality."

Yet the important fact is that many people already had in their minds a negative image of public relations that made the charge against it seem plausible. This prejudice seems to be part of a large category of unfavorable judgments about the way contemporary life is organized. People readily accept the specific fruits of modernity—such as mass university education and automobiles and longer life—while rejecting the social structures and processes that have made these fruits possible. The rejection is often so sweeping that it prevents mobilization of popular support for the correction of the specific abuses that appear in contemporary social structures and processes. A citizen who believes that "property is theft," is not likely to offer useful support to efforts at clarifying the legal and moral distinctions between the valid and the invalid exercise of property rights. A citizen who condemns *any* payment of public funds to the welfare of the poor is not likely to be helpful in attempts to reduce specific abuses in the welfare system. And people who believe public relations is essentially a form of organized deceit are not in a position to distinguish between the legitimate and illegitimate practice of public relations. Each new—or greatly elaborated—activity in contemporary society requires a careful examination of the reasons for its growth. Only when we understand *why* it has grown will we be able to appraise—and possibly to improve—*how* it functions.

Historic Roots of Public Relations

Public relations is not a brand-new invention of the Twentieth Century. The function in its communications aspect seems to have been present in all societies, except perhaps the simplest. Julius Caesar's *Gallic Wars* is an information operation intended to explain his transalpine campaigns to a public that had no war correspondents, no institutionalized media, to help it keep track of events. Examples of public relations appear in the history of ancient Greece and China. Tyrants and liberators, villains and heroes have all availed themselves of communications techniques. Religions have used public relations both in their missionary activities and, defensively, to guard the faith against rivals, backsliders and heretics. Great and salutary changes in the human condition have often been nourished by deliberate, organized efforts to inform and persuade the public.

Perhaps the most admirable public relations program on record is the Federalist Papers. The authors of these political essays had intimate knowledge of the drafting of the Constitution. For months they had been involved in intense discussion, leading to a complex set of compromises. The electorate knew far less than the authors did about why the articles had been formulated the way they were. The Federalist Papers set out to narrow this gap of understanding. They did so mainly by explanation, and secondarily by persuasion. The authors are obviously aware of partisan objections that had been raised against the draft Constitution, but they seem less interested in defending their work against the attacks of their adversaries than in meeting a public need for explanation, a need they regarded as natural and legitimate. The authors, in a word, accepted the burden of proof by rational argument, in a sense that would not have occurred to lawgivers (say Moses or Solomon) of previous ages.

The Federalist Papers form a kind of landmark in the development of public relations. Through the nineteenth and twentieth centuries the need for public explanation and persuasion became more and more widely recognized by the leaders of nations and other orgnizations, large and small.

This rising need is apparent in the darkest as well as the brightest chapters of modern history. Today we often use the very old term "dictatorship" without recognizing certain huge differences between ancient and modern tyranny. Pharaoh was a dictator, his power resting upon tradition, military force, economic control and religious veneration. His position, however, was not heavily dependent on a steady flow of persuasive propaganda. Modern dictatorships, on the contrary, work hard to win and hold "the consent of the governed" by persuasion as well as by older and cruder means.

In democratic contexts such modern figures as Franklin Roosevelt, Winston Churchill, John F. Kennedy and Charles DeGaulle were more important for what they said, for the verbal images of action they projected in the public mind, than for how they used the vast physical powers that the words put into their hands.

It isn't really possible to cast a balance between the good and evil that has been done by this emphasis on "public relations" in politics—an emphasis that has grown decade by decade since the Federalist Papers, which were genuinely educational, marked the beginning of a new phase in the importance of "the consent of the governed." Truth as well as falsehood has been served by the immense modern effort to inform, influence and arouse public opinion. For every miniature Goebbels there may be a miniature Gandhi.

Whether two centuries of rapidly increasing emphasis on public relations may ultimately be deemed more good than bad or more bad than good, the primary present question is why this increase occurred. What are the characteristics of modern society that called forth a multiplied effort at informing and persuading "publics" of many shapes and sizes?

Why Communications Has Expanded

The rise of public relations is, of course, only a segment of a much broader movement, the rise of communications. If this category is understood as including education and organized entertainment, it now ranks in the U.S. economy far above the production of food and shelter in the number of workers involved. It's hard to find a country where communications is not the fastest growing activity.

The revolution of rising communications is usually discussed in terms of technological advances: telegraph, photograph, cable, telephone, cinema, radio, television, computer, etc. But these conspicuous new tools only help to explain how the rising social demand—or need —for more communication has been met. They do not explain why the need itself has multiplied.

Although it is impossible to imagine a community without *any* internal communication, societies before the modern era had to invest only a tiny fraction of their total effort in transmitting messages among their members. Some message contexts (e.g., Chinese administration, Greek drama, and the folk arts of many peoples) reached superlative qualitative levels, but no pre-modern community approached our degree of dependence on a massive day-to-day flow of signs and symbols.

Political decision-making was highly centralized in most pre-modern societies. Commands and laws were transmitted to the people from the top, but very little political message-load moved in the opposite direction—or horizontally among the people. In such societies "amateur" communication (as, e.g., conversation, entertainment, courtship, prayer, artistic expression, the reinforcement of ethical consensus) was present and important. But in those times a society's functional need for professional full-time communicators could be filled by a few thousand nobles, clergymen, poets, minstrels or other symbol-handlers. Through the images projected by these leaders a society recognized the identity and solidarity that underlay its practical coordination.

Three intimately related trends that formed the character of modern society required the huge expansion of its communications:

1. Knowledge and work became more differential.

2. From this intensifying specialization and concentration came a tremendous multiplication of the aggregate power possessed by a society's members.

3. The ability to "do more" burst the bounds of traditional social inertia at a thousand points, powering a much more rapid rate of social change.

Of course, such characteristics of modernity as specialized knowledge and the division of labor are, in origin, very old. What's new during recent centuries is their accelerating proliferation. This "mere" difference in degree developed a kind of society unknown in past ages. Among other consequences, modern society has had to find new ways of coordinating joint action among its members.

Differentiation in thought and in work powerfully encouraged the trend toward individuality that had been running for many centuries in Western culture—a trend that now affects all the world. In today's U.S. the overwhelming majority of people have developed, through formal education and otherwise, specialized modes of thinking and particular skills. We pursue millions of life paths, and our varied experience sets up a wide range of individual viewpoints, values and goals. These different paths separate us from one another. We are not, however, an atomized society. On the contrary, each person's differentiated knowledge and work have little utility or even meaning unless they are brought into coordination with the knowledge and skills of others.

Our individuality, in short, is very different from that found in the kind of society idealized by Thomas Jefferson. The small farmers of his day had a high degree of economic and social independence of one another. They proudly learned to respect and to cultivate differences in views and values. Underneath these differences, however, lay a set of life experiences that tended toward homogeneity. Such coordination as American society of the eighteenth century needed could start from a common pool of knowledge, a similarity of occupations and of life style. Even then, however, the social need for communication was already rising because the Americans were less bound by tradition than their European ancestors and because they had rejected certain traditional forms of political coordination from above.

Trends already visible in the eighteenth century were to run so much more strongly in the next two centuries that the modern maze of communication networks would be needed to maintain the cohesion of the new societies marked by rising individuality and interdependence. These two qualities, apparently opposed, are in reality two faces of the fundamental trend toward greater differentiation in knowledge, work and life style.

The growing power available to modern man is usually attributed to technology—but that is only the most obvious element in the causation. Most of the technology would not have been possible without specialized science and most technology could not be deployed without the development of organizations more elaborate than any seen in past ages. Charles Reich's plaintive demand in *The Greening of America* that we keep modern technology and scrap modern organizations indicates his failure to understand that the two are utterly dependent on each other. A telephone, standing by itself, does not imply elaborate organization, but the ability to use the instrument to call millions of people does.

Organizations Work through Communications

Organizations, as the word suggests, are made up of distinct parts, or organs, whose specialized activities have to be coordinated. Today's organizations are more like biological organisms than they are like machines. A very simple organism (say, an amoeba) without much differentiation of parts requires little internal communication. But highly differentiated organisms, such as animals, have elaborate nerve systems through which they achieve coherent action. This metaphor, applied to organizations of human beings, illustrates why the increasing specialization of function within them requires the elaboration of internal communications networks. The evolution of modern management is, indeed, the development of communicative functions needed to maintain coherence in the face of specialization.

As recently as the first quarter of the Twentieth Century, the typical "modern" industrial organization was envisioned as an assembly line at the bottom, designed and readily controlled by a tiny management at the top. This model had obvious similarities to many pre-modern forms of social organization: power within it was concentrated at the apex and power was exercised by relatively simple commands; most members of the organization merely had to obey.

Fifty years later organizations that follow this model have become rare. A subtler and more elaborate structure has appeared. The top has expanded numerically and usually works by consultation among leaders who have specialized responsibility, such as marketing, production, or finance. A huge "middle," made up largely of specialists, has bulged. Even at the bottom, workers' tasks are likely to be more differentiated— and to depend more on their personal qualities—than was the case in the 1920s.

The joint action of the more recent type of organizations cannot be achieved by simple command, any more than the coordination of a modern army can be symbolized by commands like "Fire!" or "About face!" Today's organizations require an enormous flow of information from part to part and from man to man. Some of this information is raw data, but much of it is cast in the form of explanation and some is in the form of persuasion. The simple command is seldom heard because it is functionally inappropriate for members who have their own specialized skills and responsibilities, their own spheres of "power" which the organization must respect lest it shatter the effectiveness that it derives from the differentiation of knowledge and work. This objective condition—and not the subjective desire of people for more "democracy" or "participation"—is the basic reason why organizations become less hierarchical, whether or not their leaders wish them to move in that direction.

We have been talking about specific organizations (e.g., a corporation, a trade association, a foundation, an army, a university). In any advanced nation most of the action is generated within and among such organizations. Some of these organizations are huge in numbers of people and other resources. But none of them is big enough or broad enough to prosper or even survive by itself. Therefore, each of them must develop systems of external as well as internal communications. Public relations form is one of the principal forms of external communication.

An Organization's Actions Need Explanation

Because no organization is an island, because even the proudest and strongest are dependent on outsiders, they must seek to explain themselves to the world around them. When they try to do so, objections are raised in antique accents: "Good wine needs no bush" or "If a man makes a better mousetrap the world will beat a pathway to his door." Any validity these sentiments ever had has long been destroyed by modernity. No matter how meritorious his product, the vintner now had better be prepared to defend it against consumer advocates and taxing authorities. The mousetrap inventor needs to prove his brainchild really is better—and also free of environmentally negative side-effects. And to handle such communications he may well need the help of people who concentrate on developing a special competence in public relations.

In popular myth public relations is often seen as an arm of corporate power, an arrogant manipulative device for subjecting "us" to "them." But the growth of public relations takes on a very different aspect when it is considered within the context of modern life. Essentially, the need for public relations arises not from arrogance or greed but rather from recognition that in our world everyone's power is limited by the increasing powers possessed by others. Sure, public relations tries to create or modify or dispel "images" in the public's mind. Sure, there are many instances where this has been done cynically, deceitfully and arrogantly. But in essence, public relations proceeds from a respectful and even humble recognition that we need to explain ourselves to people whom we can no longer either ignore or coerce.

My understanding of this began (dimly) more than forty years ago when a highly respected colleague told me he was resigning as an editor of a newspaper to become public relations officer of a university. I did not conceal my bewilderment and shock. My friend was not one to seek an easy job, and the university in question seemed above any need of public relations assistance. It enjoyed national prestige, and was slavishly venerated in its own city where we worked. Local newspapers and the politicians treated it as the most sacred of cows. Why did it need public relations?

When I expressed some of this to my friend, he reminded me of several instances during the previous year when I had mentioned the university to him. For instance, a handout about some scientific advance had been written in language so technical that even scientists in a closely related field had been unable to understand it. On another occasion, I had told him that many of the poor people living near the university's superb hospital habitually endured trolley rides to distant clinics because they thought of the university's clinic as cold and inhuman. At the time I did not blame the university hospital, but rather cited the aversion of its neighbors as an example of the ignorance of people who would put themselves to great inconvenience in order to avoid a superior level of medical treatment. My friend, however, saw the hospital's reputation in its neighborhood as a responsibility of the university. He was suggesting that intrinsic excellence was not enough, that there was a further duty involving communications or, as we would now say, the modification of an image in the mind of a public.

Now, suppose that the unfavorable image had arisen because the university's clinic did in fact have a tendency, as its neighbors said, to "treat people like guinea pigs." Possibly a serious public relations operation might have brought this home to the doctors and modified some of their attitudes, procedures and policies. In short, attention to public images does not necessarily stop with the images. Frequently, the image cannot be improved without improving the substance.

This incident came forcefully back to my mind in the mid-Sixties when I was for a while writing about student unrest on campuses. The protest, which was later directed against the Vietnam War and "the corrupt society" in general, was at first largely focused on university policies and attitudes. Those complaints about the "impersonality" of the university, those picket signs reading, "I am a human being. Do not fold, bend or mutilate," were uncomfortably reminiscent of the patients who had fled by streetcar from "scientific" medicine.

Moreover, when I poked around troubled universities, I got the distinct impression that their public relations departments contained a far higher sense of responsibility toward the human needs of the under-graduates and other "publics" than did the university faculties, most of whose members did not seem very interested in problems of the images projected by universities as institutions. Many of the professors, of course, despised their public relations departments, no doubt on the ground that "Good wine needs no bush"—a sentiment in which a certain lack of humility can be detected.

In the decades of its enormous expansion, American higher education might have improved its substantive quality along with its image if it had taken more to heart the concerns of the administrators and public relations men who had the responsibility of connecting each "community of scholars" with the larger community on which it depended—socially as well as economically. This is not to suggest that universities can be operated exactly in accordance with the will of undergraduates, or parents or legislators or any other outside publics. In academia as elsewhere the principle of concentration and the principle that power follows knowledge are valid. From those principles comes the right of a biologist to design his research without interference from any public. But this right—like all rights—has limits, of which the most obvious is the public's right to withhold financial support. An intelligent exploration of where the limits lie in any set of circumstances cannot occur without communication inside and outside the "community of scholars." They, too, will need public relations. And, again, serious attention to public relations may improve the substance of policy.

Enlarging the Framework of Decision

Most public relations efforts are engaged on behalf of business. Before considering these in a capitalistic context it might be well to note that the need for public relations also occurs in socialist economies. A few years ago I was doing on-the-ground research for a *Fortune* article on the economic development of Siberia. Everywhere from Novosibirsk to Yakutsk one passionate topic dominated the conversation of most scientists, journalists, industrial managers and local party leaders with whom I talked. They were outraged by the construction of a paper mill on the banks of Lake Baikal, a huge body of water of unbelievable beauty and purity. Not surprisingly, Baikal carries a high symbolic charge in the minds of Siberians. That it should be wantonly polluted seemed a kind of ultimate bureaucratic insensitivity.

Yet when the history of the error was examined it was not hard to understand how it had happened. Moscow planners had wanted to increase paper production. The ministry responsible for that activity assigned a manager to pick a location for a new mill. Implicit in his responsibility was the goal of getting the most paper for the least cost. For that he needed a site with good access to timber, water and electric power. The shore of Baikal was a logical choice within the framework of his specialized economic concentration. Yet any half-competent public relations man might have made him aware of countervailing considerations outside of his framework of concentration. Because none did so, a major scandal erupted. Enormous and unplanned, antipollution costs were belatedly imposed upon the mill, and plans for the further industrial development of the Baikal area had to be drastically modified.

This story can be misread as antisocialist propaganda. Its real meaning transcends that debate. Like the university story above, it calls attention to a danger inherent in any kind of concentrated framework of decision. "The public" cannot decide either in a socialist or capitalist framework where to put a paper mill. For that decision special competence in pursuit of narrowly defined goals is necessary. Yet if this power is not somehow related to interests outside the framework of competent action, the result will reflect a larger incompetence.

The socialist habit of thought would conclude that the root of the Lake Baikal atrocity lay in delegating authority to locate the mill to an industrial manager or even to a ministry charged with responsibility for paper production. Had the location decision been made by Moscow central planners, whose responsibility extends far beyond paper production and far beyond economic efficiency, they might have made a wiser choice. But the centralizing bias implicit in this view ignores the fundamental nature of modern society. Even in the U.S.S.R. practical men know that most decisions cannot be centralized in a small group at the top simply because the relevant knowledge cannot be centralized there. In practice, the Russians seek to construct networks of horizontal communications that will compensate for the functional defects of the vertical planning structure which is embalmed in official theory. In the Baikal case, the decision on plant location was properly delegated to specialists, but the malfunction occurred because they were not tuned in to the values and wishes of people outside their area of competence.

Business Is Vulnerable

If we transpose the Baikal example to a capitalist economy and a democratic polity, we begin to see why business has a huge and growing need of public relations. In our kind of society we are not burdened by an unrealistic theory that all economic decisions should and can be centralized. But we are nevertheless stuck with the inescapable modern conflict between "the general good" and particular goals formulated within narrow areas of concentrated knowledge or action.

Every modern society will have multiple power centers, and the more advanced the society, the more power centers it will have. The general social problem of modern life is how to reduce conflict and to maintain cohesion without destroying the economic efficiency and (more important) the growth of personality that are fostered by the wider distribution of power. It would seem unarguable when organizations cannot coerce or destroy other power centers they must seek to improve their two-way channels of communication.

U.S. businesses, including the biggest of them, are vulnerable not only to the power of the federal government, but to thousands of other "power centers." These obviously include national governments abroad and state and local governments in the U.S. They also include all other businesses; even those that are not direct competitors are dipping into the same pool of consumer dollars and the same pool of capital. Business is also vulnerable to such "power centers" as universities and journalistic media which can influence the minds of customers, employees and citizens. Artists of all kinds are "power centers" because they have a hand in shaping society's perceptions of reality.

The many-sided vulnerability of business today isn't, in itself, a situation to be deplored. But it is one that demands far more effective external communication than American business has thus far achieved. Communication, of course, is a two-way street. A business in the formation of policy has to pay attention to outside views of what the public interest demands. As business seeks to improve its communication its first need is to understand that the public relations problem arises *primarily* out of the basic trend of modern life which business itself has promoted. No doubt the easiest—though not the best—way to sell public relations services to corporations is by emphasizing the threats to business that arise from the power and malice of its enemies. There are several traps in that approach. One is the temptation for business spokesmen to match their adversaries in stridency and exaggeration. Such a debate could drive significant segments of the public into a plague-on-both-your-houses reaction. Another danger is more general and more serious. Even if business had no enemies it would still face a tremendous need that it explain itself. Nobody is born knowing why corporations act the way they do. Neither formal education nor ordinary experience does much to diminish this area of ignorance. To the extent that business locks itself in combat with its disclosed enemies it runs the risk of neglecting the really basic reasons why it needs public relations.

In the Prologue to this book, John W. Hill has written a passage that provides a kind of keynote to any serious consideration of public relations. "Today in America there is a widespread search for the 'what and why' of things. Nothing escapes questioning. Nothing is sacrosant, whether it be Religion, Big Business or the Establishment in any of its manifestations . . . Candor and straightforward talk to people is the only way to achieve credibility, and that applies not only to business, but also to government, education and anything else of public concern."

If more public relations practice proceeded from that premise and if the public accepted the legitimacy of the public relations function, the social discourse of this troubled society would be less confusing than it is.

OVERVIEW

1

American Attitudes Toward Big Business

By Richard W. Darrow

Before The Opinion Research Corporation
Conference for Corporate Decision Makers,
New York City, August 21, 1974

SUMMARY: The steep decline in the U.S. public's opinion of American big business is traceable to failures in public relations counseling: failures to provide counsel and failures to accept counsel. Technical problems alone will make it very difficult for big business to reestablish its former standing through media communications solely. Creative alternatives are called for, such as regular use of the "town meeting" approach, with leading corporate executives meeting people and answering their questions face-to-face.

Richard W. Darrow, chairman of the board and chief executive officer of Hill and Knowlton, has also served as mayor of Scarsdale, N. Y., and as chairman of the board of trustees of his *alma mater*, Ohio Wesleyan University.

As our hosts, Opinion Research Corporation and its executives, have documented for us, American attitudes toward big business are more than bad; they are worse. Even if we could ignore escalating inflation and the looming shadows of a business recession, the already observable trend in public confidence indicates that it will continue to decline unless business itself takes action. And it is now evident that what needs doing must differ in some dramatic way from what businessmen have done in the past.

The remedy that will be required cannot consist simply of "more of the same."

When I refer to "more of the same," I am talking about the whole mix of communications efforts recommended to businessmen by practitioners of public relations and public affairs during the same years in which business' reputation has been declining. If I may speak for the many competent and conscientious public relations men and women I know, I'd like to point out that public relations counsel is just that: counsel. And counsel need not be sought. And, being sought, it need not be welcomed. And, welcomed or not, it need not be followed.

Of course, these realities of human nature do not absolve public relations practitioners of the obligation to continue their efforts to provide their clients and employers with the best information and advice within their own capabilities. Today that obligation dictates that public relations men and women take a fresh look at business' problems and potential.

Those of us in public relations did not bring on the problem. But we must share responsibility for not recognizing it earlier for what it is.

One fact cannot be escaped: much of the public relations effort of the last 50 years has been diluted by lip service or applied as a cosmetic. How often has our public statement not been the clearest revelation of truth but the most self-aggrandizing, or even the least we could get by with?

The emphasis—not always, but too often—has been on what management hoped people would accept rather than what they needed to be told to permit a fair judgment based on all the pertinent facts.

Too seldom have public relations people been consulted at the policy forming stages. This is true although their fundamental role is one of assessing and advising on the public opinion consequences of contemplated plans or actions.

Business Environment Is Changing

If we probe behind the rather gloomy statistics that ORC has gathered for us, I think we'll find there have been some changes in the public's expectations. The public still looks to business for performance;

that is, for the delivery of goods and services of acceptable quality, in adequate quantity and at reasonable cost. What has changed here to business' detriment is the context—the environment, if you will—in which business is expected to perform its traditional functions. ORC's statistics reveal a considerable gap between public expectations and what the public thinks it is getting in socially responsible performance from business.

Business' functional need is to adapt to this new environment and I shall speak in a little while about the changes which created this environment. Business management's other need, its public relations need, is to gain public understanding of its competence to make the adjustment successfully and sincerely—without the necessity of governmental guidance that verges on harassment, without the necessity of governmental supervision that verges on control.

It is the lack of that public understanding in a democracy such as ours, that is so perilous to business; because the decisions to shackle—or free—private business will finally be made as a result of public satisfaction with business' performance or of dissatisfaction with its perceived or imagined defects. That is what rings so ominously through the numbers we have heard here this morning.

I do not want to leave this point without recalling what John Hill said at the Annual PRSA Institute:

> "Now, it is a perfectly logical question to ask: 'Why hasn't the great effort by public relations on behalf of private enterprise kept it in better standing with the public?' Since no reliable method has been found to measure the results of public relations, another logical question may be asked: 'How much worse off would business have been without the effort?' "

The whole validity of John Hill's observation is based on the application of logic to history. And it is to the recent history of business in America that I now turn. By "recent" I don't mean just the 15 years covered by most of ORC's statistics. I want to go back through the '50s, the '40s and the '30s. I want to remind you that business' reputation has been worse, much worse, and *that* during the lifetimes of many or most of us.

We tend to forget that in many eyes the American businessman became the after-the-fact villain of the '20s and the tragic failure of the '30s and was rehabilitated only by his civilian service during World War II. His reputation grew in the postwar prosperity, with its marvelous cornucopia of goods and services showering down on a delighted public. It is against that standard of popularity that we tend—consciously or unconsciously—to rate business' standing today.

If American big business suffers today from sinking ratings and sinking feelings, those prosperous years between the war of the '40s and the rebellion of the '60s, those years were the years of euphoria and celebration. But euphoria is often followed by a painful letdown, and a celebration often brings a painful aftermath.

Basis for Criticism

One of my colleagues, a penetrating critic, albeit a friendly one, of American corporate performance, says that "American business today, especially big business, is being criticized and condemned because of five mistakes or misdemeanors." I quote him because his points so closely resemble the challenges indicated by ORC's discouraging report:

> One, that business took credit—or permitted the American public to give it credit—for material prosperity furnished by mass production and mass marketing of products, some of which offered defects that were only gradually detected and protested by long-complacent consumers;

> Two, that business took credit—or permitted the American public to give it credit—for material prosperity energized by a speculative stock market whose fragments now clutter the channels of finance;

> Three, that it took credit—or permitted the American public to give it credit—for material prosperity based on underpriced fuel and raw materials from less developed countries, many of which have ceased to cooperate;

> Four, that it took credit—or permitted the American public to give it credit—for material prosperity provided at the cost of mismanaged solid, liquid and gaseous wastes;

> Five, that it took credit—or permitted the American public to give it credit—for material prosperity measured largely against the illusory statistics of spiraling wage and price inflation.

This critic believes that almost every legitimate charge now leveled against American big business is based on one or more of these mistakes or misdemeanors. He feels that most businessmen were captives of the illusion that such practices could be the basis for continuing prosperity. But, if they were not dishonest, he concludes, they were certainly unrealistic.

This is a pretty harsh assessment but worthy of reflection. The record is not entirely clean.

So long as the economy was vibrant, employment kept reasonable pace and the ravages of inflationary costs did not seriously exceed increasing personal income, the euphoria lasted. This is clear in the ORC figures we have just seen for the '50s and early '60s.

But with the disillusionment and divisiveness of the Indochina War, the campus confrontations and anti-establishment upsurge of the '60s, came a parallel escalation in skeptical attitudes toward and virulent criticism of "the establishment," especially business and industry. Consumer reaction to advertising excess, together with declines in product and service quality, opened the door to consumer activism. Abuse of the environment and wasteful use of natural resources brought organized ecological forces onto the political scene.

Things weren't going well. Family budgets were feeling the pressure. And when the energy crisis threatened both their jobs and their leisure pursuits, the public had to have its identifiable villains. Business made an easy and vulnerable target. It had reaped the earlier credit; why not the current blame?

No business is entirely immune. Ironically, in ORC's statistics we now see the telephone companies, deservedly credited with the most consistent devotion to sound, organized customer and public relations efforts over the last 50 years, suffering one of the greatest percentage drops in public approbation—victims of the general decline in quality of personal service on the one hand and mounting inflation on the other.

Critics' Shortcomings Impede Communication

Turning now to the critics of business, I must conclude that many of them too are at best unrealistic and at worst dishonest. And that combination of incompetence by some and vindictiveness by others has at times distorted the public dialogue in which American business must communicate with the American people. As Irving Kristol noted in his essay on "The Credibility of Corporations":

> "In the debased version of democratic politics which prevails today, political demagoguery and popular paranoia—both, as it happens, so congenial to the melodramatic temperament of our mass media —demand that blame always and instantly be assigned to shadowy 'profiteers.' After all, if things go wrong, what other possible explanation is there? It can't be public opinion, which is always right, or the politicians, who are always dedicated to the commonwealth, or misfortunes of historical circumstances from which Americans are supposed to be exempt."

Those are strong words from Professor Kristol, but they are words of constructive criticism. They warn us that something is awry in the democratic dialogue today. I wonder how far we have actually advanced in the two centuries since the scattered Colonists communicated in town meetings or by laboriously printed pamphlets or by letters carried over the rough miles in saddlebags.

Among the assumptions at which Irving Kristol strikes with his criticism of today's public dialogue is our reliance, more or less comfortable, on the public media to serve as arenas for the opposing factions and as channels of communications between those factions and the public. The burden which history has placed on the media today is awesome; and the media are hard put, in practice, to carry it.

Businessmen forget at times that the media are themselves businesses. They have problems of staffing, of equipment purchase, of maintenance and obsolescence, of revenues and allocations. It has, at times, been more profitable for them to màke do with news coverage and analysis that were less—quantitatively and qualitatively—than editors or publishers, or listeners and viewers, could have desired. Much of the confusion surrounding last year's energy crisis was compounded by the concurrent shortage of energy experts on media staffs.

The media problem is, moreover, complicated by the unrelenting competition of all news and opinion for the same editorial space and viewing time. Even when a journalist or commentator has gained a firm grasp on his subject, there is usually a tight limitation on how much of his knowledge he is physically able to pass along to the public through the medium for which he works. The average business news story is a few dozen to a few hundred words in length; a two-minute time frame is about the maximum available for the average TV news item.

Businessman Is Penalized

The sophisticated hardware of today's print and broadcast media is expensive, and the result is that the allotments of time and space to the journalistic software—the real news that those same media are expected to deliver—are restricted.

It is tragic but true that, because of these practical limitations, the media are often unable to present in adequate depth or detail the positions of participants in our democratic dialogue. And that handicap penalizes the American businessman at least as often as it does his opponents. I do not lay this to journalistic bias; it is in the nature of our overloaded and conflict-oriented media themselves.

The shrinking availability of print space and broadcast time, dictated by the commercial realities of the communications business, has increasingly placed a premium first on succinctness, then on shallowness and finally on glibness. And a growing public appetite for news-as-entertainment has discouraged, when it has not forbidden, probing and thoughtful analyses of complicated public questions.

So we might as well recognize that the most popular media techniques, in print or electronics, are much more suitable for the presentation of an emotional and inflammatory accusation than for a detailed and reasoned defense.

Strange as it must seem, all these circumstances of today's journalism can at times convert the media themselves into effective barriers to the same communication they were designed to foster. Recognizing such strictures on the effectiveness of editorial time and space, some businessmen have turned to advertising to convey their public relations messages. But even here they have encountered the complexities of the Fairness Doctrine, further compounded by broadcast policies that reject messages dealing with controversial issues. And they are increasingly threatened by possibilities that the Internal Revenue Service will deny deductibility to such corporate expenses.

Frustrations of the Public Relations Counselor

It is at this point that the public relations man, in his role as a communicator, has to shake his head in disbelief at his own inadequacies. Here he stands, frustrated in his most energetic attempts to transmit his client's or employer's message in this, the age of communications miracles.

In his frustration, the public relations practitioner must face the reality that the mass media, with all their speed and span of coverage, might not—I'll even say do not—offer a clear channel toward regaining quickly or easily the credibility business has lost.

In an address to the PRSA Institute, John Hill expressed his doubt that the attention of the bulk of the American people could be captured by anything that couldn't be reduced to simple terms or, better yet, a slogan. Unfortunately, the message of American business does not lend itself to slogans. How can you explain productivity's importance in stemming the tide of inflation—but using only simple terms with meaning to the people ORC interviewed? How do you convey to them, in a few believable words, the importance of corporate profits to the well-being of the average American family?

The sobering analysis of public opinion we have just seen and heard offers little room for optimism. Our best creative efforts, applied to the most potent media combinations we can organize, offer us little hope of persuading a public so definitely turned-off, so skeptical, so incredulous.

I cannot personally—any more than my peers or my betters —produce such a miracle. There simply is no magic bullet. There is no easy way out of this situation—not at any price.

Give up the ballgame . . . ? Of course not. On the contrary, I believe that we do have a useful and promising course of action available to us. Not a panacea, not a picnic—not even a really new idea. Maybe we have overlooked it just because it is so old.

In fact, it's straight out of our American Colonial history, and even then it was a development based on man's first halting efforts at social communication. It is every bit as old—and every bit as strong—as a New England town meeting. I am suggesting a technique modeled on those face-to-face confrontations, those historical meetings of minds, so that businessmen today can defuse—by directly handling—the toughest and most embarrassing questions the American public has to throw at them. The very immediacy of that interface of business with those it claims to serve cannot help but generate a better climate of acceptability. Credibility will be improved by the fact that the businessmen will be talking with people, in their terms, about the problems they present to him as worrying them the most.

Direct Talk Works

The New England town meeting, with its point and counterpoint, neighbor to neighbor, seldom achieved unanimity, but it did produce a working consensus. I am encouraged to hope that something similar can be achieved for American business, if businessmen are willing to make the necessary effort. I propose that American corporations, as represented by their upper-level executives, reach out to their communities on a regular and continuing basis through this dramatically direct medium, to supplement the communications effort they have typically used—maybe a regular monthly round-table where business leaders meet the issues and the people, head-on, community by community.

Some variations on the town meeting have already been utilized by a few corporations and industry associations. Eaton Corporation, for example, has given special training to more than a hundred of its management people and made them available to discuss business problems and potential with students, housewives, union members, professional people, retailers, church groups and clubs. The Pennsylvania Electric Association makes it president and other industry leaders available to discuss business on talk shows, including those which feature phoned-in questions from the public.

In an analogous development, Mobil Oil has been sponsoring a weekly series of National Town Meetings at the Kennedy Center in Washington, D.C. Although business representatives have not yet been among Mobil's guest speakers, the format is promising, and much may be learned from this experience.

Feedback from such gatherings is still limited, of course. But what might prove applicable as a "pilot project" took place last month under the auspices of the American Petroleum Institute in a large southwestern city. API used a variation of the town meeting forum to make spokesmen available to answer the public's questions on the energy crisis before a local audience of government officials, educators and business and civic leaders. In a follow-up survey of audience reactions, a research firm found that over 60 percent of the attendees could not think of a better method to convey such information. Overall, 95 percent of the audience felt that similar forums in other parts of the nation would be of value for community leaders to attend.

Picture the initial and developing impact of corporate executives meeting their fellow citizens face-to-face, fielding their questions and feeling their concern on major business-public frictions—this in fifty or a hundred or a thousand communities across the nation on a regular basis. Media coverage need not be sought, but it is hard to imagine the media neglecting such events.

It is obvious that such a program will pose risks and have a cost/benefit uncertainty that will cause misgivings in any corporation that contemplates such an application of its executives' time. There will be an emotional hurdle for the corporate executive to clear in exposing himself to the embarrassing question and the harassing criticism. But it could be worth the costs. And I must emphasize that the higher the executives' rankings, the more significant the meetings will be.

In support of my recommendation, then, I urge you to recall the old political truism that the best way to campaign for any office is to shake the hand of every voter in your constituency. Congressmen are able to do this better than other national officers. They know this and practice it. And that may be the explanation of the paradox that Congress rates next to last on the Trust-and-Confidence chart ORC just showed us, while individual Congressmen get re-elected term after term.

Congress as an entity has so many faces it is faceless. And so has the American corporation. And that's what puts "Large Companies" below even Congress, at the bottom of that same chart.

There is a lesson there and, I hope, a clue to a new way up.

Notes on the Operation Research Corporation Surveys

A number of speeches in this book—including Richard Darrow's opening contribution—refer to surveys by Opinion Research Corporation, Princeton, N.J. The findings were the subject of an ORC conference on August 21-22, 1974, at which Mr. Darrow was the first guest speaker. ORC has been probing American attitudes toward business since 1943. Its Public Opinion Index Service conducts surveys for its clients and issues 24 such studies each year. Highlights of the 1973 findings—some of them mentioned elsewhere in this book—follow.

General Business Reputation

Based on responses to key statements, U.S. public opinion reveals:

	% of Public Who Agreed In 1959	In 1973
• Less sympathy for the utility of profits. "Profits of large companies help make things better for everyone."	60%	46%
• Greater antipathy to bigness in corporations. "In many of our largest industries, one or two companies have too much control of the industry."	57%	76%
"There's too much power concentrated in the hands of a few large companies."	53%	75%
"As they grow bigger, companies usually get cold and impersonal in their relations with people."	55%	74%
"For the good of the country, many of our largest companies ought to be broken up."	38%	53%

• The public's overall attitude toward business has changed between 1959 and 1973 as follows:

Little approval—This group grew from 52% to 67%.

Moderate approval—This declined from 28% to 25%.

High approval—This group was halved, 16% to 8%.

Profits

• With regard to profits, the public estimates that the average manufacturer's after-tax profit on the sales dollar is 28 cents; *actual* 1972 profit was 4.3 cents. Attitudes toward profits of business as a whole:

    50% believe they are reasonable
    35% believe they are too much
    3% believe they are not enough

Other attitudes held by public: 67% believe most companies could raise wages without raising prices; in replying to what is the most practical way to increase the standard of living, 24% believe it is to produce more, while 43% believe it is to get more of what companies make.

Business Ethics

- Corporate executives placed *thirteenth* on a list of 16 career groups rated for ethical and moral practices. Only federal, state and local government officials, labor leaders and advertising executives rated lower.

Credibility

- Large companies placed *last of all* on a list of a dozen major U.S. institutions rated for public trust and confidence—behind labor unions and Congress.

Almost all industries have declined in favor within the past five years, among them:

	1969	1973
Electric light/power	77%	58%
Tire and rubber	63	47
Electronics	58	47
Food	64	45
Automobile	63	45
Computer	47	45
Prescription drugs	51	44
Steel	47	42
Packaging, containers	43 (1971)	39
Oil and gasoline	65	34
Chemical	43	34

Social Responsibility

The same strongly negative attitude is shown by the public in the realm of corporate social responsibility:

- "Business has an obligation to help society even if it means making less profit."

	Total Public	Teenagers
Agree	70%	66%
Disagree	22	29
No opinion	8	5

- "Businessmen do everything they can to make a profit, even if it means ignoring the public's needs."

	Total Public	Teenagers
Agree	65%	65%
Disagree	29	31
No opinion	6	4

- "Business today has a social conscience—it is motivated by more than just the profit motive."

	Total Public	Teenagers
Agree	42%	42%
Disagree	42	44
No opinion	16	14

2

The Function of
Public Relations in Helping
to Restore Confidence
in American Institutions

By John W. Hill

Before the 16th Annual PRSA Institute,
College Park, Maryland, July 10, 1974

SUMMARY: Business, and especially big business, has taken some rough jolts in public opinion. Much of the problem stems from the failure of business to tell its complicated story clearly and effectively to the many public groups in our society. Management people must learn to communicate frankly and forthrightly on subjects which people have a right to know about. They also should strive for a better understanding of people and the needs of a fast-changing world.

John W. Hill, author of *Corporate Public Relations* and *The Making of a Public Relations Man*, founded Hill and Knowlton in 1927 and is today the chairman of its executive committee.

I am pleased and honored to be here as your lecturer. But I did feel some momentary misgivings when I recalled Will Rogers' comment that a comedian amused people while a lecturer only irritated them.

When I was invited here I fear the trustees failed to take into account my immaturity, in the incorrect belief that my practice covered half a century. To be exact, the figure is only 47 years and three months.

That hasn't been nearly enough time for me to catch up with the notion apparently held by some people that public relations is a kind of cosmetic device people use to hide the truth.

Of course, no human activity is flawless or devoid of its seamy side, and public relations—or public affairs as some prefer to call it—is no exception. But the responsible practitioners of public relations I know adhere to principles of integrity, ethics and forthrightness.

Without these principles, we would not have seen the great growth in public relations activities of the past few decades. This expansion has been stimulated by the mounting complexity and technological advances of modern society, by the communications explosion and the increasing recognition that public opinion is the final human power in the free world.

Business Under Fire

While we have moved forward in our work, we have no cause for complacency. Let us face up to some cold facts. Virtually all of the institutions in our establishment, as you know, have lost credibility and public esteem in recent years. Business, and especially Big Business, has taken some rough jolts in public opinion.

Now, it is a perfectly logical question to ask: "Why hasn't the great effort by public relations on behalf of private enterprise kept it in better standing with the public?" Since no reliable method has been found to measure the results of public relations, another logical question may be asked: "How much worse off would business have been without the effort?"

At the same time, public relations cannot escape some part of the blame for what has happened. There are doubtless many cases where practitioners have lacked the aggressiveness, the guts and possibly the capability to make their points stick with corporate managements.

The present is not the first time private enterprise has been under fire.

Twenty-two years ago, William H. Whyte, Jr., wrote a book entitled, "Is Anybody Listening?" Many of you will recall it. He said:

> "The free enterprise campaign underway is shaping up as one of the
> most intensive sales jobs in the history of industry. And it isn't worth
> a damn."

Mr. Whyte may have been too harsh in his appraisal, but the fact remains that business is still fighting the same battle. Early in my career in public relations, one of the big problems was that the people, according to polls of the time, thought business profits, after all charges, were 25 percent of sales. The actual figure was then close to 5 percent. After 40 years of hard work by many dedicated organizations, people no longer think that profits are 25 percent. They think they are 28 percent . . . and the real figure is still under 5 percent.

The spotlight has been put on profits because after all they are what make the mare go. But profits account for a small piece of the income pie. The biggest slices go to labor and other costs.

The public's misunderstanding of the rate and role of profits goes hand in hand with the difficulty of getting people to understand the importance of increased productivity in industry. A recent Harris poll revealed that 70 percent of the people polled think of any effort to increase productivity as exploitation of workers.

Why the Misunderstanding?

Don't these facts carry a stinging message to all of us who have been trying for many years to get a few simple economic realities accepted by the people of America?

The message *I* get is that it is time to go back to the drawing board. Reexamine past activities. Discover, if we can, what business and its public relations have been doing and saying wrong. Other institutions are worried too, but most of them are not under the legislative gun as business is.

Perhaps we should give heed to Dostoevski, who in *The Brothers Karamazov*, said, "If people around you are callous and will not hear you, fall down before them and beg their forgiveness for *in truth you are to blame for their not wanting to hear you.*"

Let's look at the problem confronting us now. We have in America a population that is one of the most highly literate in the world and, at the same time, one of the most appallingly illiterate in economics. This illiteracy is not in the everyday family sense, but quite understandably, most people do not comprehend the complicated world of big business, of finance or of the international marketplace.

Until very recent years people were inclined to accept without too much question big government, big foundations, big universities, and big unions partly because of their nonprofit nature. But big business is out for profit and therefore suspect. This doesn't mean people want Socialism in this country, and, if they stop to think, they wouldn't want Congress to abolish profits. Still, many people are skeptical.

We have some 80 million wage earners. Why do these men and women think of their pay envelopes as something of real concern to them, and of corporate profits as something of *little or no concern to them*?

Perhaps the best way to solve this problem would be to try to lift the level of economic education in this country. Some are saying that the only way this will happen is through a big depression and widespread unemployment. God forbid! I lived through the '30s and although there is much anxiety and signs of recession now, I am hopeful that we won't have anything like the '30s again.

There must be a better way for the people, especially our youth, to get more understanding of at least the simplest economic facts. Why isn't this provided by our educational system? The problem there lies in the fact that so many of our educators and intellectuals (thankfully, not all) are either lukewarm toward our system of private enterprise or they are outrightly opposed to it. Their ideas have had wide influence in our schools and throughout our society. No one can protest fair and objective criticism but the intellectual critics of business have not always been either fair or objective.

Business Talks to Itself

As I think of the past, I become convinced that perhaps the most serious mistake made over the years was that business talked too much to itself and about itself and its needs, and too little about what all this means to people. So people are not listening, and they won't listen until we get on their wavelength. We need to convince them, in their terms and by our actions, that private enterprise wants just what they want—to make ends meet and have something left over. Unfortunately, the people, during the period of economic euphoria, have had too many examples, led off by government, of heedlessly piling up debt and living beyond one's means. But that period seems to be coming to an end.

The survival instinct is normal for all of us and I suppose this is why self-interest and material goals are so prevalent among people. But many are motivated by pure idealism and totally selfless attitudes. I have seen people's faces light up with joy when they have achieved some good and kind deed which brought them no money but great inner satisfaction.

So life teaches us this simple lesson: People are different. Each individual has his own genes, his own educational and family background, his own IQ, his own likes and dislikes, his own fingerprints. In order to interest people in our problems we need to identify with their problems and interests.

That is what makes it so difficult to know how to talk to people.

The saving grace is that people with like interests, be they economic, ethnic, educational, geographical, cultural or some other, are drawn together by their common concern. The problem in public relations is to sort out these fragmented groups and find ways to attract their special attention.

We have learned that emotional appeals often win more adherents than logical and factual arguments, but with the rising literacy of people and their growing sophistication, communicators are finding it less and less productive to talk down to them. Truthfulness and forthrightness are the watchwords for people in public relations.

Even so, I doubt if anyone today other than perhaps the President could get the attention of the whole American public on any national issue that cannot be reduced to simple terms or, better still, a slogan. Political men know this well. "He kept us out of war"—"A war to save Democracy"—"Get the country going again"—"War on poverty"—"Four freedoms." What has happened to those once lofty phrases? They gave birth to no great or lasting programs.

One of the first questions is—What is public opinion? Many people speak glibly and often unthinkingly of public opinion. But because of the fragmentation of the public, the swift movement of events, the massive changes in our society, the enormous influence of the media and especially TV, public opinion has a tendency to swing like a weathervane in America.

The questions asked by pollsters cannot, by their very nature, be in great depth. Asking how one is going to vote for specific candidates in an election is one thing. But asking for opinions on continuing involved issues is quite another. How many of us are intellectually equipped or capable of even understanding the scores of national and international problems so frighteningly confronting us today? Even the best economists are not clear or in agreement on what causes inflation or how to cure it. So the average respondent gives answers that reflect his emotions, his gut feelings and, hopefully, his common sense.

And, of course, there is the consideration that some answers are influenced by the way questions are framed. Some critics of pollsters —yes, they, too, are under fire—contend that questions can be "loaded" to get desired responses.

Public Opinion Runs Deep

Opinions on current questions and events can change rather quickly. But imbedded in society is a deep underlying movement of opinion which persists over the years like currents in the depths of the ocean—irresistible and irreversible. Unperceived by most, they are gradually shaping society and this becomes apparent sooner or later.

For example, Nader did not invent consumerism, which existed under the surface for many years before it became a wide-open issue. Business has no greater problem in the area of public relations than to endeavor to discover, evaluate, and, if a threat, to anticipate the currents of opinion existing or taking shape deep in our living society.

One hundred and forty years ago, a perceptive Frenchman, de Tocqueville, wrote that the "drive for equality" was one of the irresistible forces transforming society in America. Daniel Bell calls this the "Master Key" to our society. Time has shown deTocqueville to be a true prophet. The high level of literacy in this country, the high standard of living and many other achievements evidence the vigor of the American "drive for equality." The gulf between the haves and have-nots is less wide, by far, than it was. But, of course, great inequalities still exist, and the effort to reduce these inequalities is irreversible. No one could say this is not in the public interest, yet are we *always* so sure just what the public interest is?

Actually, doesn't every group of any potency speak of its "special" interest as being in the "public" interest? Undeniably, some of them are. Yet many other issues are just as clearly selfish.

Today, inflation is the Number One problem in this country and around the globe. Also, problems like product safety and environmental pollution are in the forefront now as primary problems of "public" interest. These issues are real, but they are also complex and highly charged with emotion, and even politics. Most of them cannot be solved easily or quickly.

Demands for more truth in advertising, more safety in product design and more self-fulfillment and participation in jobs and improved quality of life are consistent with the dynamic underlying, forward movement of our society; and so long as these demands are within reason, business is misguided when it fails to give them serious consideration.

Heeding the Claims of the Public

One way business has alienated people over the years has been by sanctifying the status quo and opposing many of the measures which people, rightly or wrongly, believe to be in their interest. Often, demagogues have presented frankly anti-business and punitive legislation and regulatory measures as good for the people when time proved many of these to be tragically just the opposite. The result is today that business is caught in a mass of regulations which are hurting the whole economy, at a time when the economy needs support. Yet it is true that some of the laws passed over the opposition of business have turned out to be good for the country, such as the Federal Reserve Act, the SEC and others.

In retrospect, it seems quite clear that whenever business adopted an adversary posture toward government and failed to make effective efforts to help shape legislation constructively, it not only usually lost the legislative battle but the esteem of the people as well.

I think all of us are aware of past mistakes by business and its public relations. The need now is to profit from those mistakes and make a massive effort to develop the best possible directions for the future. Many able minds now are at work on this new project.

What I see is that some powerful new force is stirring in industry.

One of the most significant developments of our times is' the evidence of, let us hope, a growing change by responsible industry leaders in the concept of their goals and obligations in response to the changing values of society. Added to the profit motive, which will always remain the lifeblood of private enterprise, has been a growing recognition of still other obligations business has to the people.

There is an increasing acceptance by these same business leaders that what they do and say must take into account not only profits, but the implications and consequences to society as well.

There is also some evidence of a maturing process among U.S. businessmen in their relationship to government, hopefully a general moving from an adversary position to one of positive constructive cooperation.

A case in point is the pharmaceutical industry. After 15 years of head-to-head confrontation with government—a confrontation which had largely served to erode the reputation of an industry which had served the public well—the drug people changed their tactics. At a meeting not long ago, the directors of the Pharmaceutical Manufacturers Association adopted a positive program to change a number of industry practices which had been unfavorably highlighted in recent Senate hearings.

In policies such as these lie the hope and the way of the future of private enterprise. Business leaders simply cannot stand aside while politicians and others monopolize the ''public'' interest as their exclusive property. Business leaders have the capability and the obligation to take the leadership in broad, forward-looking issues and help shape society, not selfishly but responsibly, for the good of all.

Cooperation through Dialogue

I am convinced that dialogues should be carried on between business leaders and their powerful activist critics whenever this is feasible. If there are faults which need correcting by business, isn't it far better that these be admitted and corrected cooperatively and constructively rather than punitively by anti-business forces? Businessmen can adopt a more conciliatory role without relinquishing their option to oppose unfair and strident political attacks and impossible demands. That option can never be given up.

Clearly, there is every sound reason for business and society to come to terms. Society cannot demand or expect the impossible and the wholly impractical from business, and business cannot turn its back on its legitimate obligations to society. There are growing indications that the long period of good times and affluence have led to unrealistic expectations on the part of great masses of people and that some, at least temporary, revision may be unavoidable in the critical times facing us now.

And so we have business confronted by intensified problems in these three vital areas: serious inflation and an uncertain economic outlook; increasing governmental bureaucratic regulations, and low standing in public opinion polls.

Respecting industry's standing with the public, I see much that is moving in a positive and good direction, yet negatives do persist. We might say that there are assets and liabilities in the balance sheet of private enterprise today.

I would summarize some of the positive points as follows:

- Corporate management is giving increasing recognition to the fact that public relations and public affairs is a united function of the whole organization. Policy decisions, implementation, and communications are all closely interlocked. Policy decisions come first because fine words can never substitute for faulty acts.
- More top managements are accepting overall responsibility, not only for profitable operations but for the organization's relationships with its own publics and with society as a whole. High-level officers are being appointed with the specific responsibility of public relations and public affairs.
- Recognition is spreading in business that legitimate complaints and justified irritations of consumers regarding product quality, service, repairs and warranties require prompt and honest attention. The consumer movement is neither new nor a fad, and consumers are voters, too, with the ultimate power of life or death over private enterprise.
- A few industries are recognizing that some of the so-called "public interest" groups, which are regarded as anti-business by many companies, do serve a useful public service in alerting both government and business to valid problems. These groups are skilled in legislative work and are busy not only in Washington but in all of the 50 states. Some industries are monitoring and studying the legis-

lative proposals of these groups throughout the country and supporting those clearly in the public interest. In the case of other proposals that are unreasonable or impractical, constructive modifications are offered. When no alternatives can be worked out, then, of course, these so-called "public" interest proposals should be and often are opposed. This process has proven of value to communities and to the country, and hopefully it will become a pattern for more industrial organizations.

- Business leaders are becoming more flexible in their views and acts, in recognition of the fact that society is changing greatly and irreversibly.

- While corporate managements know that their organization cannot long exist or expand without profits, they are becoming aware of and more responsive to the people's insistence upon preserving and enriching "the quality of life." Therefore, efforts are being made to help in the solution of such problems as environmental pollution and other public issues.

Negative Points Need Correction

These are some of the outstanding actions and policies on the positive side of the ledger which are enabling business to help shape society. On the negative side where progress is still needed, I would include these points:

- Business leaders need to become more aware of the anti-business attitude of intellectuals and critics and face up to the charges that the moral standards of business are below society's standards; that its behavior is getting worse; that in its anxiety to maximize profits, it has a callous attitude toward the quality of life of the American people; that it often gives only lip service to its responsibilities to society; and that industry is always three or four years behind the people.

- Business leaders need more awareness that their motivations are no whit different from the motivations of the "little guy." The levels of expectations vary, but the principles are the same.

- More management people nationally and in the communities need to show willingness to communicate frankly and forthrightly on subjects people have a right to know about. There is every reason to be available for face-to-face discussion with the press and on TV and radio, despite occasional exasperating experiences some have had. The more people understand business and its problems in terms of their own daily life, the less they will be alienated from business.

- There is a glaring lack of management people, top and middle, experienced in clearly and effectively explaining the system under which they operate. This lack is highlighted by the fact that some companies are sponsoring management training courses to equip their people to participate in public appearances.
- Ways should be developed to present financial returns to the public which will show where income comes from and where it goes; and why profits are in the public interest. Some companies are spelling out the inflation factor in their profits.
- Corporate executives could well take heed of the statement by Irving Kristol that corporations have no constituencies, no one—stockholders, employees or anyone else—who is ready to come to their aid in a controversy. He suggests, among other things, giving incentive to stockholders to encourage them to hold their shares for long periods, also more attention to keeping them informed. This is a subject that needs careful study.

These are among the steps American business can take in support of their own cause. Many more steps will be called for as time goes on.

Range of Industry Actions Widens

The truth is that leaders of American industry have responsibilities far beyond their own companies, their own communities or their own nation. The problems of the world are coming to their doorstep. For example, sooner or later American business will have to give what help it can toward solving the gigantic problems of the "have-not" nations with their immense populations. Right now, food shortages and starvation are frightening problems in countries in Asia and Africa. In the present crisis, we are finding out that the whole world is bound together economically and financially.

The revolution in transportation and communications has created the "One World" Wendell Willkie used to talk about, with a "global marketplace," instant communications and satellite TV. Multinational companies have multiplied and the most fascinating development of all is the fast deterioration of the Iron Curtain, at least so far as our expanding trade with the Communists is concerned.

All of this local and global stirring in industry is of enormous significance for people in public relations. It is impossible to overemphasize that the public relations function cannot be a thing apart from top management. In the best-run companies it is a vital segment of management and of the organization. This is bringing an ever-increasing demand for trained people in public relations and public affairs.

The need is not only for individuals skilled in the important technical aspects of communications but even more for those who can participate helpfully on policy discussions. Since most policy decisions have public relations implications, the need for experienced counsel is of growing importance at the top level of corporate managements. In arriving at sound policy decisions, in addition to business, financial and legal considerations, the need in today's world is also for information and advice on social, government relations, public attitudes and similar matters. This applies, for many companies, not alone to our own society, but to other societies around the world as well. The call will be for people of broad competence and stature.

At the PRSA meeting in Detroit in November 1972, I suggested a public relations postgraduate course in such disciplines as the social and political sciences and other pertinent studies. I know your research foundation has given some thought to this, and I strongly urge that further study be devoted to it.

In public relations, it is imperative that we keep a perspective of history—where we are and how we got here and where we are going. The present feeling of the people toward Big Business is not new. It has been surfacing on occasion since the beginning of the century and before.

I remember as a Hoosier farm boy in 1904, when my father took me to Indianapolis to hear his hero, Teddy Roosevelt, I stood close to the speaker's platform and was thrilled by Teddy's angry denunciation of the "malefactors of great wealth." He was unfair in some of his charges, and Big Business hated him, but the people loved him. He was their champion and in public relations we need to listen to the critics of business just as we want the people to listen to what we say.

Once again business, particularly Big Business, is a political whipping boy. The times call for business statesmanship which will take the lead in forward thinking and actions in the interest of society as a whole. Public relations and public affairs practitioners must be prepared to help bring this about.

The people, including influential intellectuals, would benefit from better understanding of private enterprise, its problems and dynamic contributions to the general good. But also it is an obligation of managements to strive for a better understanding of people and of the *valid* complaints of a changing society. There is a need for more straight talk by business, but words will carry conviction only when supported by policies and acts, and by a demonstrated feeling for people.

This is the way to get people to listen. It is the clear path toward helping to restore confidence in the American institution of private enterprise.

FINANCIAL RELATIONS

3

Catch 23 for Regulated Companies

By Richard E. Cheney

Before American Gas Association
Financial Seminar, Boca Raton, Florida, May 30, 1974

SUMMARY: The nation's regulated companies face a "Catch 23" dilemma: To get investor interest they have to report high earnings, but this hurts their chances for rate relief. Without rate relief, however, they can't have the kind of earnings that attracts investors. To solve this dilemma, the companies must identify and foresee the public's needs and concerns—and convey in a persuasive way that they are out to advance the public's interest.

Richard Cheney, an executive vice president of Hill and Knowlton, and veteran of many of the major proxy fights and tender offer contests of the last 15 years, has spoken before bar associations, management seminars, major financial public relations meetings and business schools in the U.S., Japan and Europe.

While nobody likes to be dragged in off the golf course to hear a lot of bad news, I might as well warn you in advance that you're in for it. If there was ever a time to bolt for the door, this is it. I'm supposed to talk about your financial public relations, but to do so I'm afraid I must talk about a miserable dilemma facing you today—what might be called Catch 23 for regulated companies.

This dilemma, I'm sure you're well aware of. An article in *The Public Utilities Fortnightly* got at part of the problem this way: "Is it a kind of unfair 'double jeopardy' to have consumers inconvenienced and discomforted in the name of energy conservation and then thank them for their pains by hitting them with a rate increase? Why did not someone tell them that the natural consequence of truly effective consumer conservation of energy was reduced earnings for utilities and subsequent proposed rate hikes?"

Simply stated, your dilemma is this: You can't have high investor regard for your company without reporting the kind of earnings growth that causes you to run into trouble on rate relief. Without rate relief you can't have the kind of earnings growth that leads to high investor regard for your company.

This situation may very well tend to get worse, the way things are going, since to get rate relief you may well have to get into a position that will prevent you from getting the capital you need for long-term survival.

You're in a buried lie in a sand trap with a strong head wind and a carry over water to the green. I am the apprehensive caddy who is supposed to help you choose a club.

Under the circumstances, perhaps it might make for a pleasanter beginning if I talked about investor relations on a theoretical basis —uncomplicated by rate considerations. If I can only prolong this part of the talk, I may get away without any trouble at all.

One of the most common yardsticks for measuring how a company is regarded by the investing public is the price-earnings ratio. The price of a share of stock in relation to the earnings per share might be regarded as a sort of report-card grade assigned to a company in the marketplace. A company with a high price-earnings ratio might be said to be turning Wall Street on and vice versa.

Evolution of the P/E Formula

I'd like to give you my hypothesis, expressed as a formula, for arriving at how the price-earnings ratio of a company comes about. I'm still fooling around with this formula, but I think it's useful, if not yet perfect.

The price-earnings ratio is equal to the integrity of a company's financial communications plus its perceived future prospects diminished by the risk of the specific business the company is in and the risks of the marketplace at a given time. The price-earnings ratio has a floor under it—provided by the size and the dependability of the dividend. The price-earnings ratio also tends to be limited on the upside by the number of shares available for trading and by the amount of overall savings available for investment, plus the appeal of alternative investments such as bonds.

In other words, we buy stock because we think it's going to make us money (future prospects) and because we think management is going to level with us as we go along toward the goal of getting rich (integrity of communications). We hesitate if we think the business is risky or if the market is going to take a nosedive and take even the more promising stocks along with it. If the stock pays a good dividend and the dividend is reliable, we may buy it (if the price goes low enough) for the return on our money alone. But if we're a big buyer, we're going to hesitate if the supply of stock is limited—if it's hard to find a seller and—more important—hard to find a buyer in case we later want to get out. Finally, we're going into the market only if we have the money to do so and think the equity market is a better bet than other investments.

Now let's look at the stock market five years ago and again today, in terms of this formula, dealing first with industrial companies before turning to regulated companies such as yours. Supposing we turn back the clock to a talk I made in Chicago in September 1969 called "The Public Relations Lessons of the Takeover Era."

"We are now at the New York Society of Security Analysts and our principal speaker is Joe Blowhard, chairman of Consummate Management, Inc., and he is concluding his remarks. 'Gentlemen, let me say that Consummate Management has now had 26 quarters of consecutive improvement in earnings per share, averaging 22 percent annually. I believe you can see that when we talk about planned earnings growth we're not kidding. With our basic management setup—a tight-knit headquarters organization that is acquisition-oriented—we believe we can assure you a continuation. Any questions?'

"Willie Wonder, a 23-year-old analyst at the back of the room, who has just been unleashed from Harvard Business School, jumps to his feet and says, 'Joe, would you care to estimate your earnings for this year?' This particular analyst, I might add, works for Out of Sight, the fastest growing mutual fund with the best growth record of any in the industry ever since its formation three years ago. The fund's managers have their own gymnasium right in the office. As they sweat off the high living they can afford as a result of their soaring management fees, they can contemplate the fact that the assets they manage have grown to the three-quarters-of-a-billion mark since the original offering three years earlier.

"Joe Blowhard waits briefly until Willie Wonder can get his slide rule lined up and then answers, 'We should make $8.00, possibly $8.50, altogether our best year—an increase of about 43 percent in earnings per share.'

"The analyst ducks out and hurries back to his office. 'Let's add some more Consummate Management,' he shouts over the door of a shower bath adjoining the gym.

" 'Why?' comes the reply from within.

" 'Because they're going to make $8.00 this year—maybe even $8.50.'

" 'Who said so?' comes the reply.

" 'Joe Blowhard,' the analyst answers. 'Who else? I wouldn't give you a recommendation like this unless I got it from the horse's mouth.'

"So, faster than you can say horse liniment, they buy—and they buy some more. Joe Blowhard's stock goes up and he uses convertible securities to pick up another eight companies. Willie Wonder is not so young as to be ingenuous. He knows this is how Joe Blowhard works and in his way he's proud, so to speak, to be on the Blowhard team. What the hell. There's money in it for everybody.

"Joe Blowhard makes this prediction for the year in February, which takes some temerity. I'm not saying that there aren't a lot of honest, optimistic men in business who get a lot of work done in this country by setting their sights high. I also recognize that a lot of merger-minded managers in the past few years have had legitimate grounds for predicting substantial earnings improvements as a result of new efficiencies they have been able to bring to acquired companies. But Joe Blowhard doesn't belong to this particular group.

"Joe Blowhard isn't thinking, when he makes his earnings projection, about how he's going to strengthen operations. He's counting on his own financial legerdemain and the credulity of his following in the financial community. He knows he's got a lot of things going for him. He's got pooling of interest. He's also got unamortized good will. He can change depreciation charges on some acquired companies. And he can change the actuarial rates on his pension plan. He can change the way he accounts for inventories in some acquisitions he has picked up. A couple of companies he acquired have been deferring tax credits over the life of the assets. He can change that in a hurry. 'Accounting-wise,' as he would say privately, 'I'm loaded.'

"If things turn sour in the second quarter, he also has another string to his bow. Quarterly earnings aren't audited. He can defer some of the bad news to the third quarter and launch what I call a cosmetic tender, a takeover designed to improve his figures. He can get Out of Sight, the mutual fund, to buy a big block of the target company's stock ahead of time and park it for him, ready to turn it over to him at a profit when he makes his tender offer. If the offer should run into resistance, he can make a fat profit selling to another company that wants to rescue the victim. So what if this is a nonrecurring profit? He'll lump it in with operating profits and nobody will know the difference. Or, if they do, they won't care. After all, their stake is as great as his own."

Today, Joe Blowhard's company stock is selling at three times earnings, well under book. He's having a lot of trouble with his directors, who are guys who sold their companies to him. Willie Wonder is driving a taxi. Out of Sight, the mutual fund, is buying back shares from disgruntled stockholders.

In terms of my formula, what happened?

Change in Criteria

Five years ago, a stock could appear to have a great future on the strength of an acquisition-minded management alone. The accounting rules were such that a company could report higher earnings and cover up a multitude of sins on the strength of a single acquisition. Also, under the rules, a management had a wide latitude about what it could tell a trusting public without losing credibility. In that expansive market, dividends really weren't nearly so important as capital gains and often a restricted number of available shares simply served to whet the appetite of investors who should have known better.

Today, all of this is changed. Investors fear diversification so that an acquisition-minded company turns investors off unless the acquisitions are closely linked to the ongoing business. Every departure from an existing business represents a potential bad surprise. In terms of the formula, what once excited investors as additional future value now only increases risk.

An accounting change five years ago might simply have excited eager investors as somehow adding value to an investment. Today, it tends to arouse suspicion and undermine the company's reputation for integrity of communications.

Five years ago, investors were willing to accept the future on faith if a company had five years of consecutive quarterly earnings improvement. Today, an unbroken string of earnings improvements makes everybody nervous about accounting gimmicks.

Sharp earnings increases worry people, too. Recently, one of our clients, the head of an over-the-counter company, was talking before a small group of analysts and he announced a 50 percent earnings increase for the year. A market maker in the stock who was in the audience jumped up and said, ''My God, I hope you're not going to *announce* such a big increase. You'll never be able to top it next year.''

The market maker wanted management to bury some of the profits until next year to assure a smooth upward earnings curve.

As a result of this kind of pressure, we now find companies burying earnings whenever possible through what has come to be called cookie jar accounting. Five years ago, a manager was much more apt to let the future take care of itself. He figured a timely acquisition would bail him out of a tight situation.

Meanwhile, inflation has cut into the amount of money available for stock market investments. As stocks have nosedived, individuals have been looking at other kinds of investments for such savings as they have left. High interest rates are siphoning money out of equities. Back-office problems have made investors nervous about their brokers.

All of this—plus a drastic tightening of the commission structure —has caused contraction on Wall Street, as I'm sure you all know. There are fewer analysts following fewer stocks much more carefully. They have nervous stomachs. A single recommendation gone sour may just cost them their job. As a result, they stay clear of companies with volatile earnings records. They want tranquilizer-style stocks with stable growth built in.

With conditions what they are, brokers tend to try to grab so-called superstar analysts who have the best reputations for reading the tea leaves for various industries.

Once they pay the astronomical salaries required for one of these whiz kids, they can't afford to let him waste a minute on a non-productive situation—that is, a piece of research that isn't going to result in commissions.

I tried to have lunch the other day with an old friend who's an analyst, a superstar, and discovered that his firm had hired an appointments secretary for him to make sure that every minute of his day is spent generating commissions. She told me he sent his regards. He didn't even have time to send them himself. Incidentally, he's always been lousy at picking winning stocks. But he is extremely well informed on the oil industry. His brokerage firm has the best of both worlds. He generates commissions advising money managers on oil industry economics, but he doesn't run the risk of being criticized for making bum recommendations on individual stocks, since his employer doesn't let him make any.

To sum all this up, Wall Street in a way hasn't really changed all that much. It is still turned on by greed and turned off by fear. It has always wanted as close to a sure thing as possible. But today, it doesn't regard nearly so many companies as sure things as it did five years ago.

Reconciling Regulators and Investors

Where does this leave you?

In the sand trap I alluded to in the beginning of this talk. To turn Wall Street on, you're going to have to report the kind of earnings that is going to make you the scapegoat of the regulators. To avoid trouble with the regulators, you're going to have to report earnings that will make you a wallflower on Wall Street. At the same time, some troubles in the public utility business have made people nervous about supplies and edgy about your dividends.

In terms of my formula, your price-earnings ratio is being depressed because your perceived future value as an investment is far from rosy. Your business is riskier, and other investments look a lot more attractive than your common stock.

I've now come to the part of my talk that I have tried to put off as long as possible—venturing an idea on what you can do about it.

Essentially, most of your problems stem from the fact that people don't understand you and your business, they're suspicious of you and your motives, and they don't really want to see you prosper because they regard your prosperity as hurting their pocketbooks.

It's common for a public relations man in a talk such as this to conclude by prescribing an economic education for the public. Profits, he'll say, are the goose that laid the golden egg. Profits supply the motive force that enables business to give us an ever higher standard of living. Let's teach the people how important profits are to the American Way of Life.

The trouble with that prescription is that a large proportion of your audience regards your message as self-serving. As you launch into your sermon, a voice in the back of the hall says, "Look who's talking."

Don't mistake my message. I'm not saying that your argument about profits isn't sound or that it wouldn't be nice if the public listened to it and agreed with you. I'm just saying that they aren't willing to give you a fair hearing. In fact, in many instances they want to deprive you of the advertising budgets you would use to educate them.

What should you do then? My prescription is that you must become better politicians—in the best sense of the word. What do I mean? I mean you must identify and foresee the public's needs and concerns—and convey in a persuasive way that you are out to advance the public's interests. Before you can educate the public, you have to become the kind of teacher they like and trust. Increasingly, I submit you are going to have to run for your office.

In the midst of the gasoline shortage, I turned on the television to find a camera crew on location at a gasoline line. What took them there? They were covering one of our Senators who was out sticking his head through the car windows taking the public pulse and promising Congressional action. If my prescription were followed, the man on the gasoline line—and the television tube—would have been a top official of the oil company supplying the gasoline station.

"If the chairman of the board runs for his office, who's going to run the business?" you may ask. "We've got a public affairs officer to take care of the political matters."

The trouble with most public affairs officers is they spend too much time advising management on how to cultivate politicians and too little time teaching management how to be politicians themselves. Politics today is essential to running the store.

Going to the People

After the past few years of scandals over campaign contributions, any indirect attempt by management to influence legislation through politician surrogates is going to come in for sharp scrutiny and public criticism. You're going to have to go to the people.

Where should you begin?

I don't propose to give you a nuts-and-bolts program for either consumer or financial relations here today. I'm sure you've heard speeches of that kind—although I'll be glad to talk about specifics in the question-and-answer period.

I would begin by making sure you know where you are. First, I would take a leaf from the politician's notebook and do some careful opinion surveying to find out how you stand with your publics —particularly your customers; to find out what their beefs are about you, for example, and what's troubling them that might mean trouble for you.

I would then develop a program that dramatically conveys that you share the public's concerns and want to help meet its needs.

In my firm's rate relief work, which has been growing rapidly, we have found that economic concerns such as job security and new jobs for young people often make a very useful juncture point for identifying with the public interest. Throughout the country urbanization has meant that many young people are lost to local communities because of a lack of economic opportunity. There are many ways to show leadership in changing this trend in your community. Rate relief, put in the context of a broader program of this kind, may prove a lot easier for the public to take.

However carefully you plan to show your concern for the public interest, you'll come to grief if your own management and work force aren't carefully organized and trained to convey that same concern. Too often operating officers tend to think of the most efficient way to get their job done without taking public opinion into account. A high level public relations/public affairs officer must be given enough authority to make sure other company officials don't step on the public's toes. He must also have broad authority to assure that you have the kind of training programs that prevent representatives down the ranks from being quoted in public-be-damned type statements. One thoughtless or ill-phrased statement from a single spokesman on television may very well cost you your election.

Increasingly, we find ourselves counseling top company officials on how to handle television appearances and interviews. This should be part of such a training program.

As with any political campaign, you must take the initiative and make news that identifies you with the public interest. This requires careful planning and good organization. It also calls for continuing opinion surveys to make sure you're on the right track. Is your advertising too high pressure, for example? Are you as persuasive as you think you are?

Importance of Shareholders

In such a campaign one very valuable group of constituents is your shareholders. In these times, individuals are leaving the market, turned off by inflation and big losses on their investments. Some financial officers tell me they couldn't care less. The individual shareowner, they say, is a crank who owns 30 shares and writes nasty notes to the chairman. With institutions doing most of the trading, why care about the individual at all?

For one thing, a few weeks of selling by individuals can cause an institutional money manager to take another look at his block of your stock. He may decide to sell too. If too many individuals sell, who's going to sop up inventory? Down on Wall Street, things being what they are, nobody wants to position a big block and wait for a buyer. Chances are if one institutional money manager sells today, they all decide he must know something and sell too. The block houses consequently don't want to be caught with a big position in the face of such selling pressure. Under the circumstances, individual ownership helps to bolster the liquidity of your stock.

But more important, individual owners in your operating area are apt to be a receptive audience for your economic message. Far too little is being done to build local shareownership and to enlist shareowner support for objectives of mutual gain. What might I suggest? Close rapport with local brokers and visits to individual owners, for example.

Let's assume that you get the public with you and are successful at getting the kind of understanding that enables you to get rate relief and report higher earnings. Won't you run the risk of turning your customers off as you turn the investment community on?

Spending in the Public Interest

The danger here, it seems to me, comes from telling your earnings story the way Joe Blowhard might have told it. For every earnings improvement story you put out, there ought to be a dozen about what you're doing with the money in the public interest. You can't expect the editors to carry all of the news in one article so you will have to space out the capital expenditure stories over time so that earnings improvements are put in their proper economic context. But even then no earnings story should go—in your operating territory at least—without your including additional material that identifies your progress with public concerns.

What about the security analysts and the money managers? Are they going to be interested in all of that local news? I submit that they had better be. Increasingly, the security analyst who keeps his job is going to be one who knows a company that is able to get rate relief from one that cannot. You may have to educate the analyst, too.

Admittedly, all of this is going to take enormous planning and great political savvy. It will also take patience—in gaining of both consumer and investor understanding. Even though your price-earnings ratio doesn't react overnight, you're going to have to continue to meet regularly with analysts, money managers and shareowners, maintaining your credibility at all costs through talking frankly about good news and bad.

I hope you agree with me as you stare into the wind over the sand trap across the water hole at the far off green, that I've selected a promising club for you. Given the kind of sand trap and water hazard we are talking about, I want to wish you the desert stamina of Lawrence of Arabia and the navigational skills of Sinbad the Sailor.

4

Won't Anybody Listen?

By Stan Sauerhaft

*Before the American Society of Corporate
Secretaries, Cleveland, March 13, 1974*

SUMMARY: How do you convince the investment community to
consider your company when making its next buying decision? What
is it like out there where you have to compete for an audience? What
sort of audience do you want? What sort will you settle for? The
makeup of the investment community is changing. There have been
increasingly stringent disclosure regulations placing unprecedented
demands on corporate financial communicators. The security analyst
has also been changing. There are many fewer, but those left wield
greater influence than ever. Also, for those companies whose stock is
languishing, there looms increasingly the threat of takeover. So don't
ignore your current stockholders, who are after all owners of the
corporation and a potential first line of defense. And don't forget the
financial press, for it can provide a foundation and backdrop for any
corporation's financial communications program.

Stan Sauerhaft, who has Bachelor's and Master's degrees from the University of Michigan, has been
a lecturer at Columbia University, is the author of *The Merger Game* (Thomas Y. Crowell, 1971) and
of numerous articles, and is an executive vice president of Hill and Knowlton, Inc.

It was more than 100 years ago when Charles Dickens wrote about an even earlier era that "It was the best of times, it was the worst of times, it was the age of wisdom, it was the age of foolishness, it was the epoch of belief, it was the epoch of incredulity."

Well, most wise observers of the Wall Street scene today would go along with old Charlie on about half of that crusty statement: It is the *worst* of times all right (and may be getting still worse), it is an age of damned foolishness, and it is certainly an epoch of incredulity. Nobody seems to believe anything. And if they do, they want to change it.

So in this something-less-than-friendly atmosphere, in one of the worst bear markets in American business history, you consider your problem of telling the investment community that they ought to consider your company when they make their next buying decision. Why you? For that matter, *who you*?

Are you a top-tier company? Then your problem may be small. But you're in a diminishing minority. One by one the favored few have been dropping out, seemingly never to return. Xerox, Johnson & Johnson, IBM, Baxter Labs, Merck—they still hold on, but the whispers are always there and beginning to grow even about them.

Are you a second-tier company? Most companies like to think they are at least that. They're in the tier ready to step up and over the fallen top tierers. Either they've got good recent earnings performances or great near-term prospects. But all their improving earnings seem to do is lower their price/earnings ratios, and nobody seems to give a hoot about their prospects.

And what if you're not even in the second tier? What is it like out there where you have to compete for an audience? What sort of audience do you want? What sort will you settle for?

Growth of Institutional Investment

In 1963, institutional investors accounted for 35 percent of the dollar value of New York Stock Exchange daily trading volume. By 1973, they accounted for more than 70 percent, and in some stocks, more than 90 percent.

Although the 30 million individual investors still hold the lion's share of outstanding securities—some 60 percent of common shares —institutions have increased their holdings from 30 percent in 1962 to 40 percent today.

Business Week magazine pointed out that there is now even a "super class" of institutional investors, if you will—the bank trusts. They control some $330 billion of the $500 billion worth of securities held by all institutional investors. Just two banks—Morgan Guaranty and Bankers Trust—together hold more stocks and bonds than all the 500-odd mutual funds in the U.S.!

We've often heard it said that bigness *per se* is not bad, but it's just what people may do with it that can be bad. The institutions, and particularly the bank trusts, have been severely criticized for misuse of their power in recent days. Although there is a certain degree of exaggeration by their critics, it is not really unfair to say that they have elected to concentrate much of their buying power on The Chosen, a few dozen growth stocks commonly referred to as the "top tier." Among just the 10 largest bank trust departments, holdings in the 10 most popular stocks average around 25 percent of the companies' shares outstanding. In some cases, bank trust holdings run as high as 40 percent of total outstanding. And many smaller banks around the country emulate them.

In a recent poll of bank trust departments, it was discovered that 22 corporations are included in the 25 largest holdings of more than 100 banks.

Ever-expanding Disclosure Rules

Against this backdrop of a professionally dominated marketplace, we have the seeming incongruity of a growing paternalism of the SEC and the Exchanges toward investors. Increasingly stringent disclosure regulations today place unprecedented demands on corporate financial communicators. Some recent developments include:

- Increased disclosure of companies' tax accounting policies, commencing December 28, 1973.
- Identification by publicly held corporations of holders of more than one percent of their stock. Now a proposal by two Senate subcommittees.
- A more active role for the SEC in securing greater disclosure in annual reports, called for by SEC Commissioner A. A. Sommer, Jr., on November 1, 1973.*
- Suggestions for reporting the impact of the energy crisis on company earnings and overall financial position have been issued by the American Institute of Certified Public Accountants. It is likely that such a suggestion will in the near future become a requirement.
- New York Stock Exchange recommendations of disclosure of

*See page 46 for new information required.

conflict-of-interest information; five-year summaries of market performance; relationships of common stock and other securities; five-year debt maturities and summaries of earnings.

- Adoption by the SEC, effective August 1, 1973, of substantial changes in Form 10K reporting requirements including information on competitors, backlogs, availability of materials, R&D costs, new products and so on.

The list grows longer almost monthly, requiring close monitoring by financial officers and corporate counsel. The trend is toward wide dissemination of the kind of accounting information hitherto limited to that provided in 10K SEC reports, including line-of-business earnings breakouts. In our role as investor relations advisors, we generally use the principle, "When in doubt, disclose."

Dealing with the Superstar Analyst

The SEC is not the only one which is becoming demanding of corporate financial information. The top-drawer security analyst or institutional research department has assumed unprecedented power on Wall Street. Since 1969, 160 firms have folded and another 60 merged. While there are slightly more analysts today than there were in 1971, those in a position of influence have dwindled to a precious few, giving rise to a situation in which massive amounts of capital are being invested on the advice of a very few individuals.

The new "superstar analyst" has tremendous demands upon his time, and quite often upon his operating budget. He is in a profession which does not forgive mistakes, so he is quite guarded in his actions. He wants meaningful facts, and he wants them straight. He has neither the time nor inclination to pry them out of a corporation, since he now enjoys a buyer's market. In recent analyst surveys conducted for clients, we have frequently heard the comment, "Why should I go out of my way to look into such-and-such a company (generally second- or third-tier)? I've got as much as I can handle with the solid companies that have performed well for me." This is a relatively new situation and one with which the corporation will have to cope.

Time and budget limitations aside for the moment, there is another factor to be appreciated when viewing the needs of analysts today. Analysts are now in the process of attempting to professionalize their occupation (Chartered Financial Analysts Association). As in any group going through this process, there is a great deal of internal trauma accompanied by a certain amount of external puffery. It is wise to take this into consideration when assessing how to deal with an analyst.

Ways to Cope with the Raiders

For the corporation which fails to impress the sophisticated financial community and whose stock is languishing in the doldrums, there looms today a threat above and beyond the inability to attract capital investment—a takeover by unfriendly outsiders.

Conditions in the stock market ominously point to an active season for corporate takeover attempts.

First, there are lots of bargains around—stocks trading at four, five and six times earnings for the first time in decades, in fact, very possibly since the Depression. Hundreds of these shares are considerably below book value. Many are actually priced below their *net working capital* —what would be left over if the company's long-term debt were paid off. Such companies are obviously vulnerable not only to a cash tender offer, but a stock exchange offer or combination offer as well.

Incredibly, and frustratingly, many of these low P/E companies are enjoying one of their greatest profit years, which does nothing but further lower their P/E because their stock price does not keep up with their rising earnings. Out of favor with, or unnoticed by, the investment leaders of Wall Street, these companies nevertheless may not escape the eye of the raider.

New conditions in the past year compound the problem for the target company. There has been an appreciable reduction in the number of stockholders in the market, perhaps more than a million. This means greater concentration of stock holdings, which enables a raider to make fewer stops on his shopping spree and simplifies his job.

Furthermore, there are billions of devalued dollars in foreign hands looking for a good place to go. The energy crunch which descended suddenly last fall may have forced some revising of timetables. But that crisis seems to be easing now in Europe, and some foreign swingers may find they will have more operating room again. Then, too, there is the massive buildup of petro-dollars which need some place to go.

Initiating a Financial Relations Program

For all the usual reasons, but particularly in light of this takeover threat, today's lower-tier corporation should want to broaden the holding of its stock through a deliberate and aggressive financial relations program.

Such companies should first determine the kind of program that best suits their needs. We generally recommend to our clients an initial survey of financial opinion leaders, fund managers and analysts, to find out what they think of the company. What are its strengths and weaknesses? How do they regard it relative to its competitors? Is it providing the professional investment community with all required information? Does it have credibility on Wall Street? What actions, if any, would improve the analyst's view of the company?

One technique we have found effective is to bring in three or four leading analysts in the company's field and conduct an unstructured devil's advocate roundtable session on the company and its industry. The interplay of the analysts' comments simulates the kind of meeting where they might normally exchange their ideas and form each other's opinions. Listening in can be very educational.

Once the brain of the analyst has been picked—and often a third party can do that better or more objectively than a member of the corporate staff—you can begin to tailor your communications strategy to correct misimpressions, point up positive points that are being overlooked, and even correct deficiencies of substance.

But don't take your current stockholders for granted. They are, after all, owners of the corporation and a source of "buy" recommendations to potential stockholders. You also want to keep them loyal to the company and holding onto their stock. Furthermore, they are very necessary to have on your side should a takeover be threatened.

This last role of current stockholders is by no means the least. Many a close-mouthed corporation, facing a proxy fight or a tender offer, has found it awkward and often futile to suddenly cozy up to estranged stockholders. In the first place, the sudden torrent of communications looks suspect. In the second place, if you haven't been sufficiently in touch with your stockholders, then you probably have not adequately communicated constructive information which might make them willing to hold out in the face of a fat tender offer or beguiling proxy appeal.

Generally, the most effective defense against a well-organized raid or the ominous rumblings of a dissident group is a background of thorough prophylactic communicative measures on the part of management. These measures include informative and meaningful annual and quarterly reports; well-organized annual meetings and follow-up reports; regional stockholder meetings where warranted, and stockholder newsletters where appropriate. As I mentioned earlier, the trend of SEC disclosure regulations is toward inclusion of SEC-required report materials in Annual and Interim Reports to stockholders. It would be to a corporation's benefit to be in the vanguard of this movement.

We have recently been experimenting with stockholder surveys for much the same reason as we use analyst surveys. They indicate attitudes among current stockholders which might assist in their retention and in the development of programs to attract new ones.

Having taken effective rearguard action with current stockholders, you are in a position to develop and pursue an aggressive analyst relations program based, ideally, on a survey of the type mentioned earlier.

Giving the Analyst What He Wants

In recognition of the situation I outlined at the outset, your initial efforts should be in the direction of the most important analysts who are generally based in New York. They are the trend setters and provide a greater return on your investment of communications effort. If you get to the big bank trust department leaders, the major pension funds and the major brokerage houses, their research sales networks will also take your story all over the country.

A well-planned program for exposing analysts to your operations should include an information-gathering function within your company, to provide the data the analyst has indicated he wants. It should establish a corporate analyst contact who has access to all corporate information, who knows the company and its top executives well, who has ready access to the chief executive officer and can schedule the latter's time for personal analyst contact. Regularized contact should be established with the more important analyst so he knows when to expect information and whom to contact at any time. The program should solicit invitations for appearances at major analyst functions as well as offering an open door to analyst visits. It should periodically solicit constructive criticism of itself from the analyst. He should be included on the distribution list for all corporate financial communications, not only to offer information but to demonstrate your communications program's extent. Conversely, all information externally printed about the company should be presented, eliminating the need for him to "go out of his way." Only then can you expect your company to get a reasonable hearing.

I dwell on the big "superstar analysts" of New York in recognition of the fact that brokerage house research, and increasingly that of banks, is being disseminated out of New York to institutions all over the country. Smith Barney alone has over 800 clients buying its research. However, corporations cannot afford to neglect the financial institutions in their own communities. Aside from merely broadening the holding of stock, statistics show that home-town holders are generally fiercely loyal during crises. In addition, the spillover into community relations from this type of investor relations is obvious.

Role of the Financial Press

There is some debate over the role of the major financial press in the investment community. There are those who feel that favorable exposure is vital to the sale of a company's stock, while others feel that with the exception of perhaps *The Wall Street Journal*, Alan Abelson's column in *Barron's* and Robert Metz's in *The New York Times*, it is not the press but rather the analysts and fund managers who move investment.

Regardless of what motivates individual transactions, few will dispute that the financial press provides a foundation and backdrop for any corporation's financial communications program. It develops credibility and it can add impressive third-party endorsement.

But competition for space on the financial pages is severe. An aggressive, but subtle, sales program is required to get attention for your company. You must be able to interest the editors in terms of what they think their readers want to learn. It also helps to understand the special attitudes and biases of leading editors and columnists. The most salable item these days seems to be the personal interview with a chief executive officer who is prepared to discuss prospects and broad developments. If he is a good public speaker, all the better, since prestigious forums may open to him which will attract the financial press.

Since I opened this little talk on a literary note, it is only fitting that I close it with some grace notes from the same old London sage, Charles Dickens: "The winds you are going to tempt," he wrote in *David Copperfield*, "have wafted thousands upon thousands to fortune and brought thousands upon thousands happily back."

The winds these days are treacherous. You would do well to test them thoroughly before wafting your fragile corporate story.

But once you have assessed the breezes, by all means push with all possible ingenuity and determination. You owe your stockholders nothing less.

5

Your Annual Report: Verbal Thicket or Best-Seller?

By Edward O. Raynolds

SUMMARY: Many managements struggle with their annual reports as if they were writing the Magna Carta. But the end product is often a dull, legalistic document that stockholders throw in the wastebasket after a quick glance. An annual report can be successful only if you can get people to read it. Company managements would do well to take a page from the magazine publishers and attract report readership with inviting graphics, plain talk and a sense of the real drama of business.

Edward O. Raynolds brings a background in journalism, the American Stock Exchange and graduate study in business and finance to his work as vice president in Hill and Knowlton's Financial Relations Division.

At a time when business more than ever needs to explain itself, the annual report still ranks as the single most important communication a company issues all year.

Yet all too often, the annual report's message never gets off the launching pad. It's lost in the thicket of corporatese that teams of management, accountants and lawyers have hammered out in endless sessions of nitpicking. While the end product finally meets all the objections of its drafters, it fails utterly to engage its audience.

Many managements, once immersed in the rigors of putting out the annual report, lose sight of the obvious: A communications document does its job only when you can get someone to read it.

Consider the following:

- Nearly one-third of the stockholders in a recent survey agreed with this statement: "Since annual reports are so difficult to understand and read, they are of no substantial help to me."
- Forty-two percent admitted they don't understand the notes to the financial statements.
- Three-quarters of the sample wanted explanation of the report's financial information in less technical terms.
- And yet nearly 83 percent *disagreed* with this statement: "My stockbroker and the financial analysts have studied and analyzed my company's annual report and therefore there is no need for me to do so."

Clearly, stockholders want their annual reports to talk to them. But they need help from management in deciphering the message.

New Demands from SEC and Readers

Recent pressures from the Securities and Exchange Commission and the stock exchanges for added annual report disclosure make the communications job even more of a challenge. New information now required by the SEC includes:

- Breakout of sales and pre-tax earnings by lines of business.
- A special five-year summary of operation, with a management analysis of the most recent three years.
- Principal occupations or employments of all officers and directors, with principal businesses of outside employers.
- Quarterly dividend payments and market price ranges of voting securities over past two years.
- Brief description of the company's business.

The broadened social role now demanded of business creates new tasks for the communicator and places still other requirements on the annual report:

- Establishing credibility for business so that its efforts to explain itself will meet with public acceptance.
- Communicating the activities of business that spell out its wider social involvement.
- Getting across business's position with respect to the new legal and regulatory measures, proposed almost daily, which affect it.

How can the annual report meet these new demands and still be an interesting, arresting document that's easy to read and understand?

First, it's useful to recognize that a company issuing an annual report really has the same problem as the publisher of a popular magazine: attracting readership. The publisher needs it to boost circulation, obtain advertising revenue and stay in business. The company needs it to get its message to investors and continue to be able to attract public capital.

Companies don't usually think this way because most of their circulation is controlled: the annual report is sent to a given number of stockholders. But its readership isn't controlled. The average stockholder receives several annual reports every year, and those that don't engage his interest are likely to wind up in the wastebasket after a cursory glance.

Attracting readership for an annual report is much the same as attracting readership for a magazine. For starters, the graphics should be good. The overall design should be clean and interesting-looking. It should invite the reader into the report. White space should be used occasionally to relax the eye and focus attention on the report elements. The type should be large and legible, with enough space for easy reading.

The writing should be clear and crisp. Short sentences are best. Language should be direct. Technical and financial information should be presented in layman's terms. Active voice should be used most of the time; it indicates that management is doing things rather than having things happen to it. Short paragraphs and active-verb subheads are useful in leading the reader into the report.

Readers tend to approach written material in layers. With an annual report, for example, the reader looks at the cover, takes in the financial highlights and leafs through the rest of the report. He may then come back to read the president's letter and go on to the main text and financials. A good annual report invites readership by encouraging the reader to go from one layer to another.

Graphics, text and even financial information combine to do the job. An attractive cover makes a reader want to see what's inside. Good headlines encourage him to read the underlying text. Interesting photos and captions can summarize the year's story for the casual reader and whet his appetite for more detail.

Financial and other numerical data can be presented interestingly in charts and graphs. The charts and graphs then become a way of attracting attention to the rest of the report. This technique converts the problems posed by more financial disclosure into an opportunity: the new financial information becomes a focus of attention rather than just that much added detail.

A review of the best recent annual reports reveals a strong trend toward more imaginative use of graphics to highlight quantitative information. It appears certain that we may expect an even greater use of graphics to present financial information in future annual reports.

Good graphics also get at the much-discussed problem of making annual reports useful both for people with financial training and for the unsophisticated layman. Obviously, putting quantitative information in a chart or graph makes it easier for the untutored person to assimilate.

Differential Disclosure

Of course, much financial information can only be expressed by words and statistical tables. How, then, do you do this without losing the layman?

The SEC has been exploring a concept called "differential disclosure." Essentially, this means making detailed technical disclosure in a source used by sophisticated investors, such as an SEC-filed form, and presenting less technical, summarized information in a "popular" source, such as an annual report.

Differential disclosure can be accomplished *within* an annual report, as well. For example, a report can employ a financial review section which places the most detailed financial information in a single place in the report. Sophisticated investors can go there to find it, but an average stockholder doesn't have to read it if he doesn't want to. (The New York Stock Exchange has recommended the use of financial review sections.)

This doesn't mean that the appearance and presentation of the financial review should say, "for sophisticated readers only." On the contrary, the information in the review should be made as clear and as readable as possible to encourage the average stockholder to peruse it. So should the data in the financial notes. Naturally, the most significant financial facts should also appear in the financial highlights, or be explained clearly in the president's letter.

In making financial information palatable to the average investor, management may wish to consider what else may be on his mind. They might put themselves in the stockholder's place and ask what they'd like most to know about the company if they were looking in from the outside. For example, mightn't they, as stockholders, want to know what's going on in *management's* mind?

Mightn't they want to know what is management's philosophy for running the company? Where they want it to go? How they plan to get it there? This kind of thinking, incidentally, has a benefit outside the annual report. It can sometimes be a useful exercise for management in more clearly defining its own goals and objectives.

Making the President's Letter Work

All too often, the president's letter in an annual report simply gives a bland recitation of what went on during the year, expresses hope that business will be better next year and thanks the employees for their loyal service. But a president's letter reaches investors better when it asks them in effect to sit down in the executive suite and listen to management's thinking. For example, it should set forth goals and strategy and give a concrete example or two of how management is implementing its strategy. This tends to engender investor confidence, while painting a picture of a ship being buffeted by the waves of chance causes concern.

Of course, such a delineation must be believable. Problems, and a plan for solving them, should be discussed candidly—along with the year's accomplishments. There should be an indication of management's progress in meeting goals that were set forth in the past.

Bad results should be dealt with openly, so that the reader knows management has told him the worst. He shouldn't feel there are surprises that can surface unexpectedly.

Believability is crucial in the president's letter. since it represents management talking directly to shareholders and sets the tone for the report. But the rest of the report should be no less credible.

Simply showing a willingness to communicate can go a long way. Being generous with information indicates an open, candid management that wants investors to know as much as possible. Being stingy with it betokens tight-lipped secretiveness. Investors naturally place more trust in managements that communicate.

Going beyond Disclosure

A management that goes beyond disclosure requirements, includes pertinent information from SEC-filed documents, gives progress reports on various operations, describes research and development activities, discusses competitive conditions and market shares—this kind of management informs investors and establishes its desire to communicate.

With critics currently questioning the role of business in society, nowhere is credibility more essential than in discussions of corporate social responsibility. Broad, unsupported statements of do-goodism in the annual report turn people off and may even suggest a cynical management.

But annual reports cannot avoid addressing the social role of business, either. Even for the industrial company with little impact on consumers, questions like environmental impact, plant safety and hiring practices are on people's minds and should be dealt with.

Discussions of social questions succeed best when management gives some notion of what it believes its social responsibilities should be. It then places itself in the active position of setting its own social goals and describing its progress in meeting them. Otherwise, it's on the defensive trying to meet standards others have set for it.

Management shouldn't try to pretend its record is perfect. Problems encountered in meeting social goals should be discussed fully. An acknowledgment that the company needs to make more progress in a given social area enhances credibility and disarms critics. Management might even consider setting forth what it believes should be a proper balance between incurring economically nonproductive social costs and fulfilling its fiscal responsibilities.

Management's best efforts to get its story across will, of course, be futile unless it can tell it interestingly enough to engage people's attention. There's no reason, however, why the story need be dull.

Most companies' affairs involve a good deal of excitement over a year's time. There are deals negotiated, new products introduced, new processes perfected. Even a management information system that flashes data from the divisions to headquarters for better decision making embodies a sort of excitement. Unfortunately, little of the suspense comes across in the annual report.

Management usually is reluctant to lay bare the real drama of its operations. It may fear that shareholders would interpret excitement as instability, or that doing so would undermine the impression of dignity it is trying to project. Possibly so.

But it might well convert the annual report from a dry-as-dust dissertation to a corporate best-seller.

6

Tender Offer Anxiety?
Good Stockholder Relations
Is the Best Tonic

By Richard E. Cheney

*Before the AMR International, Inc. Conference
on Tender Offers, Sheraton-St. Regis Hotel,
New York City, January 22-23, 1975*

SUMMARY: Companies concerned about possible raids can't sit
back and relax after they have prepared a "black book" battle plan.
Planning won't do any good if company shareholders are not willing
to support management. The best way to encourage support from
shareholders, and employees, too, is through a continuing communications effort.

Richard Cheney, an executive vice president of Hill and Knowlton, and veteran of many of the major
proxy fights and tender offer contests of the last 15 years, has spoken before bar associations,
management seminars, major financial public relations meetings and business schools in the U.S.,
Japan and Europe.

Far too many managements today react to the possibility of a tender offer with what I call Maginot Line mentality. They try to bind up all their anxieties in a black book full of phone numbers of their fight team, boiler plate ads and letters to stockholders plagiarized from *The Wall Street Journal*, and detailed schedules of who calls whom after the offer is announced. Then they either lapse into an ill-advised sense of security or wait like sailors in the hold of a transport listening for the gurgle of an oncoming torpedo.

In all their frenzy to get prepared, they fail to address themselves to a basic question, the answer to which is essential to their defensive effort: "Why should anybody keep this company's stock anyway if somebody makes him a decent tender offer?"

A year or so ago, in an effort to help a company prepare for a possible tender offer, I asked the financial officer, "Would you buy your company's stock at current prices?"

He replied, "Pragmatically speaking, I wouldn't."

Pragmatically speaking, he would have been in a terrible fix if he were faced with a tender offer, no matter how many phone numbers he had written down.

Emergency Plans Are Not Enough

I am not arguing against an emergency plan in the event of a tender offer, although I would caution you that the wrong kind of plan, if subpoenaed, might prove embarrassing, or worse, if your board were charged in court with not giving a raider's offer fair consideration. What I am arguing is that a valid defense effort should extend beyond the limited scope of most emergency plans currently being devised to ward off corporate raids.

In fact, Maginot Line mentality may be what gets a lot of companies into the tender offer predicament in the first place. Many such companies, before the onset of panic over a raid, have regarded their stockholders as adversaries. They've deluded themselves with what I call the Aunt Jane fallacy, stereotyping the owners as little old ladies in sneakers looking for a free lunch or cranks who write fractious and irrelevant notes in the margins of proxy cards, despite the fact that such owners make up an insignificant minority of the shareowner group as a whole. They ignore the fact that they themselves own stock in other companies and have legitimate expectations from the managements of those companies.

The chairman of one Maginot Line company I know used to take director candidates to lunch before proposing them for the board and tell them, "I want you to know that our board isn't a debating society." The fear of second-guessing from outsiders has led such managements to cut themselves off from the very people whose loyalty they will have to seek when a raid comes.

Like it or not, such companies are well described by John Kenneth Galbraith in *The New Industrial State:* "In the outermost circle in the mature corporation are the ordinary stockholders. This for all practical purposes is a purely pecuniary association. The typical stockholder does not identify himself with the goals of the enterprise; he does not expect to influence these goals. He has a share in the ownership; normally his only concern is that it return him as much money as possible. If he can get more income or capital gain with equal security elsewhere, he sells and invests there. No sense of loyalty—no identification with the goals of the enterprise—normally prevents his doing so . . . The relation of the ordinary stockholder to the corporation is the purest case of pecuniary motivation."

Stockholders as Adversaries

When stockholders are adversaries, it isn't surprising that they remain cynical when management calls them up to inform them of a raid and asks their support. It doesn't take much imagination to picture the stockholder putting his hand over the receiver and saying to his wife, "*Now* they call me . . . " But, based on our experience, the stockholder is so starved for attention, he is delighted about being called concerning his investment even *after* management is under attack. Bear in mind, however, that by then a broker dealer may also be calling him suggesting he tender or sell.

The adversary nature of the management/shareowner relationship is perhaps best illustrated by the fact that most companies have taken surprisingly little trouble to learn who their shareowners are and what they think. A recent report by the American Society of Corporate Secretaries indicates that fewer than 10 percent of U.S. corporations have undertaken stockholder research studies, most of them years ago.

As a further illustration of what I mean by an adversary relationship, let me cite some corporate annual reports. How many corporate annual reports reflect an honest desire on the part of management to communicate with investors about how the company is really doing? How many really come across as showing real concern for the owner? Many of the recent requirements of the Securities and Exchange Commission arise out of this lack of concern for the owner's investment. They reflect the tendency of government to seize any opportunity for expansion by identifying and moving into vacuums of business neglect.

You and I may decry this kind of government intervention and may properly condemn it as opportunistic expansionism at the taxpayer's expense. But the fact remains that the abuses of the Sixties opened the door for such encroachment. In a democracy, politicians get votes by looking for abuses they can rectify and regulatory agencies get political support the same way.

For too many companies the annual report is still an exercise in arms length obfuscation, done with little conviction that the stockholders will read it and sometimes with the hope that they won't read it—at least carefully enough to be aware of its inadequacies.

Think of the consequences for a management which has communicated in such a standoffish way and then finds itself confronted with a takeover attempt with its livelihood at jeopardy. While relatively few individual companies, as I have noted, have tested the reactions of stockholders to their investor communications, I can cite at least one survey which contained some alarming statistics viewed from the point of view of managers who find themselves at bay.

The survey was conducted by Marc J. Epstein, associate professor of accounting at California State University. Professor Epstein sent questionnaires to 2,000 randomly chosen investors, all of whom own at least one round lot of a company listed on the New York or American Stock Exchange. He got 432 responses, which gives the survey a fair degree of reliability.

In this survey nearly 78 percent of the respondents said they would like to see an independent evaluation of management's overall effectiveness—a management audit as contrasted with a financial audit —included in the annual report. If shareowners would like an outside evaluation of management's performance, whom are they going to turn to in the case of a tender offer for advice on whether to keep their shares?

Employees Represent a Neglected Opportunity

Turning from shareowner relations, employee relations is another important area where many managements neglect an important opportunity to strengthen their defenses against a takeover before the threat arises.

A few months ago I was on a plane going to visit a client. Seated behind me on the plane, I discovered from the conversation I overheard, was a member of upper middle management from my client company. He introduced himself to his seat companion who happened to be an investment banker I knew, but who didn't remember me. Most of the conversation from my client company's middle management representative consisted of an apologetic defense of the company we both worked for. He called the company a "sleeping giant."

The fact was—and he really knew this if somebody had forced the truth out of him—that his company has turned in an exceptionally fine improvement in earnings every year for more than five years. Earnings per share are far and away the best in history despite highly conservative accounting policies. The management is tough, innovative and cost-conscious. They don't happen to be glamorous after-dinner speakers, but their performance should speak for itself. But nobody in the company, possibly even including top management itself, is fully convinced of its own ability.

Even if the president and chairman steel up their courage and tell the financial community what they have accomplished, however, they have a lot of their own associates undermining them will ill-advised apologies.

"What difference do such apologetic or critical employees make?" you may ask.

I happened to be on the floor of the New York Stock Exchange talking to a specialist at the time the Arabs ended the oil embargo. This specialist happened to have a private aircraft manufacturer's stock assigned to him. I watched while the stock moved up from six to nine dollars on incoming orders and almost all of the orders came from the small town in the Midwest where the manufacturer's headquarters were located. The people buying shares I'm sure were either employees or investors heavily influenced by employees. Stock in their hands might very well be a lot safer for management in the case of a tender offer than stock in the hands of some institutions. In fact, it might be argued that any stock has a retinue of followers who may be in or out of it at any given time, but who are an important, if unrecognized, influence on investment decisions in case of a tender. They're like fans who may or may not be in the ball park on any given day. Employees are an important part of this fan club and too many managements fail to regard them as a force worth cultivating. When management is not a hero to its own valet, so to speak, it may be hurting its reputation more broadly than it thinks.

Your work force can be a help in a takeover. In a recent fight in which I was involved, the chief executive officer had made a determined effort to build the loyalty of all his employees, including the men and women who worked in the plant. He invited them to company headquarters for beer and a barbecue and got to know them firsthand. Incidentally, I might add this didn't hurt his labor relations either.

When the fight first started, he dropped the employees a note describing the firing practices of the hatchet man who was after the company. All hell broke loose among the work force. Soon there was trouble from the local Congressmen and other government officials who knew votes when they saw them.

Perhaps I can sum up this somewhat sketchy treatment of why a good defense against a takeover embodies more than an emergency plan by asking you a question: If you're attacked by a mugger, would you rather be in New York City or surrounded by friends?

Suggestions for a Defense Plan

Now that I have argued for the need to build a defense that extends beyond an emergency plan, let me make a few suggestions as to how to go about it. Before I get specific, let me make an overall recommendation about your basic attitude. Decide that you're going to treat your stockholders with respect. You may need them sometime—possibly for capital if not for support in case of a raid. You can't afford to have an adversary relationship with them. Now to the specifics:

1. *Learn as much as possible about your stockholders.* You can build a strong information bank on your stockholders by broadening the data you store about them and the program you have for retrieving it. Your transfer agent already has considerable data at hand, so it's really just a matter of organizing the information properly. You'd be surprised at what you can learn. For example, you might be able to get a notion of those stockholders who bought or sold in connection with certain significant news events or brokerage recommendations. All this could be determined within certain limits from the transfer sheets. Many of our client companies appear to be receptive to this kind of effort. Apart from this kind of intelligence, which is mainly arrived at in a mechanical way, we also try to urge clients to conduct surveys to learn from shareowners what their investment goals are, if they have a price objective, whether they read the annual report, what they like and don't like about management and so on. Such surveys are costly, but not so costly in my opinion as communicating in the dark. We are currently field testing yet another kind of survey, which can be much less expensive in the short run—a survey of shareowners buying and selling stock, which we hope will tell us about what is happening in the marketplace at any given time.

In the case of another client company, we announced in a quarterly report that we would like to communicate directly with owners who held their stock in street name. Then we included a return card that enabled them to send us their names and addresses.

We found that unfortunately some brokers require that you send such an inquiry to all stockholders, including owners with stock in their own names, even though doing so is a waste of money.

Obviously, such a mailing is going to involve duplicate effort since those stockholders who respond will get two sets of reports, proxy statements and so on—one from the company and one from the broker. Moreover, if they sell they will continue to get material from the company until the company sends out a subsequent inquiry to cull its mailing list. But in the case of this particular client, despite all these disadvantages, we felt it was still desirable to make the effort since substantial stock was in street name.

In the event of a raid there is always an unhealthy delay between the time management makes a hold recommendation and the owners of street name stock get that recommendation from management. In the meantime, the broker has plenty of time to urge the owner of street name stock to sell or tender. The effort to get a line on names of street name holders will help such a company get through more quickly to the street name holders who identify themselves.

2. *Treat your stockholders the same way you treat important customers*. Recently I've been getting through the mail personally addressed letters asking me to subscribe to *Reader's Digest* and telling me that I have the opportunity of making money in a raffle whether I sign up or not. They're offering me the Digest for what looks like an astonishing low price for 12 issues. I contrast these personal letters with the kind of letters to shareowners that I frequently encounter—letters that remind me of the fishy-eyed officers who used to squat behind the granite facades of banks in the 1920's rousing up the radical farmers in the Midwest with foreclosures. If *Reader's Digest* personally addresses letters promising a chance for big winnings aggregating $400,000 to thousands of registered voters to try to get a subscription at $2.97 a head, thereby gaining a bigger base for advertising charges, what's wrong with managements' making a similar effort to gain stockholder trust and regard?

Does such an effort work? I have some evidence that suggests it does. The manager of one of our client companies going through tough times started a program of writing brief letters to stockholders whenever he'd solved one of his problems. As he reached letter three, he got a nasty letter back from one stockholder asking ten tough questions in an abrasive way. Our client rephrased the questions to take out the nastiness without changing the substance and made them the subject of yet another letter to stockholders. He said he thought the questions were excellent and he wanted all of the stockholders to have the answers. He called the man who asked him the questions originally, answered the questions and told him what he intended to do. The stockholder was so astonished and impressed, he bought 500 more shares.

In another instance, a client was trying to get approval for a merger against the bitter opposition of a minority stockholder who had designs on the client's company. I was astonished at his resistance to sending thank-you notes for proxies. When he did, he was surprised at the favorable comments he got from stockholders and their resistance to revoking their proxies when they were solicited by his adversary.

Chances are a lot of your company's stock has been sold to your shareowners by brokers who are now driving taxicabs. To the stockholder you're a blind date he's been stuck with. He may feel the same way about you that he felt about the guy who sold him your stock. If you want to keep his regard, you'd better ingratiate yourself.

Why go through all that nuisance for a lot of troublesome stockholders when so many of them own little more than odd lots? With earnings the way they are, why not cut the postage bill? Let me ask you—if you're looking for prospective investors in your stock, who are your best prospects? Who is apt to be influential in the formation of public opinion about your company? Don't underestimate the power of the individual stockholder in influencing your stock price either. With volume as slim as it is for many stocks on any given day, the addition of a few more buy orders in the market can be an effective force in improving your price/earnings ratio. A lot of chief executives have run off chasing money managers and security analysts in the last few years, ignoring the stockholders. They never woke up to the fact that the analysts were looking for stocks to recommend that had shown some action in the marketplace.

I'm not arguing for your ignoring the institution that owns 100,000 shares in your pre-emergency efforts. Obviously, money managers responsible for big blocks need care and attention. But one of the important forces shaping their attitude toward your stock is what is happening to the price of your stock in the market while they are holding on. If enough odd-lot stockholders decide to sell, they may push the price down to where the big money manager decides to sell, too, lest he look like a chump.

With times the way they are, your next question may very well be, "It's all well and good to talk to stockholders, but what if I only have bad news for them?"

While there are always periods of corporate activity in which it's tough to communicate with investors because all the news is bad or the company faces threatening uncertainties, it's been my experience that when managements cite such reasons for not communicating, they may be involved in an internal power struggle or in the majority of instances don't really relish the communications process at all. It is always possible to point to problems, indicate you are working on them, and promise to keep the owners informed. It's better to do this before a raid than it is after the raid is begun.

In a stockholder relations program, there is no substitute for direct meetings with the stockholders. Our clients are beginning to hold such meetings where they have areas of stockholder concentration—inviting both street name and beneficial owners wherever possible. One client recently used retirees to do follow-up calls to stockholders after invitations were mailed to assure a good turnout. This retiree group incidentally has now become an easily mobilized force for proxy solicitation or telephone communications in case of trouble. Obviously any script used in such communications must be filed with the SEC. But, in the event such a script is needed, it will be delivered with feeling.

3. *Encourage investor interest in your company from people who are predisposed toward you.* When I was a bachelor a number of years ago, I learned an important lesson: to take out only the girls who liked me. This saved everybody's time. A lot of managements waste time trying to impress investors who have very little reason to follow their company for various reasons—the size of the float, the character of the business or whatever. They should look for their investing public to people who have a reason to know and possibly like them.

Employees are such a public. Many of you may be dubious about such an assertion, reminded of the employee disaffection encountered by companies that started employee stock purchase plans in the late 60's when stocks were at inflated prices or in the late 1920's when the potential problem was even worse.

May I suggest that you look into the Texas Gulf program of giving all employees stock based on their seniority with the company. Such a program calls for a lot of careful preparation. The SEC has proposed that such gifts require stockholder approval. You can't go forward with such a program if you have preemptive rights. You must file an S-8. There are many other technical problems, particularly if your employees belong to a variety of unions. But such a program should gain employee understanding of profits and also should enhance productivity. The number of shares given away in this fashion will undoubtedly be relatively insignificant in case of a raid—at most, Texas Gulf will distribute 90,000 shares out of 30 million. Yet the support for management this may create should not be underestimated.

Other potential sources of support for management are suppliers, for example. Naturally inclined to be friendly, they may also be good stockholders provided you take the pains to keep them informed about your progress and objectives. Or how about plant town banks and their trust departments? I'm not arguing here for any sort of quid pro quo arrangement with such banks, but simply an information plan to make sure your friends are aware of your accomplishments. I'm sure that other potentially receptive investor audiences will come to mind if you think about it. In this connection, don't neglect the press, particularly the business and trade press. Carrying as it does the authority of objectivity, the press can have a devastating impact on the outcome of a tender offer. It's vital to treat reporters and editors fairly and with respect at all times, and to build with them a relationship of mutual trust and regard.

Finally, in all that I have said, I would hope that nothing implies that I am advocating that you whitewash a hog. You really won't get very far trying to convince your investing public that you shouldn't be kicked out in the snow on the seat of your pants unless you're really striving to be exceptional managers—even constructive members of society. Look at all your actions in terms of their consequences in public opinion if the raid comes off. Does your proxy statement show a raise in management compensation when you've shut down plants and cut your dividends? Do your Form 4's show management sales of stock when you've been urging the world to buy? If any of the members of this panel happens to be on the other side in the event you're raided, rest assured they will use anything they can get against you. An emergency plan neatly typed up in a black book, a red book, green book or a yellow book isn't going to stand in their way.

GOVERNMENT
RELATIONS

7

Come on Communicators— Communicate

By Robert K. Gray

SUMMARY: Not since the great depression of the 1930s has Washington held business in such low esteem. While Watergate has left business under siege, it has also turned the spotlight of public attention on business and created a new audience. Now that business has the public's attention it should move quickly to take advantage of the communications opportunity to sell its best story.

Robert Keith Gray, who served President Eisenhower first as Appointments Secretary and later as Secretary of the Cabinet, is executive vice president of Hill and Knowlton, Inc., in charge of the Washington office.

It is unfair for those of us who call Washington home to imply we had more at stake in the churning wake of Watergate. But perhaps we can be forgiven for the speed with which we went into political shock and our difficulties in coming out of it. After all, Washington is a one-company town. Government just happens to be the company. The President of the Company just happens to be the President of the United States. And the players in the drama happen to be the men we had dinner with last night, attended a meeting with this morning and whose wives are playing bridge with ours this afternoon. Under the circumstances it is impossible to be objective.

One point upon which objective observers do agree is that the fallout from Watergate is not limited to Washington but like radiation from an atomic blast, it has touched every individual and institution within its range.

The credibility of businessmen and business institutions has taken as much of a shellacking as government in the deterioration of general confidence. Every institution in American life is under fire from its constituency.

From the federal government to business, to organized religion to free press, even to professional sports, some have lost the faith and others are questioning. Do the three branches of government really work, or worse yet, will they survive? Is business really only concerned with profits with a basic "damn the consumer" attitude? Are clergy more concerned about budgets than human needs? Is an irresponsible free press about to tyrannize us all? Why can't you buy a Redskins football ticket without denying your family dinner for the football season?

Even God, flag and motherhood, the safe subjects of old, will draw an argument on any street corner. The Supreme Court has outlawed prayer. If you fly the flag, the neighbors think you are opening a Post Office, and overpopulation has given motherhood a bad name, or as some put it, made it a bitter pill to swallow. It's become a lollipop world with everybody trying to get his licks in.

Business in Low Esteem

Polls show that after 40 years of effort, business has failed to get Americans to improve their notions of business challenge or profits. Sure, we are trying to tell the public the truth about business earnings, but Watergate has bent all credibility so severely that we have difficulty at times believing ourselves, much less each other.

Not since the great depression of the 1930's has Washington held business in such low esteem. This is so even though we have a trillion-dollar GNP increasing at more than $100 billion a year. Business executives are rightly anxious about this. Many are frankly discouraged as proposals mount for new legislation and regulatory actions that would hamstring their freedom of action, raise their costs, narrow down their options and bring government more deeply into partnership with business.

Taken together, many of the proposals now under study, and many of the laws and regulations now on the books, amount to official skepticism about both the will and intent of American business to improve the standards of life for the nation. Faith in free competition as a force for good has faded.

What are some of the proposals on Capitol Hill that business must be concerned about? Except for a few pieces of legislation, it would probably be unfair to characterize any of the bills being considered by the Congress as purely "anti-business." However, many supported in principle by the business community have provisions that tinker with the free operation of the marketplace. These intrusions, while still predominantly in the traditional area of taxation, now range well beyond that, and under the guises of energy, environment, and consumer protection the government continues to complicate the decision-making process and increase the cost of doing business.

Politics vs. Economics

Clearly Watergate has left business under siege. Look at the legislation on tap, the opposition, public reaction to the oil industry's problems of this year. Now it is obvious that consumer advocates are decrying business products and prices; labor officials denouncing multinational operations, and environmentalists limiting the building of new energy sources and manufacturing facilities. They are all clamoring away and that's bad news for business. But the worst news for business is not the opposition, but the mindset of the business community from within.

As long as business stays in a defensive, shoring-up posture, others will assume leadership roles. Unless business determinedly enters the arena of public debate and does so immediately, politics will rule over economics. The solution that has all too often been proposed will become an institutionalized solution to all the problems ahead—increased restraints on free enterprise.

It may be that Watergate has not brought new problems to business so much as it has turned the spotlight of public attention on our old ones. In either case, we can benefit from it. Benefit first by a new realization of the problems which face us and second by the public's new level of interest in hearing our story. There is a new readiness among many to listen. Now that the political processes are under heavy fire, that shortages and economic crises are being felt, many who never seemed to be paying attention or cared about hearing, are eager to learn and to be part of the decisions so vital to our future.

Public Concern Creates New Opportunities

A new audience is a definite plus-result of Watergate. We could talk at length about the political science aspects of Watergate, its effects on the modern Presidency and the tri-partite system of government. What Watergate has done to the people's spirit is a more important point. Faith in the democratic model is not dead or dying. While many bemoan the current situation, there are signs of intense growing interest in the political system—this growth from the people themselves. Common Cause is increasing membership at 20,000 per month instead of the pre-Watergate rate of 5,000 per month. People want to be concerned.

Men who never thought of running for Congress are tossing their hats in the ring, and citizens who never dreamed of campaigning for anyone are telephoning, shaking hands, and being informed enough to present their candidate's views. The Watergate jolt to our political system has engendered a groundswell of grass roots participation in government and attention to things governmental, and that includes business.

The public is concerned, which means we have their attention. Now let's give them the message. We have raised a whole generation of young people who have no idea what their parents do for a living. Let's search out the ways to sell the message that business is not sitting on the sidelines looking at the movements of our time, detached and insensitive. Let us tune in on the wavelength of the average workers and voters. Let's report our earnings in dollars and cents per employee. Let's consider the techniques that are being used around the world to get the worker to listen. Let's find out that makes Volvo in Sweden the model company from an employee's standpoint. Let's study the system of co-determination required by law in Germany. Let's be sure we recognize that the marketplace is multi-colored and multi-sexed when we question whether our Board of Directors is truly representative.

We must bring to the problem of selling the message of business the same level of creativity and interest we bring to new-product marketing and advertising. It is ironic, isn't it, that we in business with our sophisticated market apparatuses can forecast precisely how many boxes of what size can sell in which supermarket, yet only now are we beginning to appreciate either our political or public muscle and how we can flex it.

We must develop spokesmen the public can identify with and trust. And sometimes trust is best evoked by admitting some bad news and giving some tough talk, such as convincing the public that resources do and will run out, that some aspects of our lifestyle must change, that prices and profits are justified and government intrusion into the free enterprise system is counter-productive.

Business technology thrives on a mindset that sees nothing as impossible. We will conquer cancer as certainly as we went to the moon. We will eliminate auto pollution and recycle industrial wastes. We will bring oil to the market from shale and we will develop new forms of energy. The "can do" is there as always it has been.

Why our embarrassment at being businessmen and our apologia about the profit motive? Out of the profits of the free enterprise system come the investment incentive which creates 82,655,000 jobs for America and the revenues for everything from social programs to national defense.

Is it conceivable we in the business community can succeed with such challenges yet fail totally in the challenge of communicating to our government and private publics?

We should move quickly to take advantage of the communications opportunity we have. Our need is imminent and our opportunity is perishable. To paraphrase a famous politician, we soon may not have Watergate to kick around any more, and to put it another way, the public may not always be tuned to every newscast, devouring every printed page and searching for every answer.

8

Larger Stakes
in Statehouse Lobbying

By Martin Ryan Haley and James M. Kiss
(in association with Patricia A. Revey)

Published Originally in
Harvard Business Review January-February, 1974

SUMMARY: "Whereas 20 years ago there were perhaps a few hundred rather weak state administrative agencies, today there are more than 1,500 with considerable clout." That statement of the authors offers a hint of the new era in state capitols that necessitates a more energetic, better planned, and better organized response on the part of corporate government relations departments seeking to retain a voice there. From Washington's revenue-sharing programs and from a citizenry demanding expanded services, power and money are flowing into local government offices as never before. Many state legislatures are dominated by young, socially conscious lawmakers who care less (and often understand less) about business than do their older, more conservative colleagues. Public interest advocacy is a potent force in nearly every capitol. This article analyzes the new era in the states and shows how business must frame its lobbying efforts today to influence local legislation.

Mr. Haley is president of Martin Ryan Haley & Associates, Inc., a firm specializing in government relations and public affairs services. He is writing a book on lobbying based on his vast experience. Mr. Kiss, as executive vice president of Hill and Knowlton, Inc., heads its state and local government relations service. The firms have a close working association. Miss Revey, a former Hill and Knowlton account executive, is currently an international economic consultant.

Executives in one U.S. retail business estimate that they have irretrievably lost nearly one-half billion dollars in sales—not for any legitimate business reason, but because their competitors curried favor among legislators in state capitols while the retailers minded the store. In no fewer than 22 states, competitors who sell the same product, only in different ways, have succeeded in getting this retail group legislated out of business. In several other states, it has been crippled by restrictive legislation.

When the injured retailers finally began to fight back by hiring political experts and dispatching lobbyists into legislative halls, they did it intelligently and unstintingly. The retailers have been largely successful in containing their rivals since then, but they are convinced that, had they acted earlier, by now they would have at least doubled their current $300 million business.

Examples like this one of business ineptitude in state government relations are commonplace. Certain retail opticians, encyclopedia publishers, real estate developers, undertakers, foundry operators, and casualty insurance companies are among the businesses that have lost or are in the process of losing substantial portions of their markets because they are unaware of how important to them state legislation is.

It is folly for a company or trade association to assume that representation in Washington alone suffices. In matters that concern the government relations function, Washington has little to do with state business. Lobbying power flows from the state to the federal level, never the reverse. Whereas the state legislator rarely needs the senator or congressman, Capitol Hill usually relies on the states for political support. Moreover, there are 50 state capitols to cover (51, counting San Juan). And in all of these, legislation that is adverse to business and of a type that rarely merits national consideration because of its ostensible narrowness and specificity, is introduced in every session.

If business has been sluggish in response, if it has practiced self-elimination from the state decision-making process, the difficulty lies as much in a failure of perception as in a disinclination to act. A lot has changed since the days when smoke-filled club cars rattled toward state capitols, their occupants clutching cash-filled black bags to "do a little business" with the legislature. Gone are the days when lobbyists set up card tables in the rear of the house chamber in Wyoming, for example, to pay for votes as they were cast.

In the 1890s, when states were the focus of business concern, a state lawmaker was worth as much as $20 in gold per vote. In the early part of this century, as the federal government increased its power, state legislatures received less corporate attention. The New Deal for a time almost monopolized power in Washington, but in the last few decades the states have steadily gained in influence and money to spend. Nevertheless, business has too often ignored the altered composition of state government and the powerful new forces working at that level.

Rise of the Public Interest Advocate

The consumer and conservation movements of the 1970s trace their origins to the agrarian and urban ferment of the 1890s, when corporate power constituted a shadow government. Unlike their progenitor, the Populist Party, however, today's consumer and conservation groups aim to influence the content of government decisions without organizing to gain office. They have become special interest groups. Lumped under the loose heading of "public interest advocates," and drawing their manpower and money from the middle class, these new interests today provide more than effective checks and balances against business and industry. Their rapid rise to power can be attributed to two elements common to other popular causes throughout history—a charismatic leader and fertile ground in which to grow.

The leader is, of course, Ralph Nader. He had been working on behalf of the consumer interest for some time before he burst into the national limelight. General Motors inadvertently catapulted this spartan, almost ascetic man from the obscure position of a "public interest" lawyer to the status of an American institution. Cast in the role of the underdog fighting against tremendous odds, he appealed to the Puritan strain so deeply embedded in our character and tradition. And his victory in the General Motors affair, with its consequent publicity, encouraged like-minded persons and groups that had been floundering in obscurity and weakness.

Thus emerged a new force in U.S. political life. Or so it seemed; it certainly had a new look. In fact, however, the power wielded by the new public interest advocates is no different in effect from the power wielded by private interest.

But is it different in kind? To the consumer, public interest advocacy looks more wholesome and more legitimate than that of private interest. With a constituency larger than that of business and industry and with noneconomic or nonmaterial objectives, the public interest advocates are accorded great attention in the press. All this notwithstanding, public interest advocates *are* special interests and are not immune from interfering with political accommodation that is defensible and necessary for the general welfare. Even though the "public interest" is not exactly another form of private interest, neither is it free from pursuing the particular at the expense of the elusive, transcendent common good.

Pluralization and Power

Public interest advocacy has found fertile ground for the growth of its movement in the changing nature of government, particularly at the state level. A quiet revolution has taken place in the past decade. Part of this transfiguration is the pluralization of government—the spreading of power in the decision-making process. Emerging before World War II and accelerating markedly in recent years, it is evidenced by a proliferation of power structure at all levels of government.

Witness the mushrooming administrative and regulatory agencies. Practically every state now has its own environmental protection agency. In 1972, at least 63 bills establishing or giving greater power to environmental agencies were introduced in 38 states. Many states also have land use agencies, and, along with many municipalities, have created consumer protection offices. Zoning, once the exclusive province of local political subdivisions, is becoming a concern of the state. Established governmental bodies are either spawning new subdivisions or are themselves assuming new roles and expanded functions. Whereas 20 years ago there were perhaps a few hundred rather weak state administrative agencies, today there are more than 1,500 with considerable clout.

While the public interest groups have shared in the development of state and local pluralization, business—preoccupied with Washington—has not. Public interest advocates, maturing as pluralization has spread, have geared themselves to operate effectively in an atmosphere they understand. Most new state agencies and commissions are created to fit today's social conditions and to serve the "public good." When conflicts arise, this charter gives public interest advocates a decided advantage. Often appearing to share the same goals and values, they and the governmental units form a natural alliance.

According to political scientist James David Barber, pluralization is self-reinforcing. With the creation of each new unit, Barber explains, new interrelationships multiply. They must be coordinated to produce action. The more units there are, the more difficult it is to produce or manipulate reactions and proposals. New agencies vie with the old for jurisdiction. If one unit cannot stop a rival from infringing on its jealously guarded prerogatives, at least it can often block the rival's action.

To get significant proposals adopted, Barber says, a special interest group must exert pressure at an increasing number of points. The group able to sustain its attack over months and even years enjoys an immense advantage over opponents. Without active members, money, time, skills, patience, and especially dedication, an interest group has little chance for government action in its behalf. Therefore, pluralization increases the demand for, dependence on, and power of persons with extraordinary political talents.[1] This is the context in which the rules of the game have changed.

Changes in the Political Arena

But not only the rules have changed; the arena in which the game is played has been all but torn down and rebuilt. Through most of U.S. history, at least up to the 1930s, legislatures conducted their business in a casual and leisurely manner. The atmosphere, when they met for 30 to 90 days every other year, was like that of a comfortable club. With very little communication from one state to another, conducting a nationwide state legislative campaign was so arduous that few undertook it, if indeed they saw the necessity for it.

Information on one of these few national campaigns, one conducted in 1915, shows that typically the national coordinator stayed in New York, Washington, or Chicago and kept in touch by letter or (rarely) by phone. If he visited his lobbyists across the country, the train trip to the Pacific Coast, including stops at the state capitals, consumed at least 45 days. But now, because of advances in communication, local issues arouse national interest, and lobbyists can act promptly on information that was in earlier times unavailable or useless.

Another critical aspect of reconstructed state government is the accretion of power—that is, the ability to influence and modify behavior at the state level. Since 1965, three major changes have transpired:

1. The "one man, one vote" decision of the Supreme Court, which mandated continual reapportionment all over the country.

2. The emergence of the "new politics," which has been aptly defined as a process of campaigning around and outside of established parties and structures.

3. Cycling of decision-making from Washington back to the states, in part through the Nixon administration's revenue-sharing program.

With the elimination of categorical federal grants and their replacement by general and special monies, state legislators and governors have been given not only added power but also the unpleasant responsibility of allocating the amounts and uses of this unspecified bounty. Revenue-sharing is complicating the elected state official's life at the same time that competition for funds among agencies and public and private in-

---

[1]"Some Consequences of Pluralization in Government," in *The Future of the U.S. Government*, edited by Henry S. Perloff (New York, George Braziller, 1971) p. 242.

terests is increasing the value of largely undeveloped lobbying talent. This new fact of political life, along with pluralization, is altering the climate of state affairs.

Despite these changes, political life in many ways remains the same. Today as in the past, state government is essentially ruled by interest groups. Ours is the best system of representative government yet evolved, but the fact is that between elections, the citizen, organization, or corporation that is not part of a special interest group does not have, and by definition cannot have, much to say about what happens.

New Look in the Capitol

We mentioned earlier the relaxed, clublike atmosphere that once prevailed in legislative sessions. Today, some legislatures that have failed to streamline their administrative machinery are finding it difficult to cope with the volume of work. In 1961, when 47 state legislatures met, 60,000 bills were introduced. The number reached 90,000 in 1969, 116,000 in 1971, and 140,000 in 1973.

Why this bill-drafting explosion? The enormous increase in state agencies has created a need for enabling legislation. Every agency brings to every legislative session its program, including a file of bills to be introduced. Another less obvious factor is the ever-mounting volume of new ideas and proposals and the speed with which they spread from capitol to capitol.

To accommodate the heavier workload, legislatures are meeting oftener and longer. Less than a decade ago, 22 state bodies were meeting annually, and 28 were meeting every two years (nearly always in odd years). In 1972, theoretically an "off" year, there were 38 sessions, and in 1974 only five states will *not* hold regular or special sessions. Furthermore, lawmakers who once held 60-day sessions now meet for 90, 120 and even 180 days. Some have taken the limits off entirely or have extended their sessions by revising the way the days are counted.

In many states, when the sessions end, interim committees continue to work. Once a comfortable place to bury a bill, the interim committee operates increasingly year-round. In Florida and Minnesota, for example, these committees act with full authority, so that by the first day of the next session they are prepared to take legislation they have processed directly to the floor.

Moreover, democratization has caused procedural changes—i.e., more committee roll calls, more public hearings and fewer executive sessions—which are opening up the lawmaking process in ways that reduce certainty of outcome and dilute both external and internal control.

Three of Pennsylvania's recent rule changes serve as excellent examples:

1. The majority of a House committee may now schedule a meeting against the chairman's wishes—a significant change since it vitiates his traditional one-man rule.

2. Notice must be given before a committee takes up a bill. This also limits the chairman's power because he can no longer suddenly call for a vote at a time when a bill he dislikes is certain to be defeated.

3. All committee votes must be taken in open session.

If a businessman looking at his own state fails to find confirmation of these trends in the legislative climate, it is not because these changes work selectively, exempting certain areas altogether, but because they operate at different rates of speed. Maryland, for example, is changing slowly, while Oregon has undergone what amoumts to a political earthquake. Whatever the speed at which they operate, these trends constitute what sooner or later will be the organizing framework for lobbying everywhere.

After the 1972 Elections

When the votes were counted following the November 7, 1972 elections, it became evident both nationally and in the states that the independents had emerged as the largest political "party." The independent vote jumped from a historical average of 20 percent of the total to 50 percent. If this change persists, the role of the orthodox party will be transformed from that of leader to that of adviser, from a body commanding loyalty to one merely recommending action. Moreover, disintegration of traditional party loyalties increases the leverage of the public interest advocate, who classifies his target not as Democrat or Republican, but according to a position on a spectrum running from ultraliberal to reactionary. This fact is an important backdrop to every practical approach to state government.

Like the independent voter, the new breed of legislator is both the product and the accelerator of pluralization and the new power of legislatures. Attracted by the growing importance of law-making bodies, higher salaries, and the opportunity that longer sessions provide for meaningful work, many women, blacks, youths, and teachers ran and were elected to office in 1972.

While the aggregate quantitative change is not striking, when broken down by category the new legislative pattern is significantly different. For example, there are now nine women in one legislature that previously had three. While this increase is, of course, not enough to upset any balance between parties or within caucuses, it does indicate an accelerating trend.

It should be observed, however, that these groups are not monolithic. The women just noted are of all kinds—grandmothers, housewives, and professional people, situated at the left, right, and center of the political spectrum. The same variety is true of other groups as well.

A look at three states will illustrate the 1972 results:

Wisconsin, a pacesetter among the states, experienced a 25 percent turnover in legislative membership. Urban labor and the Milwaukee city government have become the principal power centers. This fact, combined with the residue of traditional progressives from Madison and areas to the west, intensifies an atmosphere not very favorable to the business point of view.

In *Minnesota*, another innovative state, the turnover was 40 percent. The new members, 20 of whom represent what may be called a youth bloc, include such bearers of famous names as Hubert Humphrey III and Vincent Lombardi, Jr. A liberal coalition of Democrats and Republicans now controls the legislature.

Oregon's legislative turnover was 38 percent. For the first time in 10 years, the regular Democrats won control of both houses. Of the 90-member body, 34 are new—including 11 women, 7 persons less than 25 years old, and the first black ever elected to the House. The House whip is a 28-year-old teacher.

The new legislators tend to be activists, independent thinkers and strong individuals. They are consumer- and ecology-minded. While not necessarily antibusiness, they are certainly not business-oriented. They share neither the perspective nor the value judgments that come from knowing how to read a P&L statement and examine a balance sheet. Most have never been called on to weigh the costs and benefits of economic activities in terms of the community's livelihood, and they have only hazy notions about alternatives to many business practices, which they comprehend little and appreciate even less. They are prone to view with disfavor proposals from old-style lobbyists representing business.

But that is not all: the "old guard" legislators are changing, too. Reacting perhaps unconsciously to the new environment and new challenges, they are less "reliable" for the lobbyist than they used to be—that is, less receptive to established ways of communicating positions and soliciting assistance like logrolling and exchanging favors. Now that the conventional propriety of voting with traditional "friends" and against established "enemies" is under attack, many older legislators feel obliged to give greater consideration than they formerly did to the merits of any legislative proposal. Most wish to give at least the appearance of careful judgment and independent appraisal. This attitude helps make old-style lobbying obsolete.

Blueprint for Business

The altered rules of the game and the different picture at the capitol not only make business' job more complicated and more difficult; at times they exclude business from influencing decisions. Its failure can be partly attributed to the fragmentation of business. Too often the concept of free competition runs counter to the need for cooperation in matters critical to business as a whole. Interindustry struggles for markets in product applications, contests for market shares between companies in one industry, and intracompany rivalries for power frequently override the need for maintenance of a united political front.

This fragmentation notwithstanding, business can become more effective at the state level. But once a company begins evolving a new style of government relations by taking the logical first step—selecting a new-style lobbyist and developing a system and plan—management often tends to think that the job is done and that management can return to its "normal" concerns. The company must stifle this tendency, since implicit in the new lobbying is an understanding of how changed conditions relate to both the lobbyist's techniques and to the requirements for corporate commitment.

Here we shall not attempt to describe completely government relations as it is coming to be practiced; rather, we shall highlight a few departures from practices of the past.

As we have pointed out, the older forms of special access and personal relations are not very effective in the new lobbying framework. Lunches, banquets, small favors, and year-round remembrances are welcome as tokens of civility. But as techniques of influence they are being overtaken and superseded by specialized knowledge, integrative analysis, and planning.

The size and complexity of state government have reached a scale in which sound research and professional expertise rather than lay enlightenment are the critical ingredients in policy formulation. Given the tangled nature of today's problems, government everywhere is turning to policy analyses, surveys, and studies farmed out to universities and consulting agencies. State legislators want to do a good job, but they often lack well-staffed committees or good research services. For them the lobbyist can be a critical resource. Under these circumstances, his effectiveness depends increasingly on his degree of specialization and his ability to impart precise information, even on technical matters. These requirements result in extra demand on the lobbyist for his time and on the client for support in research and staffing.

The complexity of issues and the proliferation of structures dealing with them make the job of assessing the ramifications of a problem very difficult. The legislator wants to know how a particular decision will affect sectors across the policy spectrum. The intuitively brilliant horseback survey is no longer adequate. The lobbyist must have, first, a procedure to gather and process information and, second, the ability to make an integrative analysis. The more diversified society becomes, the more critical it is for the lobbyist to conceptualize (or reconceptualize) the issue and to link the various needs and demands of society's parts.

With the accelerating pace of change and the telescoping of time, planning assumes greater importance. The lobbyist must be able to assist the legislators occasionally in their deliberations on long-range future options, which should be oriented toward the way things will be or should be rather than toward the way things are. His capability is closely associated with the clarity of the client's objectives, for if the priorities of the company or group are vacillating or hazy, the lobbyist cannot proceed with confidence. His capability is also related to anticipating future developments in the corporate support program, which we shall discuss shortly.

Both lawmaker and lobbyist must try to deal objectively with complicated problems that have no easy or even "right" answers. This task requires good judgment, a sense of timing, advance preparation, and good organization. What counts most for today's lobbyist is a reputation for being well-informed and honest, being able to gather, analyze and impart information, and being able to make sound recommendations to both client and legislator.

Building a Corporate Program

Pluralization, that is, the vesting of decision-making in a multiplicity of decision-making governmental units, extends to all elements interacting in public life—private, semiprivate, and quasi-public. To keep abreast of events under this condition, a government relations program must proceed systematically, carefully structuring what once could be left to instinct. The government relations audit is a good example. This is a system for identifying groups and persons whose interests coincide with the auditor's; it is also a means of assessing the political abilities of organizations that may be enlisted to work for their mutual benefit.

An audit is necessary because no one can guess who has interests in what issues. In auditing an industry association, let's say, members may be asked the following questions: Has your company previously taken an interest in state legislation? If so, in which state(s)? On what issue(s)? How recently have you been active? What is your staffing structure for legislative responsibility? What organizations and associations provide your company with legislative information?

It is not enough to identify just the natural support groups; the government relations office should make sure it has classified, categorized and updated information on any group with a mutual, related, or ancillary interest in accomplishing the campaign objective. Later the information can be deployed as needed.

Since organization is the key to assembling power, potential sources of support must be recruited and their activities coordinated. They must be educated about areas of overlapping concern. They must be persuaded to act sometimes even when action appears to be only marginally effective.

The hearing is a case in point. The smart lobbyist will direct a sound and detailed program at the legislative committee for weeks, perhaps months, before the pertinent bill is taken up. If for any reason its fate is predetermined, if (as the old lobbying axiom goes) the votes have been counted before the hearing begins, then why pay all that attention to the hearing? The hearing is an excellent public information vehicle. The importance of making one's case forcefully and thoroughly extends beyond strengthening support on the committee or swaying an uncommitted member. A creditable performance can influence and educate the growing numbers of persons who take an interest. Even in the absence of press coverage and other publicity, testimony is a means of building the record—and one's reputation.

Moreover, a hearing enables support groups to gain valuable experience, provides them with a tangible role to play and offers a vehicle for building cooperation. In short, the hearing is an essential exercise in organization, communication and support building. In all too many cases, business neglects it or, perhaps worse, rushes into it at the last minute in a patchwork, ad hoc fashion.

Importance of Commitment

Without wholehearted corporate commitment to an effective government relations program—establishing a policy, formulating a plan, and following a schedule—much of what we have said is academic. If a company sets up a government relations or public affairs program merely because it seems to be the thing to do, chances are it won't work. Even if the company is motivated by the best reason—a desire to meet its civic and social responsibilities—the failure to involve itself actively can have costly consequences for its legislative efforts.

Unfortunately, the government relations program is frequently viewed as an intrusion into management's objectives. It does not intrude, or should not. A government relations effort can be important to a company's marketing when, for instance, it defends the company from political attack. Also, the lobbyist's surveillance activities can help locate opportunities for market expansion.

But more important, a good government relations program sensitizes the corporation to the attitudes of its various publics and helps it respond to further its own welfare. Obviously, community goodwill is as important to the corporation as customer or shareholder loyalty. The government relations program relates social problem solving to the process of nurturing the company's markets and profits. Such a program helps protect the bottom line.

It is wise to guarantee the lobbyist clear lines of access and to appoint a single individual to whom he will regularly report. It is important, on the one hand, to delineate the lobbyist's authority and grant him freedom from interference. On the other hand, management should collaborate closely with the lobbyist in a continuing process of reviewing and revising the government relations program.

A good lobbyist is an initiator of action as well as an implementer of policy, since part of his business is to watch for opportunity. Any corporation that engages a lobbyist with the hope that he will sharpen and refine its understanding of the legislative process and then proceeds to hamstring his operation because of preconceived notions as to how things should function will in the end cripple the program.

Formulation of goals that are fully accepted and readily communicable depends on a high degree of rapport between lobbyist and client. However, when program objectives seem to be agreed on but actually are poorly understood, there will be trouble. Headaches also arise when forces whose concerns have been left unarticulated silently resist program goals.

All organizations have management and communications problems. If, for example, management delays the lobbyist's recommendation for action because of an unresolved internal conflict or a communications gap, and thereby the company fails to challenge an unfavorable bill before it becomes law, the government relations program in this instance is a waste. The lobbyist is only as effective as the organization retaining his services.

A good government relations program may stimulate better overall corporate performance by inducing management to reexamine the company structure, thereby improving information flows and disclosing internal conflicts.

A Program That Worked

Since it incorporates something of the old style and much of the best in new-style lobbying, the case that follows is fairly typical of a modern state lobbying program.

At issue was a $5 million market share involving two groups of businessmen selling the same health product. The first group had built substantial political strength through its trade association, which we shall call the State Health Professionals Group. Those business interests enjoyed a captive clientele and commanded a much larger share of the market in their state than the second group, the mass merchandisers, who were organized nationally as the National Health Products Association.

The Professionals Group had a bill prohibiting price advertising introduced into the legislature. The bill's supporters claimed that price competition would result in lower product quality, thus endangering public health.

The Professionals Group, ostensibly a single-state organization, was in fact following the policy recommended by its national parent. Prohibition of price advertising was part of a grand strategy in which each local trade association was a subordinate but integral piece in a 50-state mosaic. The state we are speaking of was the twenty-third in which the Products Association joined battle over similar bills promoted by the Professional Group's parent. While the need for integration of strategy meant that the contest was nationally supervised, all but a few participants in each case were indigenous organizations with strong local interests and ties.

Because prices were higher in states adjoining our case state, the result of laws against price advertising in those territories, stores in the case state situated close to its borders were taking business away from adjacent state Professional Group members. Naturally, merchants from the adjacent states pushed for action from colleagues in our case state.

Such out-of-state involvement—whether financial, material, or moral—is typical of a major legislative campaign whose results either establish important precedents or produce other reverberating effects. The public aspect of the controversy is likely to appear entirely local, however, not because out-of-state participation is covert, but because in deference to local pride and particularisms it is necessarily subtle. No state legislator welcomes outside interference, even (or perhaps especially) when he recognizes that the issue has been defined in important ways by forces outside his control.

The mass merchandisers launched a campaign to fight the bill. Based outside the state, they had only recently entered this market and consequently had virtually no political influence. Their legislative posture was purely defensive, although their methods were not. The following 12 steps describe the Products Association's eight-week, $75,000 effort:

1. The association appointed as coordinator a legislative specialist operating nationally and accepted his recommendation that three local lobbyists—a House Democratic specialist, a House Republican specialist and a Senate specialist—function as a team. They underwent a thorough but necessarily rapid indoctrination to give them some technical sophistication about the health product in question.

2. The coordinator commissioned a research consultant to prepare a study of the retail price of an identical product ("identical" here includes quality) in two neighboring states, one which allowed price advertising and one which did not. The results showed that the consumer benefited from a 30 percent to 50 percent price reduction in the state permitting price advertising.

3. The local lobbyists engaged in some old-style tactics by reaffirming personal contacts, meeting legislators socially, and in general cashing markers for old favors. At the same time they established contact with prominent consumer movement groups that normally would be expected to support the opponent's "maintain-the-quality" pitch.

4. The lobbyists enlisted support from organized labor, which was the largest identifiable single purchaser in the market as well as the state's most effective interest group.

5. The team studied each legislator of both houses to determine how best to communicate with him. Should he be approached on the basis of friendship and past commitments or on the merits of information and research reports? The conclusions were tabulated, along with tentative assessments of how each would vote on the bill.

6. The coordinator commissioned a second independent study, this one to establish the effect on inner-city groups and on the aged of prohibitions on price advertising. He also sought the cooperation of local inner-city organizations and committees active on behalf of the elderly. These constituencies were important segments of his client's market.

7. With guidance from the coordinator, the inner-city groups joined to construct their own support operation. They won few converts in the legislature but generated publicity and provided spirit for the campaign.

8. The coordinator and mass merchandisers jointly piloted a public information campaign. Union members, consumer advocates, inner-city representatives and committees for the aged wrote letters to the editor,

issued press releases and otherwise showed their interest and circulated their opinions.

9. The lobbyist subsequently reinforced this publicity effort through meetings with the state's major print and broadcast media editorial boards. These meetings produced TV, radio, and newspaper editorials against the Professional Group's bill. Two important papers ran cartoon editorials. Impressed by this editorial outpouring and influenced by labor and consumer group pressure, the state newspaper and broadcasters' associations authorized their own lobbyists to join in the effort.

10. The coalition assailed the legislature with arguments against the bill. Coordination of the forces avoided deluging legislators with duplicate visits from the lobbyists. They included volunteers from the consumer and inner-city groups and from organizations of the elderly, as well as paid lobbyists for the unions, newspaper and broadcasters' associations, and retail merchants (latecomers, but present nonetheless). Even banks doing business with members of the Health Products Association sent lobbyists into action. A highlight of these representations was the orchestrated appearance of more than 200 octogenarians at a critical hearing.

11. The Products Association lobbyists personally reascertained the position of every legislator. At this point, however, recognizing inevitable defeat and wishing to avoid embarrassment, the Professionals Group asked its champions to drop the bill.

12. The coordinator established a continuing surveillance program, placed the principal lobbyist on retainer, and kept open the channels for periodic future contacts with all groups that had participated in the effort.

Behind the Victory

It is not easy to identify what causes victory in a legislative contest, if by "cause" is meant that which produces the effect. Many positive factors contribute, as we have stressed—information, intelligence, planning, organization. Often negative elements enter in—a poor legislative proposal and lassitude or complacency on the opponent's part. In this campaign, specialized knowledge, integrative analysis, and corporate commitment were contributory elements without which success would have been unlikely.

Specialized knowledge—The mass merchandisers had recognized for 20 years that having good relations with government is imperative, and they were aware of the changing situation in state government. Because the lead company in the group had its own government relations department and because both it and the Health Products Association had had outside political counsel for 12 years, those active in legislative matters were comfortable with the technicalities of these particular products, could interpret research, and could discuss the results of economic forecasting.

Integrative analysis—Linking the needs and demands of various parts of society made possible the coordination of support groups whose interests were otherwise disparate, if not conflicting. One output of the analysis was this: if the Professionals Group succeeds in legislating for themselves a virtual monopoly on a product, the price rise will discourage lower income groups from periodic replacement, which in this case is vital to personal well-being. Other ramifications will certainly include a sharp rise in state institutional budgets, increases in state welfare costs, a decline in occupational safety purchases by industry, and deterioration in public school performance.

The Health Products Association lobbyists considered these problems and policy implications and gave legislators comprehensive advice on the ramifications of the policy choices they faced.

Corporate commitment—Besides the efforts manifested in the 12-step description, commitment took these forms: providing the coordinator and lobbyists with free access to the top executives of the retailing companies, granting to the coordinator broad decision-making authority and independent license in implementation, commissioning of outside studies, and arranging for support from the companies' legal and public relations departments.

Barometer of Intention

To the extent that business defaults on recognized social obligations or abuses its market power, criticism—even sanction—is justified. But it is unwise to create, through demands for immediate ''answers,'' exaggerated public expectations of business performance. They could lead to widespread disillusionment with business as an institution.

The real problem in changing corporate-societal relationships is that socioeconomic diversification and interdependence have accelerated faster than institutional and philosophical means of coping with them. If business has not yet developed accounting methods to fairly assess the consequences for society of its decisions, it is because the task is uncommonly difficult—too difficult, also, to permit public interest advocates to construct reliable cost-benefit ratios for their proposals.

On the other hand, if we discard the notion that business acts solely for narrow ends and selfish purposes, the public correctly senses that business must do more to contribute to the solution of our proliferating domestic problems. In the search for solutions, perpetuation of antagonism between business and public interest advocacy often places our problems in poor perspective, substituting myth and rhetoric for badly needed constructive thought. Given the will and better understanding, both sides should be able to find the basis for working more cooperatively. Experience in the legislative arena demonstrates that business and public advocates can be partners if their assessment is based solely on merit and not on a baggage of inherited prejudices.

Furthermore, business cannot function well without the confidence of the American people. Like any other major institution, business must earn through action the public respect and trust that form the basis of its leadership and privilege. One important aspect of such action is an ongoing local government relations program to sensitize business to changing public expectations and reactions, and to bring business into a policy-making forum where responsiveness serves as a barometer of honest intention.

MEDIA RELATIONS

9

The New Era in Business-Financial Media Relations

By Walter V. Carty

Before the National Investor Relations Institute,
Detroit, February 5, 1974

SUMMARY: The business and financial pages of American newspapers and the major business magazines are going through profound changes regarding the amount of space available, the audience to which their publications are directed and the techniques of moving stories from the source to print. Most vital is that the people writing the business page stories are increasingly young, bright, well-educated. They are neither pro- nor anti-business. They want to find out for themselves precisely what comprises the corporation.

Walter V. Carty, a graduate of Boston College and Harvard Graduate School of Arts and Sciences who formerly wrote and edited for Boston newspapers and Time, Inc. and Curtis publications, is a senior vice president of Hill and Knowlton, in charge of business-financial media relations.

Several years ago, I was part of a group that was invited to the New York Stock Exchange to get a first-hand view of how this market operated. I was amazed how few of the 150 guests had ever before been to the home grounds of the Big Board.

First there was the view from the gallery down to the floor of the Exchange. This area, where thousands of shares of stock were changing hands, was a sea of motion and sound. It was a sight certainly as tingling as one's first view of the Eiffel Tower from a plane or being in the midst of the noon bustle in St. Mark's Square in Venice.

The plan was to usher us then into the Governors' Room—which looked like a miniature U.S. Senate with its mahogany and plush and the stern faces of the former Exchange presidents staring down from their gilt frames. Here we were to listen to talks from several Big Board officials.

As the president that year of the organization that had made the arrangements for this meeting at the Exchange, I felt more than a passing responsibility for the precision of the day's activities. So I stayed on in the gallery to be sure all our members and their guests knew where the next session was being held.

I saw one woman, whom I know to be a highly intelligent person and a very accomplished writer, linger on as though the scene below might suddenly disappear. I reminded her the talks would start precisely on time and there was a bit of a trip to get there.

"I wanted to look and hear a little longer," she said. "You know, this is my first visit to the Exchange. And I *know* this is the last time I will be seeing anything like this. All those men racing around with little pieces of paper in their hands! This *has* to be an echo from the past. Even where I shop there is a greater sense of automation and modernism."

Later in the week I mentioned the incident to one of the Exchange officials. "She's a very perceptive person," he said. About a month later, *he* left the Exchange for another position!

Disenchantment with Wall Street

I venture to say this little vignette might represent part of what's at the root of today's disenchantment with Wall Street. The people who had pushed computerization for business seemed reluctant to computerize themselves. Couple this with the parade of negative headlines, and it's not difficult to understand why the so-called "little man" has not hurried back to the securities market. His attitudes are largely formed from what he reads in newspapers and magazines and sees on television. What with the collapse of a Weis Securities, the shock of a giant fraud like Equity

Funding, and the exposure of an I.O.S., he wonders if anyone with a grain of sense should be investing in the stock market.

But there is, of course, the other side of the coin. We in this country may have some trepidations at the moment about our economy, the believability of business and the efficiency of our money markets, but it isn't necessarily shared by the rest of the world.

Listen to these words from a leading banker who spoke recently in New York.

Alfred Matter, Senior Vice President of the Swiss Bank Corporation, said in an address at New York University:

"Europeans, and especially Swiss, believe in the future of the U.S. . . . We regard the U.S. and Canada as privileged, especially in the current energy fix, and therefore, we have a more positive attitude toward stocks of these two countries rather than, say, those of Japan and Europe . . . but a very important and indeed over-riding reason is that we believe your economy is still very highly geared to the free enterprise system. Your unions do not question this framework, which is as profitable for them as it is for managements and shareholders. Even though you are moving toward more of a welfare state and more governmental controls—as all of us are—there are no outspoken efforts to destroy free enterprise. I think this is why Switzerland, which is also still committed to this system, and your country find so much common ground. Unfortunately, in other European countries, the trend seems to be going in another direction. This is why, rightly or wrongly, we prefer to have our customers invest in Wall Street . . . furthermore, I have no qualms in saying that we know no other stock market in the world with the same efficiency and breadth as Wall Street . . . ''

All this praise, despite the image of men running around with pieces of paper! Mr. Matter's words appeared editorially in *Barron's* and were picked up by such publications as the Paris *Herald Tribune*, but they weren't exactly the ''News of the Day'' across America.

Max Ways and I were discussing something similar at a recent luncheon, where we agreed it is the two-headed calf and not the normal calf that creates news. Even his own *Fortune* magazine is not necessarily an exception. That which proceeds at its normal pace does not a story make.

It is the derailed train, the deposed leader, the declining stock market that earns the bolder print. We are often bemused in our office when we see how fast a story read to the wires about the closing of a plant suddenly comes clicking over the ticker. We know it usually will see print next day. The *opening* of a new plant is not always quite as newsy. But, you may ask, isn't that a fact of human nature? Good news, no news. Bad news *is* news.

The Place for Positive Stories

I for one don't agree. And that, basically and primarily, is the point I'd like to leave with you today. I'm convinced that behind every human being and every human endeavor—and that means every corporation, for it consists of humans—there is a story to be told—and I don't mean the seamy or the sad, which usually guarantees an audience. I believe the positive and the constructive and the solid can also be news.

A corporation may be "Dullsville" on the surface and its chief executive may be as exciting as slushy weather, but peel away the veneers of the corporate situation and I think you'll very frequently find editorial fodder. But that opinion peeler must, at the very minimum, be *curious, probing, perspicacious*.

I recall a project with a certain client a few years ago. The company planned to make a positive but relatively unnewsy announcement—yes, the opening of a plant, this one in South Carolina. For a variety of reasons, the company wanted to "break the print barrier" and get the broadest coverage possible.

On the surface, it looked impossible. The product at the plant was ordinary, the men were unknown who would be running the operation, even the price tag for the whole complex was not that impressive. How could one create a major and *valid* story?

I sensed that a trip to the area would open up new avenues. Talking to every conceivable person—local businessmen, government people, newsmen—filled out the picture. Every person in some way provided ingredients. It was the mayor of the smallish city who presented the *pièce de resistance*. In a very casual way, he mentioned that my client's plant was situated in the very heart of an area called the "Golden Crescent" which abutted three states and would draw its workers from this section that had a history of nagging unemployment.

The somewhat "dishwater" aspects of the original story gave way to what business-financial editors across the country saw: The genuine rebirth of an impoverished pocket which might finally, through this particular corporate transaction, see the day when people there could achieve what was suggested in the name of their area. The "Golden Crescent" story, although basically local, enjoyed coast-to-coast visibility. It came only from that old-fashioned news reporter responsibility—digging for the facts.

If the editorial people shaping what we shall be reading in the newspaper this evening want "color," there is only one answer for people in our business—provide it. I think this can be done even when dealing with the weightiest figures and the most complex of subjects. Take one look at Bob Metz's column *Market Place* in *The New York Times*. It is a rare column of his that doesn't sparkle, even when it analyzes the complexities of arbitrage or is studded with an accountant's briefcase full of numbers.

It can be done, as you who know good writing can attest. But as you must know, it also requires time, enormous care and a great sense of the concrete—seeing things in hard, visual, meaningful terms, then translating them into the right words to convey a specific mental image. In other words, you have to become a reporter again, or if you have never had that experience, then you must develop reportorial skills.

What is the most pronounced characteristic of a good reporter? Questions, of course. And what is the most frequent question? "Can you give me an example?" asks the reporter who must always keep in mind his multifaceted audience of varying levels of education, income, lifestyle.

Those of you involved in the business of investor relations must indeed live in a world of words to convey your message . . . First the rather starchy, uncolorful words of the prospectus . . . then the somewhat more vivid words of the interim and annual report . . . next the words from the company spokesman before a group of analysts . . . and finally those very concrete words to present your case to the media, and then, *their* words, hopefully clear, concise and telling phrases . . . that will be received and understood and perhaps accepted by your ultimate audience.

Five Media Changes to Remember

What about your approach to media? If you're not already aware of some profound changes in the business-financial media in recent years —and even months—you should be. From my vantage point, I see at present five fundamental changes that will affect the print side of investor relations in the immediate future.

1. There is substantially less space available owing to the newsprint shortage. You've noticed the shorter articles and the thinner editions. The shortage affects practically all newspapers and magazines. For example, the daily *Wall Street Journal* news hole has been reduced to 72 columns. The editor has to be more tough-minded. A robust earnings report from the biggest of the blue chips may end up in the financial digest. What does this mean to you who must get your company or client into print? Present your story ideas to the media in tight, terse language. Be sure you have that gut feeling that what you're presenting comprises hard news. If it falls more into the area of background news, be convinced, at the very least, that it sheds light on an important situation. What happens when you have what you believe is a valid story, and perhaps for reasons of

space, it doesn't get printed? You always have one alternative: paid space. Increasingly, we are seeing advertisements spelling out sales, earnings, per-share earnings. It is the one sure way to provide your financial facts in full. Our company is so convinced this is the wave of the future, that we've expanded our advertising activities and have formalized them into a full-scale advertising department.

2. Most publications are now consumer-oriented. If consumerism hasn't changed the texture of practically all stories—as it indeed has in *The New York Times*, for instance—then it has become a major subject for consideration, as in *Business Week*. The business pages of the *Times* were once tailored primarily for the businessman audience. Now, a housewife here in Detroit can understand practically every article and she will find more of them written with precisely her in mind: Columns on personal finance, Sunday business features written by someone like Marilyn Bender that concentrate on family-founded corporations where a woman might have been a pivotal figure. It is rare now to find a corporate profile in either *Time* or *Newsweek*. Remember how familiar they were in the Fifties and Sixties with the chief executive officer on the cover? Now it is the *trend* business story that is published most often with the consumer in mind. A few months ago, when the government published a litany of products believed to be unsafe, *Newsweek* shaped the story into a prominent feature and illustrated it with a sketch of a house with indications of where the unsafe product could give trouble to the homeowner. Mark my words, the era of the consumer is as much part of the American scene, and will continue to be, as social securities benefits. Keep the individual in mind in your investor relations endeavors and you won't go wrong.

3. The caliber of media personnel is continually being upgraded. It is not all that unusual today to find a Ph.D. writing business-financial news copy. The day when someone from the reference library will be promoted to the business news desk is part of the past. The people writing the business page stories are increasingly young, bright, well-educated. They are neither pro- nor anti-business. They want to find out for themselves what makes things tick. To provide you with a thumbnail sketch of what I mean, the last three writers employed by the business pages of *The New York Times* were an A.B. from Harvard with a Master's in Journalism, a woman from the Washington bureau of *Business Week*, and a second woman—a graduate of Smith College with a law degree. They are also well-paid people compared to previous years. The cliche of the newspaperman with his tongue hanging out and waiting for your 5:30 press party is pretty much gone with the wind. Most business page writers these days dress and think like businessmen, and when it comes to 5:30, more often than not, they're catching a train to the suburbs where they live with wife, children, mortgage and all the other little amenities.

4. The current disenchantment with Wall Street requires greater rationale in presenting story lines. I say "current" but more accurately the disenchantment has become a condition. As Bob Bleiberg, the editor of *Barron's*, said at a recent Hill and Knowlton luncheon, it's really been a bear market for five years. So when an editor or writer asks *why* did your company or client acquire another company or bring in a new director or come out with a certain product at this time, he is not trying to pry into proprietary information. He wants his story to stand up. He wants to determine corporate motivation. Nothing is more distasteful to Wall Street than a surprise. The same could be said of the genuinely good business-financial editor. He wants to know what's going on behind the scene—and behind your release. Did Gulf & Western buy into Amfac merely as an investment? Does the laying off of personnel at Disneyland mark the fading of the Walt Disney bloom? Where is that restaurant chain like Gino's picking its next location in the wake of the energy crisis?

5. The increase in speed in moving stories from source to publication. We're living in the era of the *instant*. As automation moves rapidly into the production of newspapers and magazines, news sources must keep up with the pace. You're perhaps familiar with the equipment Reuters is prepared to install in public relations firms and corporations that immediately files a release from the source right into the newsroom. No need for telephones, messenger service or the like. One New York business editor receives 1,400 releases a day but publishes an average of only 40 stories. The earlier your story arrives at the desk of the editor, the better the chances of breaking the print barrier.

You hear a great deal about coast-to-coast pick-up, but it's amazing how many corporate leaders are satisfied if they appear in only two publications, *The New York Times* and *The Wall Street Journal*. Their rationale is that the so-called opinion molders in Wall Street and Washington usually read these two papers.

What is the best way to work with each of them?

I could now wax philosophical about basic editorial premises, but I believe you're looking for practical suggestions. Some may refer to such matters as "nuts and bolts," but I think you'll agree nothing ever happens until one step follows another step—until you reach your goal. That may be termed nitty-gritty by some, but it is also the reality that can lead to success.

"The Wall Street Journal"

I'm sure you know it's best to work with *The Wall Street Journal* bureau if you're located outside New York. One of the unwritten rules is that headquarters won't try to scoop the hinterlands. Your story ideas should go along to the bureau chief or some contact there you might have developed.

Something many people in investor and public relations forget is that *The Wall Street Journal* and Dow Jones are two separate entities under the same umbrella. Appearing on the ticker does not insure *Journal* pick-up. One way to stimulate appearing in print as well as on the DJ is to phone the individual on the *Journal* responsible for a certain news category to let him know a story in his bailiwick is on the ticker so that he can be on the lookout for it. In most instances, the Dow Jones item will be directed to him, but if he's alerted beforehand he can start to make plans.

To be very specific, say your news release is in the field of banking. You read your story to the proper person at Dow Jones. It appears thereafter on the ticker. You then phone the banking editor of the *Journal* to let him know of the ticker story. He may ask you a few questions. In most instances he'll simply thank you and ask where you can be reached if there are any follow-up questions. Chances are fair your ticker story will be printed in some form by the *Journal*. Space of course will be one of the deciding factors.

"The New York Times"

It is not usually a good idea to call *The New York Times*. If your story has been transmitted over PR Newswire, it will be read. If it has made the Dow Jones, chances are it will be read again. There is no harm in sending a back-up copy of the release by hand if you're in the New York area, but the messengering of a release has some built-in negatives. There are the security provisions at a newspaper that frequently prevent the messenger from getting into the news operations. Hand deliveries can sit for some time before they arrive at the desk of the person for whom they're intended. In the case of *The Wall Street Journal*, all hand deliveries are automatically moved to one main desk *unless* they're marked "Personal and Confidential" for a particular individual.

For the feature story in greater depth, it's always best to outline the idea on paper, direct it to the individual responsible for the particular news category, or one of the editors, then give it time to be read. If you don't hear by phone or letter, it's perfectly legitimate to call at a time when you know the publication is not closing to discuss the story and get first-hand reaction.

One publication that never leaves you hanging is the Sunday Business Section of *The New York Times*. If the story idea hits paydirt, you normally get a phone call. If it doesn't, you normally get a courteous note telling you why not.

"Business Week"

Business Week, Fortune, Barron's and *Forbes* all have their special approaches which I'll not be able to provide in any detail here. Come to the New York University-PRSA Seminars I conduct each fall, and you'll be able to hear directly from the editors of these publications.

Suffice it to say, you have a ready audience in the editors of *Business Week*. And although it is a general business news magazine competitive with TV and other publications, it has a very special audience composed primarily of 735,000 businessmen. Its audience is special and its news is special. As senior editor Jack Dierdorff said at our October 1973 seminar: "If a Chinese writer were to rape a Russian ballerina in the middle of Times Square at high noon, it would not be news for us."

Take a good look at the masthead and learn what direction you should go in: Three top editors, three senior editors, 12 associate editors, five economists, 19 department editors, 11 contributing editors, one assistant editor—plus 11 domestic bureaus staffed by one to four people. If you're outside New York, the best starting point is the bureau nearest you. The next best step is to write a tight story line and direct it to the department editor closest to your basic business line, followed up a week or so later by a phone call. And in talking about changes, don't forget some of the major changes in *Business Week* that offer opportunities for you—new departments like "Legal Affairs," "Ideas and Trends," "Social Issues," "The Environment" and the Wall Street column. And don't overlook the special industrial edition going to 300,000 subscribers.

"Fortune"

Fortune is another cup of tea. Most of the ideas are staff generated, but it is a publication sincerely interested in story ideas from outside—so interested in fact that *Fortune* has an associate editor, Lucie Adam, whose sole responsibility is the development of stories from outside the magazine, mostly from public relations sources. Twenty-four corporation stories are published each year. There are in every issue management stories, corporate profiles on the more colorful businessmen and one of the best opportunities of all—"Businessmen in the News." Ideas are best presented in writing beforehand. The *Fortune* editorial luncheon is another rich opportunity. Editor Bob Lubar likes to sit down with the chairmen and presidents of the top companies in an atmosphere of relaxation to discuss business topics of the day in general, and the company and its future plans in particular. As many as seven other *Fortune* editors join him at these sessions. Everything discussed is off-the-record, but it is interesting how many of these luncheons lead to full-scale articles.

Something to keep in mind is that, although there are 70 people on the editorial staff, there are only six secretaries on the whole of *Fortune*. So phone calls don't serve any particular purpose and letters to editors go unanswered for months. Your most productive channel is Lucie Adam and her story development department.

One of the stories often neglected is the industry story, in which your client or company is setting a trend or perhaps benefiting from a trend. Let *Fortune* know on an exclusive basis for an initial period, and your chances can be good.

In recent years, *Fortune* has also been leaning toward the first-person story. One of the most widely read was Eberhard Faber's "How I Gave Up The Good Life and Became President."

Fortune is always scouting for what they call a management story. "Let's say your company or client has come up with an unusual and really innovative way of compensating executives," said Carol Loomis, one of the magazine's editors at my 1972 seminar. "That's not an excuse for a corporation story. But it just might be the reason for us to think hard about a story on executive compensation . . . we think good management stories are hard to find; any ideas you've got, we'd like to have."

"Barron's"

When it comes to *Barron's*, there is the wag who says there are only two things to know: How do you stay out of Abelson's column, and how do you get into the rest of the magazine?

The editors say they have a "singular view about any prospective story—it must be news, it must say something fresh and there's got to be a point to it."

What the magazine prides itself the most on are its thoughtful analyses on which readers can in part base decisions regarding the funds they invest in or manage.

One of the big surprises about *Barron's* is its smallness of staff; there are only 15 people on staff in New York with another four in Boston, San Francisco, Washington and Paris.

Individual company stories can get a strong play in *Barron's*. The one consistent thread running through most of these articles is that they usually concern the company on the upbeat. But, as you well know, *Barron's* does not shy from writing the obits for high fliers that have been forced down to earth.

There are industry stories, regular coverage of mutual funds, the "Talking Money" series between top money managers and *Barron's* staffers, editorials mostly written by Bob Bleiberg and the newest addition—Commodities Corner—which the editors believe will "do for the grain pits what 'Up and Down Wall Street' has done for the Big Board." Although a weekly, *Barron's* has shown it can sprint like a daily when needed. It was on the streets a full 48 hours before any other publication with the Equity Funding scandal.

Most of its stories are generated from within, but it draws a great number of its basic story ideas from two prime areas: reading and talking. Editor Steve Anreder puts it this way: "Apart from countless press releases, annual reports, market letters, industry studies, we get close to 100 trade publications—from *Aviation Week* to *Variety*—and a few from abroad such as the *London Mining Journal*, and believe me, they are read. We also do a lot of talking—to people on the street, to presidents and financial executives, to economists, to government officials. I myself once figured I speak in the course of the year to no fewer than 500 companies." And editor Larry Armour adds: "We might even talk to a PR man or two."

"Forbes"

Forbes likes to think its editors and writers are drama critics who take up where newspapers and newsmagazines leave off. "We render criticism, favorable and unfavorable, and sometimes mixed," is the way senior editor Steve Quickel puts it. "We want to know—who's helped and who's hurt."

Forbes prides itself on being concise and pungent and along the way has earned its reputation of being "unlovable." It tries to be as factual as possible but at the same time express opinion. Is the company good or bad? Has its management succeeded or failed?

Forbes is primarily interested in significant events or trends in big companies that affect their performance. The editors lean toward companies with a volume at least of $100 million, since there would be more reader interest and usually more shares around.

The magazine is not hostile to public relations people in general, but *is* if difficulties are put in the way of the reporter. Don't try to hide when a call comes from *Forbes*. They can always talk to your competition, people on Wall Street who know the company and others who might possibly do you harm. In the long run, a story with both pluses and minuses is a hell of a lot more believable than a fan magazine piece. And what characteristic is more wanting on the corporate scene these days than believability?

Television

And there is one major area of media that is almost totally over-looked or avoided by financial public relations people: television. And that's not good. You are concerned primarily with the world of print, but please don't overlook TV's capability of reaching millions instantly with your corporate message.

One last bit of advice. Do everything in your power to bring your management people face-to-face with media. We at Hill and Knowlton go out of our way to line up clients with the top editors. There is no quicker way to dissolve any possible doubts and create trust and understanding, and very often a good story can develop.

I've been told by television producers that there usually is no prob-lem in attracting government, education and even labor leaders to the various talk shows, but there is a rather consistent turn-down when busi-ness is approached. The most educated and articulate men who handle millions of dollars and control the board rooms of the bluest of the blue chip corporations often blanch at the suggestion of appearing on the home screen. Truth to tell, as the newsprint shortage tightens the print barrier, the horizon opens with fresh opportunities in electronic journalism.

Importance of the Story-Teller

No matter what may be happening in the financial community today, we know corporations will continue to seek financing and will therefore continue to seek the proper telling of their stories to those who can provide the financing. A good part of their success is up to you—the story teller!

Two final points: The day when you can sway a business-financial reporter or editor with a fancy luncheon is definitely past. What media want today are the facts that fit in with their editorial requirements. A lunch is fine every now and then to continue your contact and provide information. But don't think you can buy the editor or reporter. The only answer: study every publication carefully before you approach it.

The last point is that investor relations people tend to stress the security analyst, with the business press pushed down the line. One Hill and Knowlton shareholder survey indicated that 33 percent thought the

Annual Report was their best source of information . . . the next largest group, 17.6 percent, cited articles in business and general magazines and newspapers . . . only 7.5 percent mentioned brokers.

These thoughts might be helpful to anyone making his living in investor relations.

PUBLIC INTEREST ISSUES

10

Warning Flags
(Still) Wave
in Polluted Air

By Carl Thompson

Before the Management Policy Council,
Ligonier, Pennsylvania, May 10, 1973

SUMMARY: Despite waving warning flags, much of industry still isn't prepared to deal constructively with environmental issues —until pressured by either laws or the marketplace. It would save money and reputations if industry would take more constructive leadership in improving environments from the work place and community to the customers' homes and trash cans.

Carl Thompson, a graduate of the University of North Carolina (Chapel Hill) and of several North Carolina newspapers and the Washington Bureau of *The Wall Street Journal*, is an executive vice president of Hill and Knowlton, Inc., specializing in environmental, consumer and energy matters.

Contrary to what many industry and business people believe, the environmental issue wasn't invented in the late '60s by a bunch of eco-freaks. And contrary to what I hope only a few may still believe, the issue isn't a fad that will fade away in another year or two.

It's unfortunate that Hegel was probably right when he said history teaches only that governments and people have never learned anything from history.

Perhaps we can learn something about the future of the environmental movement by remembering what the start of this generation's concern about ecology was. In my opinion, based upon long study, two major developments in the late '40s and early '50s were important factors in setting off our concern with, and examination of, environmental quality.

One was the discovery in the late '40s that Los Angeles smog was created by a photochemical reaction of automobile exhausts with sunlight. The other was the reporting of epidemiological and laboratory evidence that linked cigarette smoking with a rising incidence of lung cancer and perhaps other ailments. Although some scientific papers had been published in the late '40s on this matter, sensational stories began to reach and alarm the American people in 1953-54.

The real significance of these two developments, as far as the environmental movement is concerned, is that they spurred a rapid increase in intensive scientific research and attention to *environmental* factors in human health problems. And little was really known about these factors.

Research in Smog and Smoking

The Los Angeles air pollution problems and the cigarette smoking controversy were quite closely linked—although this was not widely recognized at the time. The fact is that the same scientists were frequently working at the same time on the two problems. Both involved substances in the air we breathe—one self-induced, the other spread among the public, willy-nilly.

The challenges raised by these two problems opened up a whole new medical, scientific and sociological scheme of research and investigation. What was the public—the general public—being exposed to in the products it was buying and using? Also, what was the public being exposed to in the waste products—such as automobile exhausts and waste discharges into the waters—over which it had no direct control?

The problems were not easy to deal with. Dr. Arie Haagen-Smit of California defined years ago the difficulties of research: Modern techniques make it possible to identify tiny traces of a wide range of chemical compounds which could be suspect. But what we lacked then—and still lack to a large extent—are sound biological tests that will identify the harmful substances—and at what doses over what period of time they may be harmful.

Everything was becoming suspect as a health hazard—food and drink, hard and soft water, the air we breathe, and even sunlight and sex. But who in business was paying attention to this trend? Mighty few —unless their product was directly challenged as a hazard. And then there would be some scrambling, some hasty denials, some second-thinking, and finally perhaps some effort to find out something about the product or the process in question. Research into lung disease, prompted largely by the cigarette hassle, began to reveal dangers from beryllium, radiation in uranium mines, cotton dust, coal dust, asbestos—occupational hazards primarily, but some also of public concern—such as the hydrocarbons in automobile exhaust.

And what was essentially at first a *health* problem broadened when the then Surgeon General William Stewart said being healthy is not just being unsick but having an environmemt for good health and well-being. Thus environmental insults were harmful if they tended to degrade the quality of life—as with, for instance, harmless but obnoxious odors.

For two decades, the warning flags were waving—more and more of them. It certainly cannot be said that people—including many scientists—weren't shouting. But too many who should have been concerned and who had both the technical and other resources to tackle the mounting problems—too many of these either weren't listening or refused to give their attention to the issue. This was true, unfortunately, even among some of those directly involved. This was not because there were not some or perhaps many in industry who weren't aware of, and even talking about, the implications of these danger flags. But they either were not heeded, or they were in no position to make themselves heard by decision-makers.

Propaganda Hurt Research

In any event, there was a vacuum created between a growing public concern about genuine issues and the positive action the public (or segments of it) wanted to see coping with and solving these issues. Into that vacuum stepped a number of people. Many of them were opportunists who saw a chance to make a splash for themselves—pseudo-scientists, anti-business elements, politicians, self-seeking crusaders, instant experts with instant solutions—usually out-shouting the sincere and earnest scientists, the sincere crusaders, and public servants who were striving to bring about the changes needed without sensationalizing and over-alarming.

This was happening even in the mid-60s, when Prof. Abel Wolman of Johns Hopkins, an elder statesman in environmental problems, said the search for effective control measures is "severely handicapped by the repetition of statements on the subtle manifestations of unknown diseases, of unknown origins, at some unknown future date. . . It should be possible to turn aside, now, from the propagandistic to the scientific and technological issues in the environment."

It should have been possible, but the time was not yet here. And it may not be here now.

By the time industry (for the most part) was ready to get into the game, the other players were already on the field, the rules were set, the officials chosen, and the grandstands were wildly cheering the ecologists—freaks and otherwise. Then industry showed up, saying the game was being played wrong, the officials were biased, the rules should be changed, and the fans should be more sympathetic to the industrial newcomers. Well, it didn't happen that way.

As one scientist friend of mine puts it, industry's failure to take leadership was not because of any "demonology"—but rather lack of understanding and depth of knowledge about a new problem that didn't fit into the established pattern of running a business.

When we formalized our Environmental Health Unit in Hill and Knowlton early in 1966, we sought to get across one basic concept to our clients and anyone else who would listen: Elevate the issue of environment to top management policy consideration ranking with raw materials, manpower, capital equipment, sales, profits and taxes. The reason is obvious today if it wasn't then. These latter six major business considerations are seriously and adversely affected if the environment policies are not given equal or higher priorities.

I have no measure as to how quickly or how widely this concept has taken hold—even now. But it has gained; it has gained.

Up to now my discussion has been largely about the past but most of the points I have been trying to make apply to the present and the future.

Industry Must Take Lead

Where are we today and where are we going?

First, we are at a point where industry must take over more and more informed and dedicated leadership in protecting the environment and in efficient use of all resources—human and natural. Awareness of this role must influence every business decision—especially including product development and marketing.

Second, we are nearing the end—but are not there yet—of the development of a complex federal, state and local system of laws and regulations relating to control of environmental quality—and I don't mean just pollution control. Thus we will have built into our social fabric a code of environmental behavior, with penalties for violations.

Third, we have probably seen the peak of the emotional, instant-solution, propagandistic type of environmental agitation and are moving into a more rational—and therefore more effective—campaign of using laws, courts and solid public persuasion to assure environmental quality in our daily business, industrial and recreational activities. The Sierra Club's new board of 12 directors includes nine lawyers—as one indication of trends.

Fourth, the growing energy crisis is going to result in making more clearcut the choices between extreme, and probably unnecessary, environmental control measures and the drastic reduction in standards and mode of living. Industry here is again being challenged to provide more and better and safer sources of energy and also to find—and find quickly—new, more efficient and less wasteful ways of using energy. This means more than cutting off lights. Alcoa has developed an aluminum reduction process that requires an estimated 30 percent less energy—in a traditionally high-energy-using industry.

The Anaconda Company similarly has a new liquid rather than heat process for removing copper from ore. Philco has introduced a new line of refrigerators said to use 30 to 50 percent less electricity than previous models. Montgomery Ward has announced a new "Save Energy, Save Money" action program that will help its millions of customers—and others—select energy-saving appliances and take other energy-saving actions. Oil companies are advertising how to cut gasoline consumption.

And so it goes—but does it go fast enough?

The pressures are now on. Legislation forced industry to do many of the things it is now ready to brag about. Courts are bringing about compliance with common sense as well as nonsensical demands, and are delaying, sometimes unfortunately, many industrial projects until they are thoroughly thought through and proved out—but why should this be a court function? Why not a management function? Insurance firms are examining company policies and practices on environmental questions before writing insurance. Investors are looking above the hallowed "bottom line" at the capital and operating expenses for pollution control and environmental protection, as well as certain other social policies.

And there is still much to come. Occupational environment is an area where demands for improvement will continue. Consumer interests and demands will not abate.

Tough Problems Ahead

Two complex general envirommental problems really have not been cracked. Noise is one of them. And we can expect increasing attention to control of noise—from industrial sites, highways, cities and offices. This is a complex problem. One modern installation is so insulated from the outside world it has had to pipe in low-level background noise to break the deadly silences.

Solid-waste management is another area where real solutions are not yet in sight. Resource recovery may be just beginning. With due respect to various industry efforts, litter collection and can/bottle collection stations are nice, but they're not the solution. We need full systems and programs if we are going to avoid inundation by wastes.

Esthetics and people pollution are growing problems. Where are people going to live, work and play and not degrade the quality of the countryside, the cities, the beaches? One new community in Long Island is proposing either to ban auto ownership or to limit residents to no more than one car per family.

Is industry going to look ahead to anticipate coming demands of this kind or is it going to try to catch up with demands and proposed solutions that take effect either in the laws or the marketplace?

Guidelines for Leadership

Our experience and observation of companies which are taking leadership in dealing with environmental issues indicate some general guidelines that may be useful to summarize:

—They give environmental quality the same status as other major elements of doing business—raw materials, equipment, labor, sales, profits and taxes. One company's president heads the environmental committee that meets regularly to review progress and plans on all fronts.

—They assign a top-ranking official continuing responsibility for environmental quality, usually in all its aspects—air and water disposal; occupational health and safety; noise and plant appearance; solid waste disposal, including disposal of manufactured products, and for seeing that environmental considerations, including consumer safety, are given early attention in all planning for new products and processes.

—They maintain close liaison with the scientific community and either conduct or sponsor research to know more about their products sooner than others who may be doing similar research—separately and perhaps unknown.

—Such companies have well-structured mechanisms for communications on environmental developments. They keep attuned to what's happening within their organization and elsewhere. They keep their employees informed, and also local community leaders, lawmakers, customers, educators, news sources, scientists and others.

—They know what the situation is at all locations they operate. And they keep up with changes. One client has 54 sites of operations and an environmental control administrator updates quarterly a complete checklist of what air, water and noise quality status is, what equipment is being installed, what is on schedule, what costs are involved, and what are the priorities and target dates. Another with 102 plant locations is just completing a similar inventory.

—They try to keep a public relations inventory—essential for any sound and continuing program of communications. The checklist for that inventory would include a clear statement of company policy—which may exist but not be articulated. It would include a review of what the company has done, what it is planning to do, and what its target dates are. It would have understandable background papers on research being supported, on technical problems being tackled, on the complexities of as-yet-unsolved problems.

—These companies reject the notion that they shouldn't be prepared to talk about pollution problems as well as achievements. They know a company that is candid on such matters has the best chance of gaining public confidence and of not being saddled with unjustified blame.

If industry is to fulfill its responsibilities in the area of environmental quality—and I believe most industry leaders are prepared to do this—then it must also devote itself to communication with all concerned publics.

This will include a continuing and forthright program of communication for top executives and other corporate officials, as well as for other employees, stockholders, community and campus leaders, public officials, educators, scientists and especially writers and editors. We are seeing a new breed of reporters on environment and related issues. An Environmental Writers Association of America became active this year and now has some 300 members.

In all this, industry has a primary task and responsibility—to seize the leadership in an essential and popular cause and show society that it can produce goods and services needed and improve the quality of our living environment—without wrenching the entire American competitive system out of alignment.

11

How to Communicate in a Crisis

By Richard W. Darrow

Before the National Public Relations Workshop,
American Gas Association,
Miami, April 10, 1972

SUMMARY: Consumerism is here to stay and, with it, a long series of consumerist crises for the American businessman. His response must emphasize a continuing program of public education on the realities involved in serving the consumer in an artificially regulated context. This is especially true in the energy industries. Public dissatisfaction, well intentioned but uninformed, will lead to further distortions and further discontent. Business should encourage formation of and participation in community study groups in which the facts of business life can be presented in context wtih the problems themselves.

Richard W. Darrow, chairman of the board and chief executive officer of Hill and Knowlton, has also served as mayor of Scarsdale, N.Y., and as chairman of the board of trustees of his *alma mater*, Ohio Wesleyan University.

I've been asked to look at the recent survey of consumer attitudes conducted for the American Gas Association (AGA) and to suggest some ways to cope with three problem areas outlined in the study—the energy gap, pollution and consumer concerns.

That's a tall order. Each subject is complex. Each has caused its share of crises for many segments of the industry.

And there's another common point. None of these issues is a fad that will simply fade away when the public becomes weary of the problems. The issues are now firmly locked into the bureaucracy at the federal, state and local levels. Each has a growing body of law and regulation. The Virginia Knauers, Bess Myersons and William Ruckelshauses or their successors are firmly in the saddle. They must continue to justify their existence, seek new powers, more activity and new points of attack. This alone assures the issues will be with us as far into the future as we can see.

I'm not going to give you any magic formulae. Most of the keys to effective communications on crisis issues are basic, bread-and-butter, common-sense public relations. They call for a factual approach. There must be a full recognition of the seriousness of these problems. There must be a willingness to mount the adequate, consistent, long-range public relations programs necessary to cope with them. There must be an understanding that a single defeat for the critics and adversaries doesn't mean an end to the problem. It has been our experience that the critics come back again and again with new facts or alleged facts, with new allies and with new proposals for regulation and restrictions.

This means that continuing research, continuing action, continuing planning on the issues that affect your business must be part of your daily activities. When a crisis hits, it is usually too late to do the kind of background work and planning that is fundamental to a strong communications effort.

A Harsh Climate

The basic rules have not changed. What has changed is the climate of communications in which we operate. All of us here today know that we need to understand the mood of our audiences and the state of their receptivity to information if a communications effort—no matter how massive and well funded—is to be effective.

The AGA survey covers issues subject to lengthy debate and controversy. Proposed solutions are numerous and are frequently in conflict. The resolution of these problems will be hammered out in the public arena, a place that often seems more dangerous to industry than the arena of Rome did to the Christians. But if industry is to make its voice heard on the public issues of the day, we have no choice but to enter that arena armed with viable and convincing practical solutions which will meet legitimate complaints and criticisms.

In today's climate there is no place for the American businessman to hide. But there is the opportunity to become involved in the ferment and hopefully to play a significant role in shaping the decisions that will affect the future course of the nation—and, not so incidentally, the ability of business to keep on making fair profits.

What do we face when we attempt to provide information about our industry or present a point of view about today's pressing issues?

First, there is a lack of public trust and confidence. In a 1966 Harris poll, 53 percent of the public viewed leaders of major corporations with "a great deal of confidence," 35 percent with "some confidence," 5 percent with "hardly any confidence," and another 5 percent were "not sure." When the poll was repeated in 1971, only 27 percent felt "great confidence," 50 percent said "only some," 15 percent "hardly any," and 8 percent were "not sure."

It is small consolation that businessmen are not alone in this erosion of public confidence. The Harris polls show a similar slide for organized religion, education and labor. In fact, only the medical profession has retained the great confidence of the majority. Other recent opinion studies show a shocking drop in just three years in public confidence in all types of leadership.

A second problem development is the growth of critics and muck-rakers as the new public heroes. The spectacular successes of the Ralph Naders and Barry Commoners have opened the door to a flood of critics and "public advocates" who make full-time careers out of focusing on what they consider industry's weak spots. And they are formidable adversaries. Many of them have done their homework, have marshalled their arguments well and have proved to be convincing. They understand the media and use them effectively.

Frequently the critics point to real problems that deserve our serious attention. But solutions proposed are another matter. They range from Barry Commoner's plea for a total restructuring of the economic system to one I saw recently, urging that more mothers breast-feed their infants to reduce the use and disposal of materials used in baby bottles. Both proposals got plenty of attention from the media.

A third problem factor is the growth of fear and doubt about where we are going. Spokesmen who suggest the need to adopt a simpler, less affluent way of life are gaining allies all the time. A few years back, they were on a lunatic fringe of the environmental movement. Today they are front and center.

You are aware of the recent computer model projection of resources use and environmental control by some MIT (Massachusetts Institute of Technology) scientists for the Club of Rome, a relatively new international organization. These studies point to an end to growth and the probability of a collapse of our present system some time in the future.

Before that study hit the press, an impressive number of distinguished British scientists stirred controversy by endorsing a so-called "Blueprint for Survival." This manifesto says our choice is between a future of famines, epidemics, social crises and wars, or a stable and sustainable society with controlled population and controlled industrial growth.

Regardless of what we may think of the premises in these studies, the problems they pose will be with us for many years and we can look for them to surface in the political arena as backup materials for any number of proposed laws and regulations.

The rapid emergence of the "no-growth" school of thought has particularly chilling implications for those supplying the energy needs of the nation. Because energy production is a key to growth, it is a prime target for those who would stop or turn back the clock.

It is in this atmosphere of public distrust, vocal and effective criticism and a genuine fear about tomorrow that we must operate when we communicate about such issues as the energy gap, pollution and consumer concerns.

Choosing the Communications Content

I have been associated with the natural gas and oil industry for many years as a consultant. I believe that I can look at the issues as an outsider and suggest from an outside viewpoint some means of approaching them.

The industries which provide the energy that makes this country the most affluent in the world have been discussing the impending energy gap for many years, and desperately trying to get the kind of government action needed to relieve the problem. But who remembers now how much oil and natural gas reserves could have been expanded if President Eisenhower had not vetoed the bill which the Natural Gas and Oil Resources Committee fought so hard for in the mid-1950s?

Present trends indicate to me that public concern about energy is bound to grow. In some parts of the country gas suppliers already are forced to say "no" to some potential industrial and residential customers. Other industries involved in supplying energy are conducting broad communications programs to make their problems known and to suggest steps needed to relieve the situation. The natural gas industry cannot afford to leave this communications effort to other energy producers. If it does, the results could be public misunderstanding of the needs of the gas industry and a growing fear about the availability of the supply for home heating.

It is up to the people involved in the production and distribution of energy to inform the public of the dimensions of the developing energy gap and to suggest to them how it can be relieved. If we do not now—in April, 1972—mount an effective information program, when the energy crunch becomes more severe, the wrath of the public will more than likely fall on energy producers and suppliers rather than on government officials who set the policies that led to the problem.

Strong communications efforts should be conducted both by industry groups and by individual companies. The fact that every major city has its gas company provides a communications base that is nationwide.

I have reviewed some of the AGA informational materials on the energy question. The booklet for opinion leaders and the bill stuffer both do an excellent job of explaining the problem and what the gas industry is doing about it.

My question is: Are gas suppliers and distributors making really effective use of this material? I am told that some 65,000 copies of the larger booklet have been distributed to local regulatory bodies, mayors, editors and others in a position to influence the ultimate decisions on the gas supply problem. Are there other local and national audiences that could benefit from this information? How about the people who are targets for communications by the industry's critics and those who might find virtue in the energy crunch?

I also know that one million copies of the leaflet have been distributed. One million sounds like an impressive figure. But the AGA background report on the natural gas supply problem tells me there are 145 million gas consumers in the United States. With that kind of potential audience, the one million figure seems to indicate that only a dent has been made in the total communications task.

Getting the Best Distribution

Producing the kind of materials needed for effective communications is only the first step in a well-managed public relations program. If the second step—seeking the widest possible distribution of those materials—is not taken, we end up in a situation where we are talking to ourselves. And even if all the AGA materials—and I include the motion picture, the radio tapes, TV film clips, slide presentation, the press releases and speeches—are used by the gas distributors, I wonder if this is still enough to make an impact on the public in today's communications climate.

Are gas companies on the local level producing materials that relate to the home-town situation? Have gas company public relations men and executives sought face-to-face discussions with members of the local press, local opinion leaders, local civic groups, legislators and regulators who form the backbone of the decision-making process in this country?

We can't assume that people who should be most aware of the problem are getting the message. Not long ago, an oil industry representative told me of a discussion he had with a congressman about the energy gap issue. After the oil man had outlined the problem, the congressman said, "Why, this is an appalling situation. Why haven't you people told us about this problem?"

In today's communications climate, it is not enough simply to tell your story and hope that your audience retains the message. You must tell it over and over again in as many ways as possible for a lasting impact.

I recognize that the gas suppliers are in a delicate position. You don't want to frighten your customers into shifting to other forms of energy. You do want to build public confidence in the industry's ability to cope with the problem. But if you hope to see a resolution to this problem that takes into account your needs and your point of view, the issue cannot be ducked.

In the past month I have seen a number of newspaper and magazine articles which discuss the gas supply shortage, including a full-blown feature in the *New York Sunday Times*. Too many of these articles end on a note that the gas supply shortage has been artificially induced by a deliberate refusal of gas producers to develop existing resources and search for new ones.

It is obvious that others are discussing your problem and too often they are discussing it in a negative way.

With the potential base of communication that exists within the gas industry, there are thousands of opportunities available for you to tell your story nationally and locally. A full-scale effort on your part and a full, open and frequent discussion of the facts can help build the public concern and understanding necessary to reach a reasonable solution to the problem.

Environmental Issues, Real and Contrived

I'm sure that you—as I—find it curious that the survey conducted for the AGA indicates the public connects natural gas with pollution. After all, natural gas is the cleanest form of energy presently available and there is a minimum of environmental degradation involved in its production and transport.

Most surveys rank pollution just below crime and the Vietnam war among problems that worry Americans most. The gas industry perhaps has not talked widely and extensively enough about its relationship to the environment. Your activities in the environmental field are a plus that can help build credibility with the public.

Certainly the opportunity exists to point out that gas heating has eliminated the layer of soot that used to be so apparent in our major cities after every snowfall.

The AGA survey indicates that some consumers link the use of gas in the home with the production of grease and dirt on kitchen surfaces. Others have taken a similar view.

I noted in a recent issue of *Air and Water News* a report that a Chicago allergist, Dr. Theron G. Randolph, says gas appliances are major indoor polluters and along with common dirt they have an adverse effect on his patients. We have seen lesser criticisms, first appearing in relatively obscure publications, grow to the point where industry must spend endless hours in researching the facts and making these facts known to both the scientific community and the general public.

Do we know enough about pollution within the home? And can we say something useful about this problem that will be of help to the consumer, either in quieting his fears or in actually reducing any amount of grease and dirt connected with the use of gas appliances?

There are, of course, some environmental problems related to the production, distribution and use of natural gas. These, too, should be recognized and the story of what the industry is doing to solve these problems should be told in detail.

Consumer Confidence

According to the survey, the consumer's positive opinion of the gas industry is a real plus that should be developed as extensively as possible. Credibility in any area is a golden asset. I'm particularly impressed with the efforts to provide information on means to conserve gas both as an economy measure and as one that can assure that supplies are allocated properly. This is attractive to the consumer who is worried about dollars, the environmentalist who links energy production with pollution and the conservationist concerned about dwindling resources.

The consumer confidence that you have built through the years can be a stepping stone to credibility in discussing other problems that affect your industry. We should all ask ourselves: How can we make greater use of this asset? Have we established alliances with local consumer groups and local consumer officials so that they are open to understanding of the other problems that the industry faces?

In considering the issues before us—the energy gap, pollution and consumer concerns—it occurs to me that there is a means of communications that has yet to be tried by any segment of industry. It is one that would take nerve, hard, long-term effort, and a very deep management commitment. But it is one that would go to the heart of the problems that most severely affect our urban communities and the industries that operate in these communities.

Too often, decisions affecting communities are made mainly on demands of highly vocal social activitists. Not enough thought and attention are given to allowing people to make choices about their current and future wants and needs. Emotion, even hysteria, tends to take over.

There is valid concern about preserving the environment. There is valid concern also about goods and services and jobs needed by a growing and viable community. There is concern about housing, education, law enforcement and drug abuse—just to name a few issues. Too often these concerns appear to clash. There is too little communication among the groups interested in specific problems. Important decisions are made on the basis of emotion, pressure tactics, popular political issues, or because of government pressures.

Community Study Groups

The concept of making decisions based on full examination and understanding of all obtainable facts generally is not practiced by U.S. communities. I believe there is a better way for communities to chart their futures. And there's a useful role in this action for the local gas company. It involves:

1. Creation of a system or formula by which communities can make rational, informed approaches toward understanding and solving the problems that are of most immediate concern.

2. A demonstration to the community of the complexity of the problems.

3. A display of industry's concern for all aspects of community welfare.

Communities need to join in an organized look at what's ahead—the problems, the possible solutions, the choices that they face. This would not be a simple, inexpensive or short-term endeavor.

A basic step would be organization of local leadership beginning with a "core" influence group, perhaps consisting of a newspaper publisher (or other top major-media man), a college president, industry representatives, head of a prominent conservation group, a religious leader, a labor leader, and others.

This leadership group would take responsibility for arousing community interest and recruiting support. It would establish primary objectives and bring in other representatives of the communications media, municipal government, industry, civic and religious organizations, women's groups, universities, youth groups, labor and political leaders to provide broader support and assistance for study and action programs.

In the beginning, the program would operate on seed money from industry. But since this would be a community effort, operating funds should be raised by public subscription to give a sense of community participation. A United Fund-type campaign might be necessary.

There would be a need to establish task forces for in-depth studies of all the community's problem areas. A series of community forums for thorough and public discussion of the issues would have to be created. And some mechanism to provide follow-through on any action indicated by task force reports would have to be built into the program.

By providing the means for in-depth discussion of local problems, there would be an ample opportunity to communicate fully on issues such as energy supply, pollution and consumer concerns. The opportunity would be open for a direct meeting with critics, supporters and neutrals in an atmosphere where they would have to consider all of the facts, not just the ones that fit their point of view. A good way to introduce a critic to reality is to burden him with the facts and the responsibility for decisions, for choices.

I wonder if the gas distributors with their deep local roots and strong reputation for service and integrity might not be in the best position to act as catalysts for such a program?

This approach would present an opportunity for "action-oriented" public relations. In these times it is not enough to generate those "warm feelings" that so many associate with the traditional goals of most public relations efforts.

We must find the ways to acquaint the public with their involvement in our problems—convincing ways to carry our messages to the same groups that have been the major targets of those who have misunderstood and misinterpreted our past record.

But anyone who takes this route must realize he will be able to get by with no less than the true and full disclosure of the facts. This can be no cosmetic undertaking. When faced with problems that involve the public, we must be willing to explain as fully as possible what the situation is, how we are part of the problem, what we are doing about it, what it will cost us, what it will cost the public and what problems are presently beyond solution. And we should do this before the critics take the floor and demand it.

We should also insist on full disclosure by the critics who so often avoid facts that don't fit their preconceptions.

Full Disclosure Is Essential

This side of the problem was summed up by C. Howard Hardesty, Jr. of Continental Oil in a recent talk in which he said that many of the challenges facing the natural resources industries have the potential of destroying the economic ability of free enterprise to respond to society's needs. He said, "My belief arises not from a fear that the business community is incapable of meeting our nation's demands for energy and other basic natural resources. Rather, it stems from a recognition that our critics, if not questioned and held accountable for false or misleading criticism, will divert business, government and the public from the pursuit of a common purpose."

Industry's problems readily become public property, and experience has shown that silence or defensive tactics alone do not lead to understanding or solutions. The climate has seldom been worse for half-truths or a no-comment response. Taking such a course helps insure that the critics' position—no matter how misguided—will prevail.

I suggest that if industry does not accelerate its policy of full disclosure, needless and perhaps harmful requirements may be forced upon us by government edict. Rules and regulations continue to grow in the area of financial reporting. The Federal Trade Commission now requires that advertisers back up all the claims in their ads. And this has been taken a step further with the demand that equal time be allowed on the networks for those who would dispute material presented in television advertising.

Obviously the same principles could be expanded to cover other aspects of corporate activity. The objectives of these regulations and proposals are admirable. We all recognize that integrity in advertising is essential, and that all sides of any issue should be available for public scrutiny. But all of us, too, are aware that bureaucratic controls can impose tremendous and unrealistic burdens on the public and on businesses that serve the public.

This indicates there is even more to increasing our efforts to achieve full disclosure than the desire to be a good corporate citizen. There is the matter of practicality—a common-sense approach to business survival in an era of change. I am confident that we can develop a common-sense approach that will pay dividends to the gas industry, to the economy, to our customers, and to the American consumer whose welfare we serve and on whose welfare we all ultimately depend.

12

How the Chemical Industry Can Better Its Image Through Communication

By Liz Carpenter

Before the Manufacturing Chemists Association
New York City, November 20, 1973

SUMMARY: The emerging restless segments of society can no longer be dismissed as the "zealots," the "little old lady in tennis shoes." They are likely to include your wife, your daughter or your neighbor. If industry is to walk hand in hand with the public, it must know the public better. It must respond to anxieties and fears with better understanding and in a more coherent vocabulary. People are becoming noisier and more restless because they want someone to listen and to respond. In the absence of an answer, the public has only Mr. Nader, Congress, or a buyer's strike for an outlet.

Liz Carpenter, vice president of Hill and Knowlton, Inc., in its Washington, D.C. office, served for five years as a White House press secretary and speech writer during the Johnson years.

Back in the early days of the Great Society, when we were trying to see how much of a program was needed for Headstart, Sargent Shriver used to tell the story of a word-identity test given to children in a Boston slum.

The children were shown a series of flash-cards and asked to identify the object on the card. One card showed a teddy bear. Seventy percent of the children thought it was a rat.

The rat was the only furry object in their human experience.

You in the chemical industry have a similar identity problem. The first step to public acceptance is to realize the extent of the public's ignorance of the word "chemicals" or "chemical industry." What do those words mean to me or the people I know?

I took a sampling in a highly unscientific poll and tried the word identity game in several gatherings where the age and intelligence of the people are considerably higher than in the Boston slum.

One group was my own family and assorted friends. Another was the Washington Press Club pub at high noon. I simply asked:

"What mental image do you have when you hear the words: "chemicals" or "chemical industry?""

The answers ranged from "war" to "pollution."

"People in white coats with bubbling test tubes."

"Yellow fumes out of a smokestack in a city."

"Green pools of water on the Jersey flat."

"It's everything—too vast to explain!"

I have thought about those answers a lot, as well as my own, which is a hazy sort of kaleidoscope of plants with pipes to the sky and a lot of words that are too long and have too many consonants.

Why, when we talk of chemicals or the chemical industry, don't I think about:

- the knit dress in my suitcase which travels so well?
- the measles vaccine which stops blindness in babies?
- the sweet-smelling bottles and jars of cosmetics on my dressing table?
- Chanel No. 5?
- the new food analogs which are tomorrow's lifesavers on this crowded planet?
- my friend, the Supreme Court Justice, with a plastic valve in his heart?

Did you tell me they were chemicals?

We are, alas, chemical cowards because we are chemical ignoramuses. We fear what we do not understand.

As a result, you have to spend an enormous amount of money coping with the food faddists' anti-additive attitudes, making your case to the Food and Drug Administration, or trying to persuade a city zoning commission to give a permit to build a plant. And you still wind up in the negative context.

I think the time has come to let the public in on some of your positives.

I think the time has come to tell people that you are primarily Dr. Jekyll, not Mr. Hyde. I think it is time the public looked on the chemical industry as the key to life, not to death.

This will take an all-out program to explain the chemical industry and the many roles chemicals play in our lives, while at the same time recognizing problems where they do exist. It may mean revising some of our own product emphasis.

Letting the Public In

If this industry is to walk hand in hand with the public, you must know people better. If this industry is to change public attitudes and understanding, it must change some of its own attitudes. I think the public deserves to be counted in. I think they are curious, open-minded, and eager to absorb some of the exciting new solutions that are bubbling in those test tubes. Right now, the main thrust of your effort seems to play to the legislators and others who regulate your industry. This is necessary and it builds understanding in a small audience, but it really does nothing to reduce the overall negative image.

The FDA may come forth with a wise and knowledgeable decision, but it hasn't stopped the letter-writer from Duluth who worries about everything on the pantry shelf, who keeps those cards and letters coming in to the lawmakers.

We live in an ever increasing, ever restless society. In the last 15 years, we have seen society, like so many chemicals, regroup into new combinations and pressures: into caucuses, coalitions, which form and influence the great movements of our times, movements which spill out into the marketplace and the political arena.

Thirty years ago, when I came to Washington, these restless segments who showed up in their Congressmen's offices or picketed the agencies, were easily dismissed as "the crazies, the zealots, the little old ladies in tennis shoes."

Today, the protesting voice belongs to a Junior Leaguer with a stationwagon load of friends making a swing through the supermarket to check chemicals in foods. She is the young mother questioning the plastic toys she buys for her children, as well as the tires for her car, or maybe your company's stock. The "little old lady in tennis shoes" is likely to be your wife, your daughter, your son or—you.

The "zealot" is the new member of the state legislature or the city council who does associate with and respect all those noisy groups which keep forming.

The Need to be Heard

Why are people getting more restless and noisier? They should be heard. They want someone to listen and respond.

If industry fails to foresee the questions or provide honest and adequate answers, then the public has only Mr. Nader, Congress, and a buyer's strike for outlet.

That is why new voices in industry are speaking up with strong words, for these are strong times.

"The freest nation is the nation whose members, by proud habit, always do less than the law allows, always more than the law requires," said one such statesman.

"We had better spend as rapidly as we can whatever money and manpower is required to make our products socially acceptable in real terms," said another.

All too often you are too selective, too inhibited, too limited. Any project is likely to be good public relations, but it needs to be far more than just good public relations.

More new positive steps are beginning to move industry from the negative to the positive in the public mind.

One outstanding example, of course, is one of your companies which took on pollution as a challenge and simply said, "We will not pollute," and promised to meet government standards *before* the 1980 date.

Others are busy in developing products for the environmental front.

Another company, with new developments in food analogs, is holding a seminar in December where food and nutrition editors will hear from respected nutritionists from hospitals and medical schools they will trust.

Public seminars—where everyone is invited—to listen to the pros and cons of a new drug are another part of the scene.

Your own MCA consumer program has been reaching out to the grassroots to bring the company executive or the company technician face-to-face with broadcasters and consumer editors.

Commitments at All Levels

There needs to be much, much more of this. There needs to be a real commitment to this end on the part of the corporate board, the corporate bookkeeper, as well as the press office. Most press offices are making valiant efforts on limited funds and limited cooperation and understanding. Often an enlightened board doesn't convince the middle-management level. They don't comprehend, for instance, that yesterday's food editor who merely helped her readers pretty up the Sunday ham or keep the souffle from falling is today's consumer reporter on the air each night questioning the value of your products.

Today it is show-and-tell time for the chemical industry. It is going to take some real commitment on your part to make it successful.

One first step: If you are going to rap with the public, you'd better look like the public and feel like the public. The public is not all-male and all-white.

Some revisions in your board room to bring in new dimensions of thinking and reaction will do wonders for you. It will help you reach out; it will help the public reach in.

Business can take a lesson from the recent Watergate experience. You cannot run a government or a business from a mountaintop or a board room—remote from the public.

These painful lessons occur periodically in our history and generally we emerge from them stronger in our thinking and our actions.

Calvin Coolidge used to preach that "the business of America is business."

In a world of growing population, in a world of shrinking resources, perhaps the business of business is America.

We in this country are plunging into an era of soul-searching such as we have never known before.

Soul-searching can be a rewarding experience—asking ourselves, "What is our national purpose? Where is our national soul? Where do we fit in?"

In time of war, our country is bound together by the bond of patriotism and expediency. In times of relative peace, we look for leadership and answers at home.

We want something more from government and business.

The wise businessman will join in this soul-searching in a most visible way.

What is our national purpose?

I would hope it would be for all of us to be the watchful and jealous guardians of the freest society ever created. I would hope it would be to improve, really improve, life in this country for the people, all of them. I would hope it would be to reach out by worthy example and friendship and hope to the 150 nations of this restless globe. I would hope it would mean we would live in openness because we have nothing to hide.

For you are engaged in the vast, exciting, awesome business of taking the most basic elements of earth and air and combining them to produce the way we live.

So let us look with new eyes at the wealth of human resources all around us. Human resources are the most vital part of the formula. They have been missing all too long.

13

... and Candor Begat Credibility

By Vincent N. Gannon

Before the 74th National Meeting of the
American Institute of Chemical Engineers
New Orleans, March 12, 1973

SUMMARY: Consumerism has taught us that an informed, educated, concerned, and frequently skeptical public calls for nothing less than forthrightness in corporate communications, an understanding of audience attitudes, and the ability to communicate in terms attuned to their interests. A conscientious effort to reduce sources of friction will make it harder for critics to establish common cause with the general public.

Vincent N. Gannon, broadly experienced in corporate public relations, is a senior vice president of Hill and Knowlton.

W hile the title of my talk is in the style of Genesis, it should at this point in time be labeled "prophecy" to conform to truth-in-packaging standards. But it's a prophecy I feel must and will be fulfilled as more and more businesses realize they face a situation that demands new initiatives.

During the Fifties and Sixties, attitudes of the general public toward business were reasonably good. Employment was high, the economy growing, and people were enjoying increasing affluence. But the communications policies that may have been acceptable then are inadequate for the skepticism and mistrust that have thus far marked the Seventies.

Today, we are told, the public feels business is out of step with its expectations and demands. Daniel Yankelovich, highly regarded as an analyst of opinion and attitude trends, last year gave a sobering view of the dimensions of the problem. He reported that:

- Nine out of 10 people believe that consumer protection advocates can help them improve the value they get for their money.
- A two-thirds majority of the public would support the consumer protection movement, either by active participation or through money, votes and moral support.
- The public favors severe penalties for companies that do not live up to high standards: fines for polluters; prohibition of advertising if it proves to be false and misleading; suspending the sale of products altogether if necessary; and even personal liability for executives.
- The public, at that time, singled out certain industries—notably, the automobile industry, the oil industry, the chemical industry and several others as the chief culprits.
- The people's chief complaint is that products are overpriced for what they give and that manufacturers put their profits ahead of product quality, long life and service.
- There is a pervasive feeling that advertising is misleading, promising more than the manufacturers deliver, and that products which involve the public's safety and health can stand a great deal of improvement.

All in all, a stunning indictment. Clearly consumerism has become a major focal point of the problem facing business in its relations with the public.

Challenge to Corporate Performance

But consumerism represents more than a crisis in confidence. Added importance derives from the fact that it raises questions as to performance in the basic social function of the corporation—to provide goods and services for the public.

The role of the corporation in society has been debated in the past, of course, but chiefly on legal and economic points such as concentration, monopoly power and management accountability. Generally, however, it was conceded that the corporation did its basic job well. With this no longer the case, it becomes all the more difficult for business to communicate on other subjects on which it needs public support.

Periodically, too, the status of the present-day corporation is questioned. Theodore Jacobs, associate of Ralph Nader and executive director of the Center for the Study of Responsive Law, terms it "outmoded and inefficient to continue the fiction that they (large corporations) are entities created by a single state." In a paper, "Pollution, Consumerism, Accountability," presented at a conference of the Center for the Study of Democratic Institutions, he wrote:

> ". . .there must also be basic changes in the form and privileges of corporations if corporate power is to be made accountable. We must recognize that the privilege of incorporation is just that—a privileged status granted by government to achieve economic and social purposes, to be modified or withdrawn when it no longer is useful for their purposes. Specifically, it has been suggested that Federal rather than state charters should be required for all corporations doing business in interstate commerce. . . . Federal incorporation would help make our legal concepts of corporations square with reality."

A public which feels that business is letting it down in terms of product service will be far more receptive to such proposals than it would have been five years ago.

More immediately, the impact of consumerism means a continuing threat to industry's freedom of operations and its ability to innovate. The prospect is for continuing pressure for tighter restrictions on such interfaces with the public as:

- The environmental impact of its manufacturing operations.
- The environmental fate of its products, their ingredients and their packaging.
- The advertising and marketing of its products.
- The development and testing of new products.

It is the seriousness of such implications—and the evidence of the degree to which consumerism has eroded public confidence—that is the source of my conviction that business needs to respond effectively to the new communications demands today's situation places upon it.

To do otherwise, to adopt a posture of resistance and rely on purely defensive programs, would be to pursue a strategy inadequate in the past and unpromising for the future. The likely result will be greater government regulation and its inherent problems and implications.

Addressing consumerism, however, is tackling a problem not easily isolated. It must be understood, first in its historical perspective and, secondly, as both a manifestation of, and contributor to, the widespread disaffection with business.

Long History of Consumerism

Historically, consumerism in this country dates back to the turn of the century and eventually led to the passage in 1906 of the Pure Food and Drug Act and creation of the Federal Trade Commission in 1914. Later, in the mid-Thirties, public concern prompted strengthening of the Food and Drug Act and broadening of the FTC's power to control misleading advertising, false labeling and deceptive sales practices.

Today, consumerism becomes part of the movement for corporate social responsibility and, as such, represents the continued questioning of the role of the corporation in society. The rationale is familiar:

> The consumer is bewildered by a continuingly heavy flow of new products . . . Their technological complexity makes them difficult to evaluate . . . They may have potential long-term side effects . . . Modern marketing techniques induce people to buy things they do not need . . . Consumer sovereignty is eroded since the ability to make an informed choice is hampered.

Clearly, the American marketing concept is under challenge. To the critics, marginally differentiated products serve no primary social need; competition between products with little or no discernible difference is not seen as competition, certainly not as legitimate competition. We have, for example, already seen advertising labeled false for preempting an attribute—specifically gasoline advertising which gives the impression other gasolines do not contain a certain additive.

For a proper perspective on such developments, an important distinction must be drawn between consumer protection and the broader concept of consumerism. Consumer protection involves measures to protect the public against deceptive packaging, bait-and-switch advertising, loopholes in warranties and other practices judged to be misleading and unfair. But consumerism has deeper roots, being a lineal descendant of economic theories that hold competition between different brands of substantially the same product to be economically wasteful. While their theories admit a limited informative function for advertising, anything beyond that—i.e., to shift people from one brand to another—is not only economically wasteful but unfair to the consumer who ultimately pays for that advertising.

Pressure points of the future may well be in the resolution of underlying questions: Who is to define what margin of product difference is significant and how? Who is to decide by what means which needs are to be served?

General Disaffection with Business

The second aspect of consumerism which must be taken into account is the relationship it bears to the low esteem in which business is held by the American public. Whether consumerism has contributed to the problem, or whether it is the result of the disaffection—or as is most likely, both—is beside the point. Unless a major, determined, sustained effort is made to re-establish the credibility of business, the effectiveness of consumer-oriented activities will fall short of their potential. However, consumer-interest programs, which are undertaken as part of a broad, innovative approach to corporate communications, should contribute substantially to solving the confidence and credibility problems business faces today.

The need for new approaches to communications is inescapable in view of available evidence as to the prevailing mood of the public. A Louis Harris survey, for example, last year reported a sharp erosion of confidence in the leadership of our institutions. Among the findings: only 27 percent of the public have ''great confidence'' in business-leadership—a drop of 50 percent since 1966. Of America's institutions—among them education, organized religion, labor, medicine, the press, advertising—business loss of 1966 supporters was exceeded only by financial institutions, the Supreme Court and the military.*

A study released by Opinion Research Corporation provides some dimensions of the erosion since 1965:

- Among the public at large, those indicating high approval of business dropped from 20 percent to 11 percent;
- Among adults under 30, the drop was from 23 percent to 12 percent;
- College graduates showed a decline from 36 percent to 17 percent.

*Ed. Note—In the early days of the energy crisis, the slippage in confidence again manifested itself. According to a Gallup Poll taken in December 1973, the public placed the blame for the energy situation largely on the Federal government and the oil companies. Twenty-three percent judged the government in general was at fault, and another 19 percent named President Nixon or his Administration. One out of every four, however, fixed responsibility for the crisis on the oil companies themselves.

Moreover, there is evidence that this erosion has taken place even within the ranks of business itself:

- Among people in professional and managerial occupations, high approval skidded from 28 percent to 16 percent.

Nor are youth attitudes encouraging. Another ORC report shows that among people between the ages of 15 and 20 years overall favorability toward 18 major industries has declined more than that of the rest of the population. In the case of the chemical industry, 51 percent of youths in the survey claimed to have very or mostly favorable attitudes in 1969; in the most recent survey, this percentage dropped to 34 percent. Much the same is true of the oil and gasoline industry, which dropped from 69 percent in 1969 to 43 percent.

Responding to the Warning

To disregard these warning signs, simply to do business as usual, would be a mistake; corporate communications which are just "more of the same" may not be only unproductive, but possibly counterproductive, if not damaging.

There are some, of course, who feel consumerism is only a temporary phenomenon. They welcome the prediction of some Washington observers that this Congress will enact legislation to set up an independent consumer protection agency empowered to intervene in proceedings of other Federal agencies and that, with its passage, consumerism will fade as a political issue. Very possibly they may be right. But the agency will still be with us and, regardless of its political heat, consumerism will have been further institutionalized.

Just as previous consumer movements left new laws and regulations to function in behalf of the consumer, the current movement has already left us an impressive legacy: Truth-in-Packaging Law, Truth-in-Lending, an Auto Safety Law, the White House Office of Consumer Affairs, the Environmental Protection Agency, and greatly broadened activities on the part of the Federal Trade Commission and the Food and Drug Administration. Whether or not additional legislation is proposed, many of the premises of consumerism already have been built into our legal and regulatory system. And because the consumer movement touches on the daily bread-and-butter concerns of the public, and appeals to the affluent and influential middle class, continuing public attention to consumer issues seems likely in the future.

Some companies take a defensive position and concentrate their efforts on refuting what they consider unwarranted criticism. Others accept as a fact of life this new concern about values, prices, longevity, durability and hazards, and they have moved to accommodate it. Some, in fact, view consumerism as an opportunity to find new grounds for competition.

All business, of course, has a competitive and responsible interest in responding as quickly and as positively as possible to concerns of the consumer—the final judge, after all, of industry's products, its warranties and its methods of sales and promotion. As the private consumer movement has expanded and as government has become more deeply involved, the consumer has grown more sophisticated in his knowledge and judgment—and more demanding.

Industries that recognize this at an early stage and develop strong programs to anticipate and meet emerging demands will be in a far better position to avoid both unfair and unwarranted attacks and the continuing move for tighter control of all phases of business by government.

Accomplishing this will take a strong, conscious and continuing internal and external effort by business. In view of the grassroots nature of the consumer movement, intensive communications must play a vital role. Necessarily, public relations has an important place, but public relations programs must reflect a thorough understanding of the government's involvement, the private consumer movement and the needs of industry.

Consumerism in a Public Relations Program

Public relations aspects of the undertaking would include:

- *Programming*—Consumer concerns must be identified, and positive constructive programs developed, including responses to new legislation and consumer criticism.
- *Organization*—Consideration should be given to establishing high-level, permanent, internal organizations to deal with consumer complaints and desires.
- *Internal Audit*—Operations, products, sales methods and other aspects of the business should be examined to spot potential pitfalls and determine if better means can be found to respond to the desires of consumers.
- *Monitoring*—An early-warning system should be developed to follow legislative activities on the Federal, state and local levels. Similarly, the activities of consumer groups and specific media should be watched to determine emerging trends and possible problem spots.
- *Consumer Education*—The development of classroom units for

consumer education programs and the distribution of materials to consumer groups and others.

- *Publicity*—The development of consumer-oriented material, for editorial and/or advertising use.

The specific objectives of any such effort will, of course, vary from company to company. But general goals would be to:

- Re-establish the integrity of a company's products and services.
- Demonstrate—not simply assert—that the company is responsive and responsible.
- Defuse potential problems by bringing them out in the open—not prematurely but when the gestation period is about over.
- Build a reputation for the company as responsive and progressive: aware of its sensitive interfaces with the public . . . open to reasonable point of view . . . sincere and conscientious in seeking ways to eliminate potential points of friction . . . reasonable in its reaction to new issues . . . forthright and complete in discussing problems and issues.

In the past, corporate communications have tended to put their emphasis on success, without admission of problems, partial successes or failures. Many feel that this approach has encouraged the public to have unrealistic expectations of business.

While it is only natural to try to hide your warts, the tendency to tell only the good—or to hold back on some aspect of the situation—may offer only temporary benefit. Any good that may be realized is often undone when other facts are brought to light . . . and presented in terms, and under circumstances, chosen by others.

In light of the prospects for continuing consumerism pressure and the general disaffection of the public for business, a re-evaluation of total corporate communications, policies and practices seems not only worth while, but imperative. If ways can be found to eliminate sources of friction and criticism, the effort would probably be repaid many times over in avoiding further arbitrary controls on a company's operations and its freedom to innovate. Future attacks, whether economic, legalistic or legislative, will stand far less a chance of success if critics cannot establish common cause with the general public.

14

Promises, Promises!

By Faith Prior

Before The Savings Banks Association of New York State,
Marketing and Public Relations Forum,
New York City, January 26, 1973

SUMMARY: One key to improved consumer relations is more and better communications, free of jargon and ambiguity. But sound communication must be based on positive and innovative action to improve consumer services. Strong management backing is necessary to develop the type of consumer affairs department that can seek out problems, devise solutions and maintain strong contacts with appropriate government and private groups. Knee jerk reactions to consumer demands can only lead to the type of confrontation that business usually loses.

Faith Prior, Extension Family Economist at the University of Vermont and the originator of Vermont's pioneering consumer protection law, serves as a consultant in consumer affairs to Hill and Knowlton, Inc.

Whatever the word "consumerist" means to you—that is what I am likely to be called, so we might as well start at that point. "Consumerism," as any historians among you will know, is not new. What is new is that this is a new kind of consumerism. It puts to the test many of the basic concepts which business and industry have lived with for a long time.

For one thing, the consumer interest extends far beyond adulterated food and unsafe cars. I am personally involved in such a variety of areas as health care, insurance, anti-poverty programs, housing, power, legislation, nutrition, debt counseling, ecology, drugs—yes, and banking. And there are some common denominators among all of these.

One common base, certainly, is the fact that the American consumer has high expectations. Business has, in fact, promised us a rose garden. But while individual products and services may be a great deal better than they were, say, at the end of World War II, we all buy and use so many more products and services that our total impression is that nothing ever works the way they promised it would. "If we can land on the moon, why can't the computers get my bill right?" is the plaintive cry from San Diego to Presque Isle.

A second common denominator is that the valid interest of the consumer is not sufficiently served by existing mechanisms. There has been, in general, far more acclaim for new formula detergents and computerized billing than for dealing substantively with the complaints the new marvels generate.

Given these two observations, plus a whole new social climate in which the market's ability to absorb the products of industry is suddenly seen as finite, it should be quite clear to any student of economic history that the age of the producer has quietly become the age of the consumer.

Government Backs Consumerism

That this is the view of many public officials is evident. Those of you who heard or read Superintendent Albright's address at Boca Raton last November found the message spelled out unmistakably: "So that there will be no misunderstanding," he said, "I should emphasize that the new Division (of Consumer Affairs) will not only respond to consumer complaints, but, wherever such complaints bring to light needed reforms, the Division will press vigorously for these reforms within the banking system. I assure you that it is very much in your interest that the Banking Board and the Banking Department play a much more active role in insuring that people doing business with banks are fully protected. If we do not, others, without any understanding of your problems, will.''

It can't be said much more clearly than that. But I suspect that your reaction is much like mine when I hear a speech on the challenges of being an educator.

There's a great book of photographs with brief captions called ''Vermont is Where You Find It''—some of you may be familiar with it. One of my favorites is the picture of two old boys listening to a Fourth of July speaker; one cups his hand behind his ear and asks ''What's he talking about?'', to which his crony replies ''He don't say.'' In case that *is* your feeling about consumer interest in the banking business, I thought we might talk a little bit about what *I* hear them saying. (And underlying my comments I want you to understand that I think this is all in your own interest and that that's a perfectly valid reason for making certain changes if you can't get it done for nobler reasons.)

Then let's think about the promises you make—and how you say them.

Consumer Expectations

It is a fact that clarity and simplicity make some people nervous. Advertising and publicity releases often tend to try to create a sense of importance through the use of jargon—and this is as true for professions as it is for business and industry. (Did you ever listen in on a meeting of a Bar Association?)

Once upon a time I taught English to French-speaking people, and simultaneously taught a creative writing course to an English-speaking group. It was no contest. Those writing with English as their native language produced infinitely more verbal garbage and I can only conclude that the more words you know the more words you feel compelled to use.

I had come this far in putting down some notes for today, when the word ''disintermediation'' drifted into my mind as the sort of thing that crops up from time to time in your business. But before I used it, I thought I'd better check out my own understanding, so I phoned a friend who is a senior bank officer. He worried the word around a little and then asked if he could call me back. After a while he did, and said he'd called New York just to be sure he gave me the right definition, then went on to talk about ''disinvesting as rates fluctuated.'' Finally I said ''John, are you talking about shifting money around to take advantage of better interest?'' There was an uneasy silence, and then a cautious reply ''Yes—I guess you could say that.''

Now I'm not suggesting that you shouldn't be free to speak any professional language you like; I'm just warning that the consumer has now been conditioned to suspect jargon, and that you can at least *seem* more honest and believable by taking the most direct route to the public mind.

You may think you already *are*.

I'm on the Board of Directors of Blue Shield and at a meeting one of the staff was complaining that the public wrongly expects that each health insurance policy he pays for will pay off if he's sick, no matter how many policies he has. I asked if they'd developed any ads or informational pieces to tell the public *why* they wouldn't pay if another company *did*, and he said they'd mentioned it in ads. What exactly had they said? The ads had pointed out that "duplicate reimbursement is actuarially unsound," he told me!

We consumers have learned the hard way that the "legal" phrase is generally the one that confuses and weasels—and that the protective coloration seldom works out to our benefit.

I've seen the Kenyon and Eckhardt report on the public's view of savings banks, and one of the most interesting things in it to me is the conclusion that the greatest potential for increasing your share of the market lies in developing young adults as your customers. Young adults, perhaps you're noticing, are putting a high premium on simpler life, lack of discrimination as to race or sex, and much plainer talk. "Sunshine laws" are breaking open hitherto closed meetings, and such complex documents as statements of condition are beginning to say things like, "This is what we own," and "This is what we owe." Not because people are less knowledgeable, but because they are more so: they want you to say what you have to say and get on with it.

You have the knowledge and skill to do this; all you need is to look at everything you write or say from this point of view—I urge you to do so.

What else does the consumerist expect of you? He expects *his* problems to have very high priority in *your* hierarchy of concerns. Too long has somebody told a very junior officer, "And by the way, Henry, would you also take care of any complaints we happen to get?"

That just isn't good enough any more. Bankers are still respected in the community, and the price you pay for that respect is the anticipation that you will take community leadership in solving problems. If you are in a policy-making position, make the policy that at the senior management level you will have a consumer ombudsman who does something considerably more than run a complaint department. And if you're not in a policy-making job, appoint yourself to be your bank's official gadfly until such a policy *is* developed.

Innovative Bank Programs

I'd like to tell you about one New England bank's Consumer Affairs Department.

First, the senior officer in charge has the authority to act. One of the first things he did was notify the Attorney General, the State Banking Commissioner, the State Consumer Association, the Better Business Bureau, and the Federal Administrator along these lines: "When you have problems that involve the consumer and our bank, get us into the act immediately so that we can take whatever action seems appropriate." This was not an effort to bypass the commissioner's office, but to solve the problem at once.

Second, they found that they had to do some in-house housecleaning, moving complaints rapidly up through the lower levels instead of sweeping problems under the rug. To do this they developed a simple duplicate sheet on which to record a problem; even if it is solved at the point of origin, it is recorded, with one copy sent up through channels for general information, and one directly to the bank's consumer officer. This permits an analysis of where and how often problems are developing.

The Consumer Affairs Department answers all complaints in 48 hours—even if it is to say they have to go into the archives and an answer will be sent in a week.

They set—and met—a goal of 10,000 customer contacts in 1972, contacts both written and personal. Pick-up opinion cards are available in all offices, and are used in mailings on a staggered basis. The cards ask about staff friendliness, efficiency, convenience and so on. If somebody returns this card, and signs it (as most of them do), and the comment is quite general, the bank sends back immediately a printed letter that says "Thank you" to show that it didn't just go into the circular file. If a comment requires a separate letter, that is written.

The program showed up a number of areas where policy has now been changed: minimum quarterly interest payments, for example, for small savers. After the policy was amended, everyone who had communicated about it received a letter saying thank you for your interest and for helping us see this problem. This, it seems to me, is evidence of real People Banking.

There's not time to go into all the consumer programs banks have developed: taking leadership in response to holder-in-due-course legislation, meeting with voluntary consumer associations, working for schools and community groups, providing lobby space for consumer information desks, selling consumer books at cost. Even such simple devices as queue lines so that you don't have to guess which teller is going to be free next. Sylvia Porter lists some innovations. House calls, even to businesses —an idea that's spreading. Person-to-person counseling, particularly for those heavily in debt. Newcomer services, furnishing information about the community that extends far beyond the field of banking. An "SOS" (Survivors' Optional Service) that helps a surviving family make sure that every available benefit from Social Security, Workmen's Compensation, insurance, credit life insurance, etc. is collected. These are the kind of things that can make your bank unique in a market where regulation doesn't permit you much uniqueness beyond the choice of premiums you offer.

People Are Watching

We shouldn't conclude without some mention of the Hunt Commission Report. There are few secrets from the public any more. I think you would be astonished to realize the number of laymen who ask knowledgeable questions about the Report—not just what it will mean to them as consumers, but what it will mean to different kinds of financial institutions. We in New England are watching the current confrontations over checking accounts in Massachusetts and New Hampshire. I urge you not to underestimate the public's awareness of your posture as you respond to overall programs affecting your industry. As consumers become better educated, they become more critical of all institutions; this is predictable and, in my view, highly desirable in a truly functioning democracy. You promise us that you are People Banks; well, we're the people and we're watching.

So—to sum up:

1. Consumerism is a force whose time has come, and if you insist on spinning your wheels you'll only succeed in wearing down your tires.

2. Take the initiative, and when you do something good don't consider it immodest to take the credit.

3. Keep it simple, and let the sun shine in; you'll seem more honest, and you may even be so.

4. Develop an in-house system that really gets hold of consumer problems, that finds out what they are, how widespread, how they can be solved. And let all the appropriate agencies know what you're up to.

5. Be innovative in ways that people can see, and feel the benefits of. They may not all work well the first time—but learn by doing. Your service is the only really unique quality you have to offer consumers.

6. Avoid that kind of knee-jerk reaction to change that I have come to think of as one more association circling the wagons. The outcome can only be a confrontation in which your own interests are not served.

Thank you for inviting me to talk to you, and thank you for letting me speak as honestly and directly as I can.

Go thou and do likewise.

15

Youth—A Fractionated Audience

By Dr. Paul A. Wagner

Before U.S. Defense Information School,
Fort Benjamin Harrison, Indianapolis, Indiana,
September 12, 1974

SUMMARY: "Youth" is not a monolithic public, but is as fractionated as any other group in our society. If the leaders of American institutions hope to communicate with this important and vocal but shifting series of publics, they must learn to target and monitor youth activities. The author urges "youth-watching" as an effective method of understanding the diversity of, and the contradiction in, the attitudes of eighty million young Americans.

Dr. Paul A. Wagner, a senior vice president of Hill and Knowlton, Inc., is a former director of public relations for the Bell & Howell Co., president of the Ford Foundation's Film Council of America, and faculty member at Columbia University and the University of Chicago.

The awesome statistics surrounding any discussion of "American Youth" have served to reinforce the notion that the young people of our country are a monolithic group of great power, to be sold or courted or feared. True, there are over 80 million Americans under the age of twenty, many of them wielding discretionary power over the spending of more than 20 billion dollars. (Teenage girls alone buy several billion dollars worth of clothes.) And the purchasing influence they wield in the family, even on big-ticket items, is impressive. And since one in every three Americans has a close relationship to the educational process involving young people, their influence in the marketplace of ideas is even more impressive.

But it has become a truism of public relations during the past decade that the leaders of American institutions have been singularly unsuccessful in communicating with this public. The young people have seemingly turned their backs on the traditional loyalties to parents, college presidents, and political leaders; to the church, the military, and the business world—despite a counter-barrage of speeches, advertisements, commercials, and books explaining the established order to youth, and vice versa.

Veteran youth-watchers have come to the conclusion that this lack of communication with one of the largest segments of our society is due to a fundamental error—that of perceiving youth as a monolithic whole. In a communications sense, there is no such thing as "Youth"; for youth is as fragmented and as pluralistic as any other segment of our society.

Any grid of American youth, involving as it does a wide range of age groups, educational levels, racial, ethnic, socio-economic, and sex divisions—will reveal the staggering permutations our society has made possible. And even as such a grid makes the task of the professional communicator more difficult and more demanding, so it makes his messages more effective, by pinpointing them.

Anyone who has had occasion to communicate with the youth of other more traditional and tightly knit countries has already gained an insight into this communication problem. Messages to young workers regarding greater productivity, or less absenteeism, or 100 percent participation in the community fund drive are much simpler where the working day begins ten minutes before the opening of the plant, and where management and labor literally stand side by side to sing the following pep song. (It might be added that they sing it loudly and enthusiastically, 300 days a year, at the large plants of Matsushita in Japan.)

> For the building of a new Japan
> Let's put our strength and mind together,
> Doing our best to promote production,
> Sending our goods to the people of the world
> Endlessly and continuously,

Like water gushing from a fountain,
Grow, industry, grow, grow, grow!
Harmony and sincerity!
Matsushita Electric! Bonsai! Bonsai! Bonsai!

If it is obvious why such a simple and direct approach would not work with the young workers of Lordstown, it is equally obvious why the mosaic of our youth groups must be studied, analyzed, and dealt with on a tile-by-tile basis. There can be no hard and fast rules for dealing with such a dynamic situation, but some working hypotheses may help in grappling with what at first appears to be a communications puzzle.

Just How Different Is Youth?

Youthful sub-groups may appear to differ radically in their attitudes toward life, but in reality may continue to cling to some traditions of their elders, even while espousing radical change in others. This apparent contradiction between demand for change and support for the past will be of great aid to the communicator seeking a middle ground on which to explain the reasons for corporate or institutional policy. Take the case of the present university freshmen. In one prominent university, 60 percent of the entering class has announced an intention of pursuing a medical education. The reason? Partly idealistic ("to help my fellow man") and partly pragmatic ("doctors earn more"). Such young Americans want to lead the "good life" in both the religious and the materialistic sense of the word.

And although it is obvious to even the sexist (of either sex) that Women's Lib is here to stay and that its impact on all of our institutions will be considerable, it is interesting to note that surveys on campuses, where the modern suffragettes are in full force, indicate that the number one goal of young women is still mate-finding.

Studies of young factory workers belie the popular belief that "all the union member wants is more money." The young workers are confounding their own union leadership with demands resounding with "quality of life" phrases that parallel the undergraduate manifestos. If most college students avoid Friday classes in order to go skiing, so do a large percentage of young blue-collar workers, and often for the same reason.

Of course the greatest contradiction of all is that age is not a useful factor to consider in an understanding of American youth. In recent political contests, observers have been startled by the voting patterns of first-time voters. They are quite similar to the patterns displayed by citizens thirty or forty years older. And studies of attitudes toward advertising show that young age groups are no more critical of television commercials than the "55 and over" groups. Sociologists at a recent conference of the American Sociological Association finally concluded that "children, by and large, mature in the image of their parents."

Youth Covers a Wide Spectrum

This may require us to re-think our hypotheses on who holds "youthful concepts." Is it just the 14-18-year-olds; or the "under 25"? Such a spectrum is cropped too closely, on either end.

Anyone who waits to communicate with young Americans until they arrive in high school is misjudging the interests and the intellectual abilities of students in the lower grades. Thanks partly to television documentaries and partly to the young teachers, the pre-teenagers have become involved in social issues ranging from environmental health to alcoholism; and from pension plans to the plight of migrant workers. They may have no immediate political leverage (save what they have on their parents), but the basic attitudes they form at such a tender age often endure into later life.

At the other end of the standard youth scale—past the days of apprenticeship and professional study—is a large group whose ages extend from 25 to 95, and who can only be described as youthful-minded. That is, their attitudes toward political and social issues are similar to those held by junior citizens still imbued by the idealism of the classroom and the Sunday school. Their ideas and ideals may not always be practical, but they are wedded to social change. As one prominent sociologist has observed, "For many Americans, youth is a state of mind that permits one to adjust quickly to the high velocity of change."

Rapid Acceptance of Change

Despite the pluralism and the contradictions of American youth attitudes, there is an underlying unity that has begun to spread from the chronologically young to all older segments of our society. It is commonplace to comment on the rapidity of social change in our time; but few observers have commented on the increasingly rapid acceptance of that change. There is far less future shock than we have been led to believe.

Take the matter of sex. Five years ago, the administration of a major American university announced new parietal rules, allowing women to stay in rooms of the men's dormitory until midnight on weekdays, and until one o'clock on Sunday morning. The ensuing public relations crisis was the worst in the school's 120 years of existence. The administration barely survived. But this year, the administration of the same university saw fit to announce a new set of regulations, in which there were no restrictions set on visiting hours for females in the men's dormitories. Around-the-clock freedom. The announcement was received by the parents, the press, the pulpit, and the politicians without any public outcry.

Or take censorship. In 1970, an opinion pollster found that the public was 62-30 percent in favor of *total censorship* of revolutionary or pornographic material. This year, the same analyst found the public to be against censorship *in any form* by 59-36 percent.

Traditionally, the thought of impeaching a President of the United States was unthinkable. And yet with the virtual impeachment of the 34th President, the unthinkable became the acceptable.

Not many years ago, state legislatures were dominated by lawyers, because many thought they were the only ones who could handle the knotty problems and the still knottier legislation. Today, fewer lawyers are going to the state capitols as legislators. They are being displaced by school teachers, ministers, women with causes, and quite often by youthful change-seekers.

Whether such evidence of rapid acceptance of social change is good or bad depends on who and what is being changed, and the degree of that change. But one thing is certain. Any public relations counsel who hopes to serve his clients effectively must design and maintain an efficient system of social radar.

Watching the Youth Scene

Since much of the demand for social change will originate from certain sectors of American youth, it will become the prime responsibility of the public relations counselor to alert his clients to the demands being made; to distinguish at an early date a fad from a significant shift in attitude; and to trigger a fast reaction to any demands that might affect the client in any serious way.

This is a big order. And ironically, only rarely can it be filled by a young person. The reason is simple. Anyone just out of college, building a career, starting a family, paying attention to all of the pragmatic details that will spell success, is too engrossed in personal challenges to stay in touch with younger sub-groups. What is needed is a youth-watcher, of any age—one who is fascinated by the subject, and is willing to glean those special inputs that can be gained only by close observation of the youth scene. Serious youth-watchers engage in many activities, including the following:

1. Books on the college best-seller lists are read with special care, to discern the new appeals, or the new packaging of old ideas. Some are on politics, others on sex, still others are escapist literature——but all are clues to youthful thinking.

2. The films most popular with young moviegoers are screened, not once, but several times. Motion pictures are not only the special province of youth, but they are regarded as visual literature by the aficionados, and as with good books, are "read and reread." It is not unusual for a popular film to be seen six or seven times by a young viewer. The value of such a film as a sociological tool becomes apparent to the youth-watcher when he finds, after a second or third screening, subtleties of body language and other non-verbal communication, or the semantic subtleties of lyrics being sung in the background, or the levels of meaning in the dialogue. The visual language of youth is one that a print-oriented professional may find difficulty in following, but such literacy can be of utmost value in dealing with youth groups.

3. Professional and intellectual journals (numbered in the hundreds) are monitored regularly, to obtain the insights of analysts in over a dozen disciplines. Books by and about youth, sometimes as many as a dozen per week, are also scanned.

4. College newspapers are regarded as good barometers, particularly in their special features and editorials. Student editors may sometimes be overzealous, but are quite competent in goading both faculty members and student readers into articulating their feelings on a wide variety of subjects.

5. Student-produced films are viewed as still another source of information. Conferences of student film producers are attended in order to screen the latest and best offerings. In this same category, although more difficult to come by, are the radical newsreels and community television presentations. Again, it is not so much the content of these new media, but the way in which they are employed, that is important to the professional communicator.

6. Teaching a class or seminar on any academic level is an excellent way of staying in touch with youthful thinking. And besides, the give-and-take of modern classrooms is good preparation for confrontations with youthful television interviewers.

7. Maintaining personal contacts with student leaders as they pursue either higher degrees or new careers can give the public relations counselor a sense of the shifting modes of various age groups.

8. Cultural monitoring covers a wide variety of student activities and interests. Although concerts are not recommended for those with weak eardrums, attendance at a Jeff Beck come-back can be a rewarding experience, sociologically speaking. The fascination of the young for the blues of B. B. King becomes doubly fascinating when they are confronted with the fact that he was also the favorite of the young—in the 1930's! Special concerts, such as Bangladesh or the readings of Yevtushenko, all have a value in sensing the range and depth of youth interests.

9. The mystical and religious interests of certain youth groups can serve to position the observer as to the value systems being developed. Jinarajadasa, Herman Hesse, Jung's introduction to the Book of Changes—all speak to the followers of distant drums. Since the challenges to our clients frequently come from unknown drummers, such a study can be of great pragmatic value.

10. In order to avoid the charge of elitism, youth-watchers analyze as many attitudinal surveys of non-school youths as are available.

Perhaps the best summary of these activities is that we are listening to youth, trying to understand the real meanings of their questioning words. Only by listening to the questions can we hope to frame our answers.

Early Recognition of Significant Changes

Since prediction is an art, and a very uncertain one at that, many executives disdain long-range planning. They point to the fact that a bevy of futurists, working on predictions for the 21st century, had failed to predict the violent reaction of the young to environmental pollution—a challenge that will be with us for a long time to come. (The futurists completed their study only six months before the first Earth Week was proclaimed.)

Professional youth-watchers were not surprised by this turn of events. Many had attended the classes of youthful social studies teachers, and of junior faculty members re-discovering Ecology, and had heard about the growing membership of the Sierra Club. Predict with certainty? No—but anticipate, and be ready for the event—definitely, yes.

For those who were monitoring *The New Republic* a dozen years ago, the name of an obscure writer, Ralph Nader, began to come into focus. In a car-oriented society, he was saying things about every American's life in relation to those cars. Right or wrong, he should have been listened to, and reacted to, before he became a household word. No one could predict his future success, but any properly working social radar would have picked up the blip on the screen. Anticipation of the possible acceptance of such radical new approaches as the negative income tax, or the establishment of legal rights for women attempting to gain equal pay for equal work, or the reaction of fishermen to the pollution of their favorite trout stream by a local manufacturing plant—all of these appeared on the screen of social radar long before they hit the front page of *The New York Times*.

A youth-watcher attuned to the activities and thought processes of young America usually enjoys a high batting average in his or her predictions of what might become the public relations issues of the near future. The real question is merely how to react when the blip becomes a reality.

Reaction to Youthful Dissent

Given the speed of change these days, and the speed of acceptance of such change, it behooves the leadership of our institutions to react as rapidly as possible. But in the case of American youth, there is still another urgent reason. Many of our young people are already finding themselves over-educated and under-utilized. Over one million new teachers will be training during the '70s—to compete for an estimated 200,000 openings. Almost one million young people who have paid for their teachers' certificates will be unemployed, at least as far as their profession is concerned. Unemployment among PhD's in hundreds of other fields has risen by 60 percent in a single year.

All of this is matched by the large group of dropouts from elementary and secondary schools who are now technologically obsolete. The Bureau of Labor Statistics predicts that by the 1980s, there will be twice as many applicants as there are jobs in the lesser-skilled vocations.

Even when one agrees that America has always found its way out of such dilemmas, it is still possible to anticipate increasing·tension and bitterness among the young. They will be even more impatient about communications delays than they are now. If not given explanations within a reasonable time, these disenchanted youths might combine their political clout to force the government to act "in their behalf." What can be done to anticipate and to forestall such drastic reactions is the subject of another chapter—but it could involve the cooperation of business and education in designing new ways of providing counseling on flexible career development in a fantastically complex post-industrial society.

Once the need for speedy reaction is accepted, the next question is: what form should it take? It is an ancient truism that you can always tell a young person, but you can't tell him much. One-way communication has never been popular with the youth. Today it is even less popular. Young Americans want to be involved in two-way communication on any of their problems. To some established leaders this connotes the dreaded word, "confrontation"; to others it connotes "dialogue" (a popular word until it is discovered that in a true dialogue, one must expect not only to change the opponent's mind—but to have one's own mind changed as well). Perhaps the most viable form of communication with youth is "creative debate." This highly civilized form of interaction has rarely been practiced in the age of the mass media, but it has the great virtue of focusing the attention of the youthful participants on one contention at a time. Since one cannot expect to avoid controversy in the future, one at least can guide it into more formal channels. For even the more emotional youths, there is an element of fair play involved in a debate that has a definite appeal. For one thing, they are not dismissed by the leadership; they are treated with intellectual respect, even if their ideas are not met with unconditional approval.

There is one hitch to this strategy. Youth speaks a different language, or to put it another way, youth does not always speak the language of business, or of institutional administration, or of pragmatism. So before the debate can begin, one or the other side must learn the other's language. Since the language of pragmatism comes from long experience, perhaps it might be easier for America's leadership to learn the language of the young.

Soft vs. Hard Vocabulary

There is one fundamental difference between the language spoken by the average idealistic youth and that spoken by the leader who has been annealed in the fires of competition—the former is derived from the "soft" sciences, and the latter from the "hard" sciences. These are familiar phrases in the academic community, wherein any science that can be quantified, where every phenomenon can be expressed in numbers—is labelled "hard." And conversely, any of the sciences where quantification is difficult, as in the social sciences, is labelled "soft."

The language of the hard sciences involves technological invention; that of the soft sciences, social invention. Since the youth are particularly interested in social invention, they tend to speak in the soft, qualitative, almost anti-quantitative language of social inventors. As a result, the hard-headed leaders (also addressed respectfully as "hard-nosed") regard the soft-hearted youth as somewhat soft-headed in their use of language.

The dichotomy is often expressed in terms of a private world, of private enterprise and *private interests* on the one hand; and on the other hand, a world of public interest. The youth are talking about rapid change, with zero population growth, while many leaders are talking about stability, with constant economic growth.

And on the bottom line, the elders speak a language of economic accounting, while the youth are speaking in the as yet indistinct language of social accounting. Small wonder that there has been so little two-way communication between the two groups.

There is, however, a hopeful middle ground. It has been provided for both parties by the computer scientists. As the problems, domestic and international, have become more and more complex, our understanding of computer models has become more sophisticated. Surprisingly enough, American youth has taken to EDP as a handy research tool. More and more students are learning the creative uses of computers in everything from the study of Shakespeare to the economic viability of 19th century slavery.

In fact, many of the youthful challenges to the established leadership will come in the form of computerized models. If the Club of Rome model #1 fails in its attempt to put forth the case for zero population growth, then the researchers turn to Club of Rome model #2, refining their techniques, begging for counter-analysis. The creative debates on materials shortages, on world famine, or on control of nuclear weapons, may well take place through the use of a computer language. It will not eliminate the need to understand the soft language of youth, but it certainly will cause both sides to examine their premises with greater precision and fewer adjectives.

But no matter how wide the chasm between the two worlds may appear, thoughtful observers are optimistic that communications bridges can and will be built—built by public relations counselors who can explain the youth to the elders, and the elders to the coming generation of leaders. It is a meaningful challenge.

PROFITS
COMMUNICATION

16

Don't Try to Communicate about Profits— There's No Such Thing

By Clytia M. Chambers

Excerpted from an editorial seminar-workshop
held for communicators in the Georgia Power Company
Atlanta, December 2-5, 1974

SUMMARY: Corporations have been unsuccessful in communicating about company finances because they have focused on profits—why they need them, why they are important to employees, shareholders, customers, future generations. But in fact, profits do not exist. All that exists is revenues (what comes in) and costs (what goes out). How can this concept be used in employee communications? That's the place to start.

Clytia M. Chambers, who has a B.A. in political science from Barnard College, an M.A. in sociology from Howard University, and a law degree from the Université de Lyon (France), is a vice president of Hill and Knowlton and a member of its Creative Services Division. She is a writer specializing in industrial communications.

I am about to slay a sacred cow.

It is generally thought—I'm too chicken to admit that I too have thought so for years and years—that perhaps the most fundamental objective we should strive for in an employee publication is an understanding of the role of profits in the lives of our companies and in the survival of every single employee as long as he or she works for a company.

I see now where we were wrong.

It's not that it's a losing battle in the usual sense of trying to sanitize an unpleasant word whose smell has permeated an entire environment. No, it's that we were trying to explain the non-existent.

I don't mean to be foolish about this notion. The concept of profits, of course, has existed for centuries in several senses. But the concept we in the business world were trying to combat is the one that rests on the idea of "the pile left over." *That's* the one that doesn't exist.

I don't know whether certain words make pictures in your mind. But I notice, when people talk about profits, they seem to have a picture of a person collecting money for whatever he sells, paying his bills for all the things he had to buy or use to make his product, and then suddenly finding to his delight that he has something left over. Even the cartoons favor that vision. That's why we see the fat man labeled "profiteer" with the cigar in his mouth, counting his pile of gold coins.

That picture may have been appropriate a century or more ago. In the days when a person built and ran his own business, there *was* a pile left—and he could do pretty much what he wanted with it. Buy a string of horses, or take a leisurely trip to England, or invest it in a new plant. The money wasn't spoken for in any real sense.

Today, that view of profits is hopelessly out of date. Corporate ownership is vested in people whose principal role is to provide money—not to exercise the prerogatives of ownership. But those owners, the shareholders, don't decide how much they should receive in dividends; they own but don't manage. Corporations themselves are run by hired hands; they manage but don't own. Neither managers nor owners can make the same kind of independent decisions 19th century entrepreneurs could.

Consequences of the Old Profit Idea

As corporate communicators, we accepted the popular premise of the leftover pile—and that has seriously affected our tactics and our effectiveness. Our emphasis was on justification: *why* the leftover is needed, *why* corporate life can't go on without it, *why* it is important to employees, stockholders, customers, future generations.

But all the while, as we are justifying the leftover, outside vultures were eyeing the pile and saying: "If it's left over, then we can peck at it, too. You, as corporate managers may think your purposes are laudable, but we have other notions in mind. We think we should tax it and use it for social change. Or, we think too much is left, so let's set a limit by law, and that will be a good way to enforce a no-growth policy. Or, we will decree that beyond a certain rate of return, you must reduce prices."

I am not commenting on whether those purposes as given are good or bad. All I'm saying is: There is no money available for those purposes outside the context of a particular corporation's objectives and commitments.

Where Does the Money Go?

Let me pursue a little further why what is traditionally called "profits" is not leftover money. Corporate revenues come with little tags attached. By far the biggest ticket is for operating expenses. The remainder is spoken for, first, by the shareholders who helped finance you, and second, by what you might call future creditors or bill-collectors—that is, those suppliers who will be sending you bills when your construction projects get under way.

In other words, dividends are a cost of doing business and a form of paying investors for the money they (or the successors to their rights) have put into your company. As your own vice president of finance said to me once, "Dividends to our shareholders are an obligation; they are not optional. When we don't pay, we are going back on an obligation."

As for future bills, since your management knows they will be coming up, they put aside money for that purpose. That money is the other component of what was traditionally called "profits," and has been called, most unfortunately in my opinion, "retained earnings." It must be emphasized that capital investment—for which these earnings are used —is an absolute for a business. You can only kill that absolute by also killing the corporation. But as long as it is alive, it must plan for the future.

To repeat: The pile does not exist for others to dispose of. All that exists is revenues (what comes in) and costs (what goes out).

It occurs to me as I say this that there are going to have to be considerable changes in accounting procedures if we are to make this approach stick. But that's a problem for later on—and for others to solve.

Making the Concept Stick

We are corporate communicators. What can we in our particular, special roles do to foster this approach to corporate earnings? We have to start somewhere. I say, let's start with our employees, where we are not bound by legalistic terminology. We have a job to do—a considerable job—to explain utility financing. So we can begin by asking ourselves how to use our new concept. Here's what I suggest:

First, we must internalize this approach so that it becomes second nature to think in those terms.

Second, we must watch our language as we talk and write about corporate revenues to divest it of terms that imply that corporate managers have the full prerogatives of ownership that a private person does.

Next, when we discuss dividends, we must do so within the framework of costs. This means bringing in whatever is necessary to understand that this cost moves up and down just like the other costs —historical references, today's money market, the fact the investor has other options for getting a return on his money, and so on.

Fourth, we should replace the term "retained earnings" with something more descriptive like "reinvested in the business." "Retained" sounds as though management is keeping something for itself, while it's really putting money aside just long enough to decide how to use it.

Application to a Writing Project

Now let's look at the "profits" editorial you submitted to the workshop for editing. In light of what I've been saying, you can see that the "profits-is-not-a-dirty-word" approach, used by your editor, is an attempt to justify profits. I have re-written the editorial to incorporate the idea that profits do not exist. All I'm trying to do is implant the idea. Let me read it to you:

> "Profits" is not a word that rightly applies to utilities.
> At the end of the year, after we finish paying all our expenses, there is no little pile left over. Our earnings are all spoken for —allocated by the realities of running an electric utility.
> Where do they go?
> Some go to shareholders. Some go into what is called retained earnings—our down payment on construction.
> When people look at our request for a rate increase and say, "Let the company take it out of profits," they should be sure of what they're saying. It's this: "Don't provide for the future" . . . and

"Welsh on your obligation to investors who are putting their money into the company."

And what about a utility's future? Is electricity something we won't need tomorrow? Don't we need new and better plants to bring more electricity to Georgia whose needs are growing faster than the national average?

Who are the investors who bought a small piece of our company? They're your neighbor down the street who thought that when she retired, she'd get some additional income to supplement her Social Security—the middle-aged couple who use dividends to help pay their daughter's college expenses—your co-worker on the job who put his money in utilities becasue he was assured they are safe.

Ours is a free state. People are entitled to their own opinions. But before they decry utility "profits" in public forums, people should know it's their neighbors, and Georgia's future, they're attacking.*

Getting across an idea—new or old—is not a one-shot deal. **It** must be presented over and over and in many different forms and contexts. Above all, I urge you to be patient. Our objective is long-range. We must give our audiences time to understand us.

*This editorial appeared in the December 1974 issue of the Georgia Power *Citizen*. For more on this basic concept, see Peter Drucker's article, "The Delusion of 'Profits,' " that appeared subsequently in the *Wall Street Journal*, February 5, 1975.

MANAGEMENT/EMPLOYEE RELATIONS

17

Employee Communications: Sorry I Can't Hear You. I Have a Banana in My Ear.

By Lilot S. Moorman

SUMMARY: Employee communication has traditionally been thought of as a transmission system to get management's message across. But, too often, the message wasn't being received.

The problem, as many companies have learned, was often in management's concept of communications. Today, new ideas and new techniques are changing some of the banana-in-my-ear attitudes with which employees responded to traditional forms of employee communication.

Lilot S. Moorman, author of several articles on management, is a specialist in financial and employee communications and a former vice president of Hill and Knowlton, Inc.

"Hey," said the man. "Do you know you have a banana in your ear?"

"What?" said his neighbor, who did indeed have a banana in his ear.

"I said you have a banana in your ear."

"What?" said banana-in-ear.

By this time the first man was apoplectic. "YOU HAVE A BANANA IN YOUR EAR!" he shouted.

"I'm sorry," said the other. "I can't hear you. I have this banana in my ear."

For years, most employee communication has been a replay of the banana-in-ear joke. Management speaks. It speaks softly, in four-color glossy magazines with pretty pictures, or a little more directly, in tabloid sheets. And when all else fails, it shouts—in paid advertisements or banner headlines. But the employee can't hear. You see, he's got this banana in his ear.

For a long time that didn't worry management too much. Having an employee communications program was enough in itself—it proved you were a forward-looking company. And besides, it was gratifying to see that weekly or monthly publication come out, especially when it played back your ideas.

Companies that applied the strictest cost-effectiveness standards to other functions went along for years, happily pouring money into gorgeous, pointless employee communications that they could point to with pride.

Today, many of those companies are having second and third thoughts. The most encouraging aspect of organizational communications today—an area that Peter Drucker calls one of management's greatest failures—is that they are finally being subjected to normal management review and standards.

Results-oriented executives sense that there is a strong correlation between employee communication and productivity, and that the cost of poor communications can too often be measured in cents per share.

One small midwestern manufacturing company, for example, was able to increase production and sales by 60% after an attitude survey uncovered employee dissatisfactions stemming largely from poor internal communications. In another instance, the management of a large company that had prided itself on model employee relations woke up one morning to find that it had just barely won a union representation election by an uncomfortably narrow margin. In the postmortem that followed, management learned that haphazard communications had undermined its otherwise excellent employee relations.

The Communications Audit

The first step in measuring the effectiveness of internal communications is a communications audit—an inventory and analysis of all the various techniques and media that make up a company's communication system. The audit answers such questions as:

Why does management feel it needs an employee communications program?

What objectives has management set for the employee communications function?

What communication vehicles are currently used on both field and corporate levels, and are there gaps or overlaps in the system?

How much in total is actually being spent on these various communications programs?

What is the content of the various communications products? What is their quality?

Are the existing programs doing any good? Or are they, in fact, counterproductive?

A key element of the audit is an employee attitude survey. This should measure more than just how employees rate the company's present communications. The most useful survey will also show how employees perceive the company, and how far these perceptions vary from management's own expectations. This, after all, is the standard against which communications effectiveness must be measured.

An attitude survey performs another vital function. It enables management to tune in—to listen to the company's employees. A company measuring the effectiveness of its employee communications programs must be willing to answer the question, "How well do we listen?"

Most managements think of communication as a one-way process —transmission only. That's why their messages often don't get through. A communications system needs both transmission and receiving devices—an ear as well as a mouthpiece. The trend in employee communication today is to stop beefing up the transmission devices and start refining the receiving system.

Listening is more than "giving employees a chance to be heard." Listening should help provide the input for communications and other programs, making them responsive to employee concerns.

Speaking to Employee Concerns

An effective internal communications program will reflect management's point of view—in terms of employee concerns. Or, as one savvy labor relations man put it, "If what you're trying to communicate is important to them, they'll read it even if you scribble it on a scrap of paper and throw it away on the production floor."

J. Paul Lyet, Chairman of Sperry Rand Corporation, has observed that he regards communication as his most important management accountability. It's no wonder that the company he heads is noted for the depth and effectiveness of its communications activities.

The role of the chief executive is central to establishing good employee communications. He, and he alone, can set the tone for open communications and make the function a top priority for managers throughout the organization. This is true whether he is a plant manager or the chairman of a billion-dollar company.

It's also true that the larger a company is, the harder it must work to set up channels for two-way communications. The kind of interaction that takes place naturally in a plant where everyone is on a first-name basis must be carefully nurtured in a larger organization. Louis Allen, who puts communicating high up on his list of activities for management leaders, says "Communication can be accomplished best by accountable managers in a face-to-face relationship with the people who report to them." Institutionalizing this kind of communication—creating structured opportunities for this to occur—is often a necessary part of an employee communications program.

There's an old Morse telegrapher's phrase for transmitting to an unattended station—"sending to the wind." It's another way of describing a conversation with someone who has a banana in his ear.

Sending to the wind can be costly to a company, especially if its management doesn't realize no one is listening.

The cure—establishing an effective two-way communication system—is by no means simple. But, as Peter Drucker notes in his book, *Management*, communication is ". . .not a *means* of organization. It is the *mode* of organization."

Amen, Brother Peter.

18

The Message Is
the Message

By Marion K. Pinsdorf

*Before the Industrial Editing and
Business Communication Institute,
University of Tennessee, Knoxville, March 7, 1975*

SUMMARY: Our concern about communications within the corporation has tended to concentrate on hardware—the way to get the message across—instead of on the message itself. Wordiness, executive isolation, following fads and the failure to even be aware of another's point-of-view are prime enemies of communication. More attention to the quality of the message and the people involved—not ever-greater reliance on machines—will help solve corporate communications problems.

Marion K. Pinsdorf, a vice president of Hill and Knowlton, is also a member of the Managing Committee of Management/Employee Relations Counsel, an H&K division. She is completing her Ph.D. dissertation in Brazilian economic history.

Some months ago I walked through a newspaper composing room newly converted from hot type to the automated cold type method of printing. The manager who was explaining the process to me prided himself on his good communication with employees. However, as we walked about, I realized he treated them as invisible men. ''I'm OK; you're not there.'' He explained the confusing plethora of red and green lights blinking away in place of jolly, friendly linotype operators, completely ignoring the technician responsible for the new equipment. This ignoring was mutual until the manager made a mistake. At this point, the technician interrupted, startling the manager, who psychologically, simply had not seen the worker.

Far-fetched and insensitive as this example may sound, it is repeated daily in many plants and offices. Managers walk past secretaries, executives ignore subordinates. This is one illustration of what I mean by, ''The message is the message.'' The quality of the people involved, the messages they send each other, the quality of what is said, all are vitally important, much more so than the media on which we have over-concentrated in years past.

We have all sat through seminars, meetings and discussions which focused *ad nauseam* on the hardware—in-house television, who controls the bulletin boards, even down to keeper of the thumbtacks, and many other mechanics of communication. Nor is this only a recent fad. Many years ago, Sherwood Anderson, at that time editor of two small newspapers in Virginia, went to New York City to view new printing equipment. After looking at it, after reading what it was producing, he commented: The machines are more magnificent than the men . . . and their message.

In a book now over 25 years old, but ever green, William Whyte noted: ''Never before has the businessman had so much paraphernalia with which to communicate to those around him, and never before has he spent so much time using it.'' And yet, even then businessmen were wondering, ''Is anybody listening?'', the question Whyte took for his title.

Therefore, today, I would like to concentrate not on the means of communication, but on the ends. On one side, the quality of concept, of the material communicated and of the individuals involved. And on the other, how messages are actually received.

Understanding Our Terms

Before we look at the assumptions that fuzz up or render communications ineffective, let's define what we mean by ''communication.'' Whyte points out it is an *inter*change of thought and opinions. Communication bridges the gap between human behavior and management. Peter Drucker in his *Practice of Management* says information is a manager's main vehicle for operating. The leader can motivate, guide and organize people to perform their own work most effectively through the spoken or written word. Communication is an integral part of many problems: Of productivity and turnover. Of morale and absenteeism. Of extravagance and efficiency.

Words themselves may be a stumbling block. Every person brings to the communication process an accumulation of past experience, of attitudes and motives. As S.I. Hayakawa points out, "The meanings of words are not in words; they are in us." Peter Drucker puts it this way: "One cannot communicate a word; the whole man always comes with it."

Today, words change their meanings very quickly, or mean different things to different groups. One must be unusually careful that the word used is understandable to all involved. A humorous, but nevertheless good example of this is given by former Canadian Prime Minister John Diefenbaker. When he became a member of the Canadian parliament years ago:

"Pot" was a cooking utensil.
"Rock" meant a stone.
"Pig" was an animal kept in a pen.
"Swingers" were hammocks, and not in the East Block. East Block in itself means nothing to most U.S. citizens.
"Grass" was mowed, not smoked.
A "Pill" was for relieving pain.
"Gay" meant happy.
People never got "hung up" except on the telephone.
"Turned on" had to do with electric power.

Careless, insensitive use of language breeds suspicion and mistrust, fear and insecurity. To avoid such semantic problems, a person should be more word-minded. He must question and paraphrase, check for feedback, and be sensitive generally to words, their meanings and consequences.

Learning to communicate well and effectively in any medium is hard work. Literacy does not descend on us spontaneously. It must be learned through assiduous attention to the smallest details, through a willing apprenticeship and the habit of work. I am sure you have all met pseudos who consider work and creativity antonyms, or think precision isn't important as long as somehow you grunt or motion your meaning. To understand the tomfoolery of this, just translate such laziness to a music student unwilling to learn his scales, or to play in the right key.

Along with hard work, managers must obey the cardinal rule of communication: that its effectiveness tends to be directly proportional to the degree to which both sender and receiver regard and treat each other as humans, with mutual respect. If ever there was a time when trust in communications was important, it is now. Watergate, last year's oil shortages, the ritual fandango of labor negotiations, and many other examples, document this need. Today's employees, in some cases rightly, are suspicious, skeptical, increasingly disloyal . . . and they want a bigger piece of the action. In his book, "Is Anybody Listening?" Whyte wrote:

> "Only with trust can there be any real communication. Until that trust is achieved the techniques and gadgetry of communications are so much effort. Before employees will accept management's facts, they must have overall confidence in its motives and sincerity. And conversely, those companies whose day-in, day-out actions have fostered that confidence, are precisely those companies that need worry least over techniques."

"Is Anybody Listening?" My reaction is indeed they are, but they aren't going to be easily gulled or fooled. So, let's look at the assumptions and vices that keep people from listening.

Communicating like Lemmings

The first vice is what Timothy Crouse has dubbed "pack journalism." Crouse, a *Rolling Stone* editor, was put aboard the 1972 McGovern campaign bus to watch his colleague Hunter Thompson, but became intrigued instead by the gaggle of top press people. Crouse found them writing pack, herd, or fuselage journalism. Bred of their traveling and drinking together, of their story-swapping and poker playing, of the bone-wearying pressure, stories filed by these reporters came to a consensus. They provided answers even before the right questions could be asked. The result? Shallow, obvious, meretricious, misleading and dull political coverage.

Without belaboring Crouse's points, I do think this example can help us understand why corporate journalism also can fail. The same imitativeness afflicts corporate communicators. They must learn to dig for information in many sources, including the opposition's, and trust their individual judgments. Corporate editors cannot follow a fad and use buzz words inappropriate to the situation they are reporting without doing a disservice to their readers.

Not Profound, Just Turgid

If there is one thing that wastes time and obscures meaning in the business community, it's using a thousand ill-chosen words when a few blunt ones suffice.

Most of you know that after suffering much criticism during his presidency Harry Truman is emerging as a great leader. There are many reasons—his decisions, his stable mid-America image, his humanness—but I dare speculate one of the strongest reasons is his blunt talk. We all have our favorite phrase. "If you can't stand the heat, get out of the kitchen." "The buck stops here." And he didn't delete the expletives, especially when talking about music critics! Sometimes it seems blunt talk went back with Harry to Missouri.

I remember once capsulizing my critique of an awful speech in one mild four-letter word. It bothered many, even the twx operator, until I asked if it was accurate. Now, I don't advise more four-letter words in business. Our language is already vulgar enough. I *do* urge direct statement. For example, when Brazil's former president Medici was asked about his nation's economy, he replied, "It was doing fine, but the people were not." Contrast that with any corporate statement that crosses your desk tomorrow. Or with this barb: "If Nixon were captain of the Titanic, he'd be telling passengers that he just stopped to pick up some ice."

Chameleon words, those vague phrases that cloak meanings, do everyone a disservice and often lead to mistakes. Too many chameleon words are probably the biggest time waster around.

"Talk About Us"

In a recent survey we made of readers of a company magazine, there were surprisingly strong and prevalent pleas to "talk about us," particularly from hourly, retired and non-management respondents. Typical responses included: "Write about people who live and work for the company, not just the front office." "Recognize foresters, for without the man in the woods procuring raw materials, paper making would be difficult." These people called themselves "peons;" they termed the company "cold" and its management "secretive." Many felt older employees were being forgotten after 30 years or more of valuable contribution. However, among the pleas to "talk about us" were suggestions from a person in a very menial job who urged that an article be written on his dedicated superintendent. "If you had more people like this," the respondent wrote, "you would have fewer problems and nothing but praise." What these pleas point up is the need for effective, credible, face-to-face human relationships between manager and employee. An employee recognition program, which honors a good job, a valuable suggestion, or a job done well over a long time, is one good solution. It also suggests that the audiences must be really understood in all company communications: publications, memos, radio, and most important, face-to-face.

Freedom from the Press

Two other criticisms of the general press—misreporting and the communications glut—should be heeded by anyone building a communications program within a company. Henry Fairlie, a British journalist, in his perceptive and highly critical study of the Kennedy presidency, points out:

> "The more one reads the newspapers and magazines of the recent past, the more one realizes how little they know of the society which they affect to report and how they understand even less. They seem to pass around each other's information until their voices become one and they succeed in creating a wholly artificial national mood."

In a *New York Times Magazine* article that scored daily addiction to news, Mark Harris points out that middle-aged and older people in general underestimate their own powers of observation. They devour the media, when they might preserve both time and energy by listening to the outer world with partial attention only. "Those of us who have seen the cycles round so many times need no longer be diverted by repetition . . . the older we grow the more shrewdly we draw sound conclusions from minimal clues."

Need I make the all-too-obvious extrapolation from this criticism to the corporate editor who writes in polished jargon for the assembly line worker, whose work situation the editor is not even vaguely aware of. This may result in William Safire's two categories of overlooked stories: MEGO—My Eyes Glaze Over, or a really significant story that evokes little reader interest called MPTR—More Published Than Read.

The Body Talks

Many discussions of body language border on banal, sensual tips. However, there's much that should meet the eye of the person responsible for communication within his company. He should at least have a glimmer of what people say with their bodies and sensitize others to its importance.

Body language or the older term "silent language," means many things: how we handle space, how we approach and sit on chairs and at desks . . . confidently or hesitantly. Whether territorial imperative is important. Body language also means the masks men wear. What posture tells. Many parts of the body reflect a person's feeling state. Jerky movements, for instance, usually connote frustration. The shrinking body suggests an attempt to hide oneself, and perhaps more seriously, indicates depression.

Normally, body language is not as controlled as a person's dress or verbal communication would be. As the manager learns by watching people, so do employees learn by watching him. Remember the manager who walked by the invisible worker. Or the CEO who touts his democratic, open-door management style, but with a finger-wagging, *"Now* I'm telling you,'' gets his real, autocratic message across loud and clear.

Assuming in Splendid Isolation

Perhaps the two worst enemies of good company communications are assumption, ''I know without asking,'' and, even more seriously, executive isolation. As long ago as the Hawthorne study, managers were assuming they knew exactly what their employees wanted to hear and what was important to them. When surveyors actually asked employees, the great discrepancies were obvious. What manager thinks employees are more interested in new products than in personal notes? Yet they said so in a recent survey. Alone in his own office, what executive thinks about the need of a steno pool member for privacy to call a doctor? Some of these assumptions can be corrected by reading union publications and, when they exist, the corporate underground papers, but even more simply and effectively by asking those involved.

One of the insidious factors in assumption is that an editor or manager is anxious to change other people's consciousness but not his own. Sometimes the fervor with which he holds a position hardens his hearing against any others. The existentialist philosopher Soren Kierkegaard warned ''you can't see a blind spot.''

I would like to digress for a moment into my own discipline —history. For a long time I've realized how valuable the historical method—be it Rankian or Annales School—is in reporting and public relations counseling. It has taught me, for example, that it is infinitely easier to grasp the extent of a material change such as technology than it is to appreciate shifts in ideas and relationships. Fernand Braudel, current luminary of the Annales School, divides this into a conspicuous history, which holds our attention by its continual dramatic changes, and a second, submerged history, which is almost silent, always discreet, virtually unsuspected, either by its observers or its participants. The second is little touched by the erosion of time. However, it is very often important, especially when it breaks through to the surface. We must constantly shuffle the pieces of the jigsaw puzzle we think we have put together so adroitly and be ready to look anew as whether we really are being accurate.

Perhaps the most useful historical technique for editors and managers is learning not to take too much of themselves into the analysis of a situation— learning to lay aside their own egos. An historian can be immersed in another period precisely to the degree that he recognizes his own times as part of himself. If he's too intimately into his own experience, he cannot enter another. The very discipline of transferring himself into strange surroundings and states of mind is a broadening and objectifying influence.

If you will permit me one more historian's example, Barbara Tuchman has written that doomsayers are often wrong because they work by sheer extrapolation. What is true today will be just as true by the turn of the century. But . . . the "doom factor" sooner or later generates a coping mechanism. Or, more frivolously, someone sneezes, someone gets sick before a battle, and the trend is altered.

Another weakness akin to assumption is abstracting—selecting some characteristics at the risk of eliminating others. "We see as we see because we miss all the fine detail." Communicators should learn to distinguish fact from observation, inference from assumption. This is not an easy task to perform. As Charles Kettering once said, "Some minds are like concrete, all mixed up and permanently set."

But it is isolation of editor and executive that concern me most deeply. In his prophetic and bluntly written book, *The Twilight of the Presidency*, George Reedy worried about how isolated and monarchical the presidency was becoming. The prince tends to hear what he wants to hear. This was true of Kennedy's Camelot and Nixon's Watergate. An editor or executive is in trouble when someone is poisoning the in-box, either by feeding it insufficient information or only with what the boss wants to hear. He's in trouble if he isn't asking enough questions, or enough basic, tough ones.

Executives appear increasingly aware of this communications breakdown. *Industry Week* interviewed some top business people on this point. The magazine noted:

> Many presidents eat in private dining-rooms, fly in private planes, and spend their free time in private clubs. In an effort to run a tight ship, they sometimes structure their companies so rigidly that only a few subordinates have access to them.

Top corporate officers are apt to lose touch, to their own detriment and that of the companies they manage. They may be unaware of new management tools, or of their customers' actual needs, or that their own operations have become fat and lethargic.

Those quoted offered the CEO solutions including: a daily coffee break with his top managers; letting executives tear his thinking apart; not relying exclusively on the men who report directly to him; having contact with outsiders who ask questions to alert him to problems he didn't know he had. One executive I know regularly schedules a day every few months for visiting New York media and for other interviews. Although his operations are away from the East Coast, these sessions help him keep in touch.

Supervision by shoe-leather prevents many problems, and that's every bit as important as detecting them. It also removes the managerial insulation blanket which some would pull around them, as important to them as Linus's is to him. Actually, that's as much security as an unknown minefield.

What To Do

We have explored and criticized corporate communications. Now comes perhaps the hardest part: to advise on what to do. The place to start? Don't assume. Ask the people involved; listen. When you are talking, you can't be learning. Observe behavior and report what you actually see and feel. Respond to people with intelligence and integrity. Get employees talking to each other and to you.

There are a number of ways to do this. One company ran a speak-easy experiment, to determine feelings in a specific plant. Meetings were held between one manager and three employees, none of whom reported to him or was in the same department as the others. Invitations to the sessions were prefaced with the promises that the company would listen and lunch would be free.

The results? Problems were not only identified more accurately, but also quantified. Many key problems were not the major and less controllable ones, such as lay-offs, wages and benefits. Rather, they were the little things, which could be more readily controllable and corrected. This speak-easy program produced such comments as "I don't see managers in the plant any more; I don't even know who they are." "I'm just a number." "I'd like to know more about how the company is organized." "Nobody ever listens to my suggestions." "I don't know what they're making in other areas any more."

Secondly, the eye-to-eye basis, the in-person discussion, opened the way for real problem-solving and eliminated some of the employees' frustration. Not surprisingly, the managers learned more than their employees. Finally, and this concurs with surveys we have conducted, the largest percentage of comments in the speak-easy experiment, 32 percent, concerned ways productivity was affected and could be improved. Twenty-six percent concerned reasons why morale was low; 23 percent dealt with poor communications, and 18 percent related to the work environment. Only one percent concerned the company's image in the community. And one thing that all of us must remember as we talk with people: almost all the comments were constructive.

A more institutionalized example of this same type process is IBM's apparently very successful speak-up program, in which any employee can ask any question anonymously. And, the question must be answered within ten days. This works because the person who runs the program has authority to go anywhere for an answer, and because top management puts its heft behind him.

An even more formalized way of asking is the audit—written and/or in-person interviews. Although an outside consultant often handles such audits, they can be run in-house. Several we have done lately include team interviews, that is, two communication specialists working in tandem with those actually invovled in producing a company's communications. The responses were then cross-referenced with managers and workers. In another survey financial and scientific experts interviewed corporate persons responsible for communications in these same fields. During one of these interviews a top manager talked about the absolute dearth of communications and contact among six members of a department. Our people envisioned graphic and multiple linguistic barriers. To their amazement they discovered these persons were English-speaking Americans on the same floor of the corporate headquarters. They just didn't talk to each other.

Audits are infinitely valuable in knowing what people think and want. It gives the interviewer pieces to put together, which individuals with a very defined part of the action usually lack. From these findings a much more effective and meaningful company communication program can be planned.

A personal, day-by-day review of newspapers and professional materials is invaluable. It may keep you from the don't do-as-I-do, do-as-I-say syndrome. A *Wall Street Journal* article recently illustrated this. It read: "For bureaucrats, lawmakers, hard times aren't here; limousines and free trips are still part of their lives." They are displaying, according to the story, a marked unwillingness to give up perks despite their appeals to the country to tighten belts, walk more, do with less.

By reading widely you also may spot general business deficiencies and even their solutions. For example, communication is usually weakest between top and middle managers. This information lack is exacerbated because most middle managers are upward striving, eager for promotion. They want and need more information than most. Ways we have suggested for handling this include newsletters, perhaps with some prestige binder to keep them in. The trouble with too many newsletters is that they repeat old information. They are dull, boring and noninformative. The news should give something of an insider's view, not just report on what the middle manager has already seen or heard elsewhere. Other topics of concern to middle managers are corporate objectives, new products, operations and the status of subsidiaries. This helps point up the fact that communication within a company has many audiences with many interests—the top man, middle manager, employees, directors, unions, families, communities.

Preparing for the Future

What other aspects must we consider in thinking through a total communication program for the future? One is to factor in elements that may be here today and changed tomorrow.

Some future employee problems have been talked to death already. Let's look at some perhaps less obvious. More people in their 40s and 50s may suffer mid-career crises when they want to choose a new career. The one they had started in their 20s may no longer be financially strong, or they may have lost interest.

Richard Sennett and Jonathan Cobb report other problems. In their study of working-class families, *Hidden Injuries of Class*, they recount feelings of injured dignity, the meaninglessness of work, a social climate that disparages manual labor and grants prestige only to marketable intellectual skills. And, I think this is increasingly true, that the education for which their parents sacrificed and which was supposed to bring freedom, turned out to be only the entrance to a boring job or one far below that expected.

Sennett and Cobb also report great feelings of inadequacy among workers, reinforced by insistent messages from the top, "My time is more valuable than yours." Some young workers still internalize the prevailing corporate myth: that a person's worth is determined by his position in the hierarchy. Aside from the difficulties of such an outer-directed nature on the job, I would ask what this poses for the communicator, what this poses for the individual, when he loses his job, or when his advancement is blocked.

Peter Drucker gives evidence of another sensitivity that communicators should understand. Drucker writes that manual workers in our society start out as losers, who feel rejected and already defeated. However, they learn one thing to perfection—resistance against being driven. "They may not be able to achieve, but they know how to sabotage," he concludes.

A Chicago interviewer, Studs Terkel, in his book, *Working*, tells a great deal about working people of all types. He reports on demoralization deriving from age and other factors. In a related vein, Dr. James Coleman, despite all the security of a college presidency and a sabbatical paycheck, describes how he was unpredictably, albeit temporarily, overwhelmed at his dismissal as a dishwasher. Terkel also warns us about the surreality of much that we call work today. He notes that more and more people are being paid to watch others than ever before, to watch for quality control, but more often for security reasons. Naturally this has caused tremendous resentment and abdication of responsibility. Terkel concludes: "It isn't that the average guy is dumb—he's tired, that's all."

What is certain in communications? That conditions will change quickly and dramatically. Not many years ago economists were bad-mouthing Malthus, urging us to adjust our economic thinking to affluence. Older classical theories built on scarcity wouldn't do. Now, we must shift again. Arthur Clarke, a highly respected futurist, has warned for some time that instead of heading into an era of full employment, we may be headed for full unemployment—that there is no function for manual labor today and may be none for executive and clerical skills tomorrow. An overstatement perhaps like Kurt Vonnegut's *Player Piano*—the grim tale of the few who work and the many who yearn nostalgically for those days when they did. As these haunt us, we should heed their implications.

What else should be considered for corporate communications? Perhaps the so-called "global nervous system" that links peer groups exclusive of national boundaries—as it did the rioting students in 1968. And how is communication going to face the task of getting across to employees that their jobs are safe, their pensions secure, if they truly are? How can basic business economics be explained better? Are we going to have to forgo the comfortable combination of liberty and abundance we have enjoyed for the past two decades? What are the implications when a major American firm is purchased by an Arabian or Japanese interest?

The stakes are high. Dr. Einar Thorsrud of the Norwegian Arbeids Psykologisk Institutt says:

> "We are getting signals that we have to make people think there's hope for them. If we are not successful in giving meaning to their lives, then we may see the terrible turmoil of the end of the techno-logical society."

My own feeling is that the decade ahead will see belt-tightening, a re-examination of the fuzzy thinking and fat of more affluent decades, some of it to the good of all, some to the detriment of many involved. But at the risk of sounding moralistic, I think the major issue, the root of all company communication, is the quality of the messages, the people involved. The hollow men spewing out phony cover stories through fancy media just won't wash any more. People will tune out, do the opposite or in Drucker's word, sabotage. Communication is no longer I-Thou, but moves from one member of us to another. Men have relied too long on their machines. Now it is men themselves and their messages . . . that are the message.

ADVERTISING

19

Corporate Advertising— Now or Never

By Thomas A. Kindre

Before the Public Utility Advertising Association, Charleston, South Carolina, October 3, 1974

SUMMARY: If there seem to be good reasons for not advertising, there may be more compelling ones for doing so—like building credibility today for tomorrow, avoiding the deadly vacuum of non-identity, and telling your story the way you, not someone else, want to. But the same old approaches won't do, and a key to fresh thinking is the total communications concept. There may be three reasons why corporate ad programs fail, and seven steps are suggested to make them work.

Thomas Kindre, a former magazine editor, ad copywriter and corporate PR manager, is a senior vice president of Hill and Knowlton and director of the firm's advertising division.

For many corporate advertisers in the energy industries, this must seem the toughest of all times.

Just when you're bursting with things that need to be said, everyone's trying to muzzle you. A coalition of activists and Congressmen would like to see all corporate advertising labeled as political so it could no longer be deducted as a cost of doing business. Their hope, obviously, is to make it so costly and difficult that corporate advertisers will stop talking.

Others have gone so far as to create and produce counteradvertising that they hoped the media would air for free. The goal? To attack and ridicule energy company advertising.

The media themselves have hardly been receptive or even neutral in many cases. Some columnists and editorial writers seem almost to have earned their living over the past year by attacking energy crisis advertising.

And if you're trying to get on network television with an energy-oriented message, the words seems to be: forget it. God knows the oil companies have tried. One of them offered to buy equal time for any of its critics who wanted to refute the company's messages. But TV would have none of it, even under those conditions.

They don't, they say, want any part of controversy. But what is controversy? I asked the chief counsel of one of the networks to define the word. He said, "As far as we're concerned, if one Congressman feels differently about things than you do and has expressed himself in those terms, the issue is controversial and we want no part of it."

On that basis, it seems to me that even motherhood is an unfit subject for TV advertising.

To top it all off, you're likely to find your own management running scared and wanting you to show cause why your whole ad program shouldn't be scrapped until times are better.

It's enough to make a communicator feel sorry for himself and wish he'd got into some other kind of business.

But no one ever said the job was going to be easy. The greatest communicating has always been done in the face of the greatest challenges, and today the challenges are there in spades.

Areas of Communications Concern

It seems to us, as we look at things from the vantage point of counseling utility companies, oil companies and trade associations, that the utility industry has at least a half dozen major areas of communications concern.

First is acceptance of the energy crisis itself. For more people than you and I would care to imagine, there's really no such thing as an energy crisis. They don't think it ever existed, or if it did, it went away when the gas station lines disappeared.

It's chilling to sit and watch video tapes of focus group research, as we've been doing, and hear dozens of average Americans, of all ages and backgrounds, telling one another blandly that the energy crisis was just an invention of the oil companies, and now that the companies have got their price increases, the crisis is all over.

It's chilling because it means there are millions of Americans who simply aren't taking seriously the vast complexity of the problems that lie ahead of them.

In the face of such widespread indifference to energy problems, how can you get these people to support your industry's urgent needs?

Who's going to tell them the facts if you don't?

The second area of concern is the fuel situation. Do most people in your area understand the dependence of utility companies on available fuel? Do they know what fuel you use and what you have to go through to get it? Do they understand the growing importance of coal as a fuel and the value of developing and using our coal resources to offset scarce petroleum supplies?

When people see the rising fuel cost adjustments on their utility bills, do they understand why?

And suppose the United Mine Workers go on strike, as many believe they will, or suppose they gain a costly wage settlement that averts a strike? The coal story will take on a new and more urgent aspect if either happens. Will people be prepared to understand what it means?

If the utility industry doesn't give them the background, who will?

Number 3 on our list would be the environment and what lies ahead for it. Are people aware of the immense gap between the present state of technology and the standards the all-out environmentalists would impose? Do they understand the significance of high-sulphur coal and what will happen if it can't be used? Do consumers really grasp the basic fact that they are the ones who must pay for environmental controls?

The story can't be told just once. It has to be told again and again in every possible way.

A fourth area of major communications concern has got to be the subject of siting. Of all major concerns, this one has been least adequately explained to the public in its broadest terms—not surprising, because the industry itself is still far from a unified policy on the subject.

The utility industry will need to about double its generating capacity between now and the end of 1984. Most industry people seem pretty well agreed on that. Yet most of the public seems totally unaware of the fact that major land areas in many locations will be needed to accommodate all that growth.

If they don't understand the overall needs—how the pieces all fit together—how can we expect them not to take pot shots at individual projects?

The fifth subject on our list is consumerism, and if you're with an electric utility you're certainly in the line of fire. The Long Island campaign, advising consumers simply not to pay their electric bills if they were unhappy about them, is spreading elsewhere, and it could spread a lot farther.

I'm sure you've all seen, too, the book issued by the Environmental Action Foundation, "How to Challenge Your Local Electric Utility—A Citizen's Guide to the Power Industry."

If you're not talking to consumers consistently, substantially and in ways that you can control completely, it's obvious that other people *are* talking to them.

And the question is, how one-sided do you want the dialogue to get?

The last and most urgent item on this list of communications problems is money.

Whatever problems there are, however the challenges intermesh and relate to one another, the bottom line always comes out the same —money.

How can the public begin to measure the scope of the construction programs the utility industry must undertake over the next ten years to meet consumer needs? How does anyone get a mental handle on a figure like $16 billion? Where does that kind of money come from, and what does it cost?

The story is so complex that it needs to be told endlessly, with much repetition, and from many directions, until public understanding begins to blossom.

And with every communications cutback or lapse, the industry is in double jeopardy, because the job of explaining the subject gets more difficult day by day, as interest rates soar to dizzier heights and earnings sink under the inflationary weight of high operating costs.

Role of Advertising

These are all problems you're familiar with, and I don't intend to use this forum just to rehash the familiar. What I am concerned about is trying to define the important role of advertising in this litany of communications needs—why it should be used and how.

A utility executive said it very well indeed in testimony before a Senate subcommittee.

"Utilities," he said, "are accountable to the public to a much more meaningful extent than non-regulated firms. The public we serve constantly appraises our performance much more closely than it appraises that of companies providing a service in a directly competitive market.

"It is of crucial importance to the utility industry that the investing public, including those who comprise and support investment institutions, have a basic understanding of the principles of economics which are unique to this industry.''

A utility, he pointed out, has nowhere to turn for expansion capital except to the investing public, and therefore a lack of public understanding could lead to the loss of vital capital.

Advertising, he concluded, was an essential part of that process, and the clincher on whether his company's advertising cost could be justified was that postage alone to reach the company's customers by mail would cost twice as much.

Granted that we believe advertising to be an entirely justifiable —actually an essential—element in doing business and serving the public, what about the thorny problem of credibility?

The surveys show that public distrust of business continues to grow, and the energy-related industries have come in for a lion's share of that distrust, as you know.

The oil companies, during the height of their advertising splurge explaining energy shortages, got a mixed bag of reactions—but mostly negative.

Can Advertising Cope with Distrust?

If research shows that nobody believes you, shouldn't you stop advertising?

I'll answer that question with a reminder that, whether people say they believe a particular industry or institution or not, the studies also show that they want the answers.

One utility company found that over 85 percent of its public wanted to know the facts about rate increases and why they were necessary. People want to know what lies behind the energy crisis, what they can expect in the future, whether and how shortages and higher costs will affect their lives.

If we don't answer their questions, others will, and the answers will be based on distortion, bias and political opportunism.

If we'd all been communicating regularly, listening to the questions and encouraging dialogue on the issues, we would perhaps have built the image of credibility that would now foster belief.

But whether we've had that kind of record or not, we can't afford not to talk now, not to make a start.

''Let's keep a low profile for now and hold our advertising off for a better time,'' is a dictum heard all too often these days in management circles.

But history isn't waiting for a better time. Change isn't waiting for a better time. People's need for facts and insights to help give the shape of reality to their plans isn't waiting for a better time.

Do we expect to be in business five years from now? Ten years from now? Then we'd better be using the next five years—or ten years—to build credibility so our public will believe us then.

Advertising Is Part of Communications

But it can't be done in exactly the same old way. Too many companies in the energy business have run afoul of a totally disbelieving audience for their advertising because they suddenly began to talk at great length, after years of spotty communications, and talk in the same old cliches.

Only a company that devotes its communications consistently to projecting its own unique identity in a believable way can derive maximum benefit from issues-type advertising.

And since the issues aren't going to get any easier as the years go by, the time to start is now.

But can't we just let advertising go for a while in this negative climate and rely on our other communications?

It's a question we hear a good deal these days, and it's not an easy one to answer. Certainly, if time, logistics and money could make it possible, it would be better to meet your public on a one-to-one basis, in small groups, or at least in situations where they could ask questions and you could respond.

But it just isn't possible to reach everyone we all need to reach in that way. Even if it were, it would take time, and the issues, the problems, and the policies would be changing too fast to make it practical.

These are the kinds of questions that have been echoing through the ranks of corporations and trade associations in recent months. In the course of seeking answers, many have been discovering that their corporate advertising needs a new approach and a new role.

The most vital trend to come out of it all is the increasing realization that corporate advertising is not a separate discipline, something to be done in the ivory tower, but rather an integral element of the total communications program, another voice to be used appropriately along with booklets, brochures, feature articles, speeches and all the rest.

Its particular value is that it gives you the opportunity not only to convey an exact message, but to control the timing, placement and exposure the message will receive.

And it becomes more important each day for a good reason. Because the opportunity to have your story told fairly in the news columns continues to shrink as available space tightens up or gets increasingly filled with coverage of industry critics, whose pronouncements always make better copy.

Since corporate advertising is one of several voices in the communications program, some of us are now referring to it among ourselves not as advertising, but as "paid space communications." It is one specific kind of element in a larger concept, an element that works to achieve the same objectives as the others in your communications package, plays the same themes and develops the same identity.

Only when that happens does a really synergistic reaction begin to take place.

Referring to it in that way may also help to overcome an unfortunate mind-set that causes many executives to automatically equate advertising with marketing.

Total Communications Concept

There's no doubt in my mind that the total communications concept is an idea whose time has come.

I see it that way from where I sit in the public relations area, but others see it too.

A keynote speaker at a recent meeting of the American Association of Advertising Agencies said it this way: "Corporate communications should employ advertising and public relations to do the job. Neither can do it as well alone as both can together."

It may help you to know that companies in other industries have been having the same kind of struggle with their communications that you are, and that companies are indeed advertising in the midst of crisis to a sometimes hostile audience and trying to do it in ways that depart from the cliches of the past.

Some have found successful formulas, and others are still trying.

Those that seem to be making it work have at least one thing in common: While they attempt to explain complex issues, including economic subjects, they approach their audience in ways that are arresting or that relate to personal interest, or both.

When the airline industry decided to use advertising as a kind of ribbon on the package for their education program on airline economics, they elected to tell the industry's story in terms of people and service. Thus, an ad describing their heavy investment in computers was illustrated with the face of a pretty, smiling girl with a headline that said, "This smile is brought to you by computer." The copy developed the theme that computers help to free up people for more personal service.

In the face of rising beef prices, the beef industry launched an advertising campaign to show consumers how less expensive cuts of beef could also be satisfying and creative. A series of ads in women's magazines featured real women who were homemakers but had also achieved some success in areas beyond the homemaker's role.

To dispel some of the myths consumers held about beef, a different series was produced. One, aimed at the price collusion myth, pictured a rancher and his wife—owners of a small spread—and copy to make the point that American beef comes from almost two million livestock farms, most of them with herds of only a few hundred head.

Getting out of your own skin and into that of the person you're talking to is the best advice in the world for any advertiser, and one of the oil companies is now considering an ad program as forceful and gutsy as any we've seen, centered on that approach.

It features the most searching questions being asked by the company's customers. The questions, taken verbatim from interviews, are the headlines of individual ads, the illustrations are real people in the process of asking them, and the copy is the company's answers.

A new campaign by a company in your own industry—Georgia Power—uses simple, arresting graphic images—an ear of corn, an egg, a concrete block—to symbolize a succession of industries and the people who owe their jobs in those industries to continued, plentiful electric power.

Each ad tells the earnings and capital formation story and ties electricity to jobs, paychecks and people.

These campaigns take different paths because they fit different situations. There's no magic key to the best creative approach. You just need all the freedom you can get from old ways of doing things, all the research you can get that tells you how your audience feels, thinks and acts, then all the additional insights you can muster to find the most acceptable way of reaching that real flesh-and-blood person you want to talk to.

Selling a difficult concept to an indifferent audience is, after all, just a slightly stronger challenge to the creative team. I suspect, though, that the creative team in many instances is not being given a free hand to do the job. Or if they are, they haven't been given the proper guidelines.

Why Corporate Ad Programs Fail

In fact, I think there are probably three principal reasons why corporate ad programs falter, dry up or disappear in times of stress.

The first occurs when communicators and their own top management are not working closely enough. This may be an organizational problem, or a personnel problem. It may be that the traditional way of working needs to be totally overhauled. Whatever it is, it can be deadly to the continuity of advertising.

Management thinking in every industry is today in a turmoil of change, and unless the company's communicators are aware, almost day to day, of how that thinking is changing, they cannot begin to be responsive to it, either short term or long term. In this era of future shock, it takes less and less time for an unbridgeable gap to develop, and when it does it can often result in the sudden cut-off of a program.

A second major stumbling block to corporate ad programs is the failure to have corporate objectives and specific policies fully elucidated. Unless policy positions are thought through, written out and given the stamp of management approval, an advertising program can become, in effect, a trial balloon for policy in the making. But it's a hard way to do things, because if a communicator's tentative brainchild doesn't hit close enough to management thinking, the messenger frequently gets killed along with the message.

A third reason, it seems to me, why ad programs flounder when they shouldn't, is a simple failure to treat them as part of the total communications package.

This has been a terrible disservice to a number of very good advertising agencies, who have been given the job, in the old way, of coming up with a corporate ad program. There is a period of input and questioning, and then they go off to activate their research and creative teams.

But in the meantime, the world is turning. Day by day, policies are shifting slightly. New emphases are showing up in press releases and speeches. New thinking is taking place in the executive offices. But the ad program, out of the orbit of all this, is not being nourished, and by the time it comes back, full-blown, it may be months out of date.

Making Ad Programs Work

How do you go about avoiding these pitfalls?

There is a way. It's a joint communicator-manager exercise that is the surest way I know to keep an ad program running smoothly so it can gradually build recognition, credibility and support.

It's not an easy process. Nothing in this business is. But if there were only one thing I could suggest to help make your advertising program work and achieve long range values for your company, this would have to be it.

There are six or seven steps to the process, depending exactly on how you go about it, and it involves both managers and communicators.

Step #1: Start with the corporate objectives—the real ones, not the ones that were printed and framed five years ago—the short-term ones and the long-term ones, with orders of priority that everyone understands. If they don't exist in that form, start the head-knocking exercise of trying to get them done.

Step #2: Define the problems that face the company as it tries to achieve those objectives. And that isn't necessarily as easy as it sounds. Don't mistake the manifestations of the problems for the problems themselves. Every management-communicator team should be doing this routinely. How many are, it is difficult to say.

Step #3: Develop company policy positions on the problems, the solutions and all matters of public concern that bear on the company's objectives.

Step #4: Research the supporting data that demonstrate why the positions the company is taking are sound and in the public interest.

Step #5: Prepare detailed position papers on every policy position. They should include the support data and in effect put forth the company's case for why it believes what it does.

Step #6: Get the position papers into the hands of all communicators—the speech writers, the publicists, the writers of booklets and brochures and the advertisers. Let their creativity work within the bounds of what they have been given, and let the objectives be used as the standard against which to measure their results.

Step #7: Keep in touch. And that's all there is to it.

But if this process were truly put to work and supported at all levels, industry's communications programs wouldn't be in some of the messes they've been in. If you can contribute in any way to making the process work, you will have done a great service to us all.

Skilled communicators are going to be needed from here on as they've never been needed before. And your managements will need your brains, your insights and your political savvy as well as your words. Don't let them down.

INTERNATIONAL
PUBLIC RELATIONS

20

The Multinational Mentality

By William A. Durbin

*Before the 60th National Foreign Trade Convention,
New York City, November 14, 1973*

SUMMARY: The era of comparative laissez-faire for the multinationals is nearing an end just as surely and inexorably as it ended for their parent domestic concerns a generation or more ago. So the question is no longer whether there should be regulation, but what kind of regulation, exercised by whom. This, in turn, will depend to a degree on the quality and persuasiveness of the facts and arguments advanced by the multinationals themselves.

William A. Durbin, formerly director of public relations of two multinational corporations, American Cyanamid Company and Burroughs Corporation, is vice chairman of Hill and Knowlton.

As one who has spent his career in the communications field, I should probably open with the observation that if multinational corporations had done a better job of communicating in the past, they wouldn't face the assaults from all sides that confront them today. I would then go on to say that although the hour is late, there is still time to "tell the multinational story" to a world public that is willing to listen.

I would then review the undoubted benefactions that the multinationals have bestowed on the world's peoples and economies, ending with a plea to all of you to do a better job of proclaiming your individual corporate achievements. The cumulative effect, as the script goes, would be a better climate of world opinion, and lessened risks of repressive rules and legislation to hamper your prosperity and growth. In other words, "Communicate and ye shall be saved."

This kind of activity is useful, in fact indispensable, but we have only to look at the strictly American experience of American companies to see that it is far from enough. Today, after more than thirty years of "telling the story of American business," public favor toward business stands at an all-time low. According to recent surveys, most Americans believe that average profits stand at an exorbitant 28 percent, that productivity gains are a production-line "speed-up" in disguise, that worker living standards can be increased solely by giving them more of the money companies are already making, and that corporations are so rich that they can raise wages without raising prices.

Let's measure the success of our rear-guard, basically defensive communications strategy in a historical frame: In little more than a generation we have moved from an essentially laissez-faire economy to one that stops just short of state economic planning. Labor unions wield power of such magnitude that the survival of collective bargaining is in jeopardy. Environmentalists, consumer groups, minority groups and others demand, and get, an increasing role in corporate decision-making. And at every hand we confront militants—militant blacks, militant youth, militant women, militant everybody.

Why? Was it just the nature of things, of forces we couldn't shape anyway? Or were we singing the wrong song all along—the one people didn't want to hear—while we tuned out the voices calling for a new score? As all of you know, a good deal of agonizing is going on in front offices throughout the country to find the answer to that one.

A Chance to Change

No one seems to have the answer, but I suspect that most of us in business share the nagging feeling that for too long we tried to stop history rather than shape it. We tended to confront the armored divisions of social change with a cavalry charge of the status quo. And those of us in communications indulged the rather sanctimonious fantasy that if only people would hear our trumpets they would join our ranks. Well it didn't work.

Belatedly today, American business is making a genuine effort to ride and even influence the tides of societal change rather than build dikes to hold them back. Those of us responsible for corporate communications have the incredibly difficult task of convincing people that this time industry really means it.

History rarely holds out a second chance, but it seems to me that the multinational corporations—many of them the overseas arms of the same companies that are under siege at home—still have the opportunity to profit from their domestic mistakes, to avoid on the international plane the kind of confrontation and debilitating acrimony that besets them at home. They can do so if their policies—individually and collectively—are derived from an understanding and acceptance of two apparently contradictory philosophies that dominate most discussions of the multinationals today.

The first is the widely held vision of the MNC as the "economic wave of the future." This views the multinationals as gradually replacing nation-states as the well-spring of economic planning and decision-making. The second is an equally strong conviction that the so-called autonomy of the multinational must be curbed through some system of regulation. Demands for some form of regulation are coming from all sides: from national governments, from supra-national bodies, international labor, consumer and religious organizations, and even from local businesses. This broadly based movement to trim the sails of the multinationals is unlikely to diminish, will probably increase, and in the long run will probably succeed at least in some measure.

At first glance, these two viewpoints seem incompatible. Yet, if you examine the evolution of the private sector within individual western countries over the past 40 years, it has been characterized by the co-existence of growth and consolidation on the one hand, and ever-increasing regulation by public bodies on the other.

We are now witnessing the escalation of the same historical process from the domestic to the international plane. However, there is one fundamental difference. The real threat to the multinationals should not be seen in the principle of regulation *per se*. Rather, the threat lies in the prospect of multiple sets of regulations involving widely differing controls, sanctions and curbs in dozens of different countries. Carried to extremes, these would be hard if not impossible to assimilate and could cripple multinational growth.

The alternative is responsible regulation under the aegis of an international authority. If the multinationals now bite the bullet and accept the certainty and the inevitability of increasing regulation, far better that this regulatory power be exercised by such a supra-national authority. In this situation, each member state must subordinate a measure of its own economic sovereignty—which in today's world all too often can be mindlessly nationalistic or utterly capricious.

Recently, we have witnessed the proposals of the European Common Market and reports arising from the UN-sponsored study on the Impact of Multinational Corporations on Development and on International Relations. In both cases the approach has been generally more thoughtful and responsible than had been anticipated, which gives cause for encouragement.

These forums are providing ample opportunities for multinational executives to state their positions in a climate where the competition, and even the adversary relationships between member states, serve to provide checks and balances in arriving at solutions that can accommodate both the mulitnational corporations and their host governments.

International Supervision Considered

Support for this approach was well summed up in a recent article[1] by Roy Blough, Professor Emeritus at Columbia University Graduate School of Business. "The MNC," he observed, "obviously is not comfortable being pulled in several directions at the same time by different host governments. Despite traditional opposition to any effective regulation by anyone, the MNCs might find it in their interest to support negotiations to develop some kind of international supervision or regulation that would seek a reasonable solution to the conflicting claims of governments. Experience suggests a 'law' of government regulation, namely, that it tends to extend its boundaries to equal those of the body that needs control. It seems to be only a matter of time before there will be international regulation of MNCs."

Some indication that business leaders are beginning to think in the same terms was summed up in a *Wall Street Journal* report on the second round of hearings in Geneva by the UN's "group of eminent persons": ". . . business leaders," the Journal observed, "are far from ready to see (the UN) set up anything like a global version of the Federal Trade Commission to 'monitor' their foreign activities. But some aren't flatly

---

[1]"U.S. Trade Policy: Past Successes, Future Problems," *The Columbia Journal of World Business*, Jan. 1973.

opposing study of some such UN function, and most are becoming amenable to less grandiose goals, particularly the UN setting up a center for exchanging information about multinationals and perhaps a system for registering those that would subscribe to a voluntary code of conduct.''

I would take matters a step further. The era of comparative laissez-faire for the multinationals is nearing an end just as surely and inexorably as it ended for their parent domestic concerns a generation or more ago. So the question is no longer whether there should be regulation, but *what* kind of regulation, exercised by *whom*.

If we accept the principle of internationally supervised regulation, the optimum would, of course, be responsible self-regulation, perhaps through a private organization of multinational corporations operating under a compact to which member companies have subscribed. But as we all know, examples of industry doing this successfully are exceedingly rare. Such agreement may be too much to expect, desirable though it may be.

If regulation must be imposed, the next step is to insure to the maximum extent possible that it will exert its authority within realistic bounds. This, in turn, will depend to a degree on the quality and persuasiveness of the facts and arguments advanced by the multinationals themselves.

And it is precisely in this area of providing quality information on the international plane—public affairs and public relations 'writ large'—where the multinationals are in disarray. There are probably not more than six—a maximum of ten—multinational companies that give priority attention to their international public affairs and public relations. And, outside of the Burke-Hartke debates, over and over again the same handful of distinguished executives appear publicly as the lone standard-bearers and spokesmen for a multinational community of corporations numbering in the thousands.

Yet, ironically, internal company studies and private surveys abound, documenting the contributions of multinationals both to host country and the world economy. There is scarcely an argument advanced by critics of the multinationals—from transfer pricing policies to employment of local nationals—that cannot be cogently rebutted or even turned to the advantage of the multinational cause. But alas, these materials rarely see the light of day. In short, there is a treasure trove of unorganized, unassimilated data in corporate archives throughout the world that needs to be codified and put to work.

A second and parallel problem is obvious to many observers: the lack of communication between corporations and the often lamentable and occasionally fatal absence of a common front in the face of political problems.

Program of Containment

I would suggest a four-step approach to begin rectifying this situation:

First, each multinational corporation should conduct an *audit of its public relations assets and liabilities* in each of the countries in which it operates. For example, what is the climate toward foreign-owned business generally? Toward the particular industry generally? What is the degree of participation in local management—or for that matter in parent company management—by nationals of the host country? What about labor relations? To what extent is the company supporting and contributing to community projects not directly related to the business? What particulars about the company are people criticizing? What might they criticize in the future? To what extent are these criticisms valid? Conversely, what opportunities to earn good will are being overlooked?

These questions are merely illustrative, for the list can be virtually endless. But once obtained from each country of operation, the answers should be collated and combined into a composite, worldwide scorecard of the company's public relations gains and losses, its strengths and weaknesses, its opportunities and vulnerabilities.

The *second* step would be a *government relations audit*, as a counterpart to the public relations assessment. Virtually every corporation possesses far greater, broader and deeper government relations capabilities than it knows it has. For example, what are local management's specific political relationships in a given country, at cabinet and parliamentary levels? What is the detailed political history of that enterprise in this country. This history should include honest, detailed background, both good and bad. What are the company's current and anticipated government relations problems? What effect, good or bad, do its labor relations have on the policies of government? What are the specific government relations capabilities of the company's suppliers? This list of questions, too, is lengthy.

Sound techniques exist for auditing a company's government relationships. The information which results from the audit is then organized systematically so that the company possesses a public affairs structure and support sytsem.

Let me add one parenthetical but important word of caution: the corporation that undertakes country-by-country audits of its public and government relationships should provide a measure of supervision by head office executives or dispassionate third parties. It is unfair and contradictory to human nature to expect the manager of an overseas subsidiary to turn a spotlight on his own public relations and political weaknesses. For example, would you expect the German manager of an American-owned plant in Germany to admit that his relations with government administrations in Bonn—his own countrymen—are less than ideal?

The *third step* is a logical sequel to the public relations and government relations audits: a *continuing analysis of political and public trends*, to monitor the forces at work at both the national and supra-national levels. These forces may be beneficial as well as adverse, and a systematic, continuing trend analysis takes both types into account.

Large business organizations for the most part suffer from a debilitating lack of medium and long-term public affairs trend analysis. This is peculiar; the same organizations frequently distinguish themselves by making eminently practical use of trend analyses in the fields of economics, marketing, materials availability, planning for expansion and technological development. It seems strange that their highly admired talent for future planning is rarely applied to the public relations and public affairs fields—especially when one considers that healthy public attitudes and government relationships are essential if the subjects of every other type of forecasting are to succeed.

Systematic trend analyses would enable corporations to take more realistic corrective actions or make adjustments in company policies or practices that may be ringing discordant bells in the minds of public authorities. They would help provide a basis for rethinking or reshaping company communications vis-a-vis the public authorities, particularly in cases where frictions stem solely from misunderstandings rather than from fundamentals. And, they would prepare companies to play a more effective role in the decision-making process—to intervene at the federal or supra-national level with cohesive positions and arguments *before* rather than *after* ill-conceived or repressive laws and regulations have passed the discussion stage and have reached the point of no return.

All of which leads to the *fourth and final step*: Some kind of mechanism, perhaps a very informal one, needs to be created to enable multinational corporations to *share and exchange information* of mutual interest. This would be a clearing house through which developments and trends at both the state and supra-national levels monitored by individual companies could be compared and analyzed and decisions taken on whether to intervene individually or collectively.

Engaging in Productive Exchange

In summary, I submit that the combination of individual company inventories of their public relations and public affairs assets and liabilities, regular monitoring of political and economic developments by each company in its sphere of operation and a mechanism for the MNCs to share common approaches to common problems could go a long way toward enabling the besieged multinationals to make their case more convincingly. Thus equipped they will be better prepared to engage in productive dialogue at both the national and supranational levels. They will also be better positioned in trying to channel regulatory actions and movements in directions that will more nearly accommodate the aspirations of nation-states and corporate needs.

Multinational reputations stand or fall on the sum total of national reputations. In order to survive, multinationals must tie their policies and practices as closely as possible to the aspirations and goals of host countries. They must increase and make known their efforts to upgrade job skills, to bring more nationals into local and international management, to seek out opportunities to provide contributions and services in the public interest—in short, to pursue the never-ending task of proving themselves honest and sincere residents rather than undesirable aliens in somebody else's country.

I began these remarks in a way that is certainly difficult for a member of the communications business. I said in effect that our corporate communications to win support for U.S. industry domestically have fallen short of success because they were grounded in a philosophy that sought to rationalize the status quo—to prevent change rather than trying to shape it.

I suggested that there is still time for the multinationals to avoid the same trap internationally if they will bring themselves to accept the principle of regulation by responsible international authority. Having crossed this philosophical Rubicon, I listed a few practical measures that the multinationals might consider taking to help ensure that the future world of multinational regulation will be a world they can live with.

What I have been saying was well summed up another way many years ago by George Santayana when he warned that "those who cannot remember the past are condemned to repeat it."

21

PR's Rising Sun—
A New Japan

By Robert W. Bowen

*Published Originally in the July 1970
Edition of Public Relations Journal*

SUMMARY: The achievements of Japan's post-war economic ''miracle'' have been widely publicized in recent years: Japan now ranks third in the world in gross national product, and some experts say the country may achieve the world's highest per capita income before the end of this century. Throughout these years of growth, the Japanese have been working together in apparent harmony. Business and government have not merely co-existed but were practically blood brothers, wages rose steadily and job security was virtually total. In this atmosphere, public controversy was minimal and the public relations profession has been regarded as little more than a superfluous commodity. In the last few years, however, all of the elements of public concern, controversy and debate which have plagued the West have been coming to the surface in Japan and are having a profound impact on both domestic and foreign business activities. Under these conditions, there is the strong likelihood that the ''Japanese Decade'' in international public relations is at hand.

Robert W. Bowen, a Yale graduate, is executive vice president of Hill and Knowlton International, Ltd., which coordinates H&K's operations overseas, and also a senior vice president of Hill and Knowlton, Inc.

With the opening of Expo '70, Japan was propelled into the headlines and onto the covers of our national magazines to a degree not witnessed since the end of World War II. The massive publicity not only dramatized the achievements of her post-war economic "miracle," but was also a forecast of new and far-ranging problems that the Asian nation and those who do business with her would face in the years ahead.

The statistics alone are awesome. Japan now ranks third in the world in gross national product, after the United States and the Soviet Union. Some experts say the country may achieve the world's highest per capita income and standard of living before the end of the century. Japan's population is now estimated at 110 million, nearly twice that of the United Kingdom or West Germany.

All this has been accomplished through a capitalist infrastructure which, in some respects, would gladden the soul of Adam Smith. On the other hand, business works in such close alliance with the government that it is hard to discern at times where one ends and the other begins. "Japan Incorporated," Tokyo's foreign community calls it.

State of Public Relations

In a nation so industrially advanced, presided over by democratic forms of government, one would logically expect to see public relations already flourishing on the scale of, say, England. This is far from the case, however. The situation is improving, but all too often life as a public relations man in a Japanese corporation can be described as The View From the Basement Floor, a comfortable resting place where Japanese managements frequently put their equivalents of "Old Joe." There are a respectable number of agencies, but their growth has been slow compared with the public relations boom experienced in other countries during the past decade. And there is still widespread confusion over the differences between public relations and advertising.

At first glance, this seems paradoxical in a nation that has a positive genius for importing foreign ideas and techniques, tampering with them a bit, and often ending up with something better than the original. Look closer and you realize that one fundamental ingredient has been missing, without which public relations as we know and practice it in the West is a superfluous commodity. That ingredient is controversy.

Like some Oriental version of the Eton boating crew, the Japanese "swing, swing, together" in dogged, purposeful harmony. Racial tensions are virtually unknown as the Japanese are largely one race. Business and government do not merely co-exist but are almost blood brothers, a bond made even closer by intricate school and family ties, personal loyalties and obligations stretching across the generations. Wages have risen steadily and, as job security is close to total, layoffs have been virtually unheard of. As a consequence, there has been little labor unrest. Proxy fights, tender offers and other corporate rows, which almost enjoyed the status of a national sport in post-1965 America, leave the Japanese bewildered and uncomprehending. It would be unthinkable for businesses to air their differences publicly, and taking them to court is a last resort involving disastrous loss of face.

Until recently, even foreign companies in Japan felt no particular need for any full-scale public relations effort. With a handful of exceptions, American participation in the Japanese economy has been one of junior partner in a joint venture. Foreign equities in joint ventures have rarely been permitted to exceed 50 percent, and usually have been much lower. With all the business difficulties this implies—and they are legion—the American businessman has benefited from the protective coloration offered by the majority partner while basking in the reflected prestige of a Mitsubishi, Sumitomo or some other great business family, or "zaibatsu."

All of this harmony and understanding is beginning to show signs of strain as Japan, like the rest of the world, is dragged screaming into the Age of Aquarius.

The Rise of Dissension

Tensions, long repressed, are coming to the surface. In Japan, as elsewhere, the fall-out of rapid, inexorable change is coming faster than mortals can enlarge their capacity for absorbing it. Within the last few years, Japan has had a preview of the same woes that have been the preoccupation of public relations in America and Europe.

Take the youth movement, for example. Much of Tokyo University, the most prestigious in Japan, was closed for more than a year. There were spectacular student demonstrations on such issues as Vietnam and the return of Okinawa. Indeed, the demonstrations became so frequent and curiously stylized that one Tokyo hotel maintained a huge war map to track their progress.

Pollution in the Tokyo-to-Osaka area makes New York seem antiseptic by comparison. Mount Fuji, always a visible and even sacred symbol of Japan in years past, is seen only occasionally in blurred outline through the smog. Until quite recently, nothing much had been done about pollution.

Then there is the area of private versus public investment. The Japanese government has recognized and voiced its concern that public services and public needs have been sacrificed for too long on the altar of exports.

There are too few schools, hospitals, parks, nursing homes; in fact, too few anything that normally falls under the purview of local or national government in other advanced nations. The country's roads are unspeakable and highway carnage ranks among the highest in the world. More and more, deficiencies in the public sector have been the subject of critical articles in the press.

Finally, in its dealings abroad, Japan has achieved such strength that it is beginning to reap the inevitable consequences. In the United States, where traditionally everybody is a free trader until his own ox gets gored, industries long noted for their liberalism are feeling the pinch from a flood of Japanese imports and are demanding stricter quotas. At the same time, foreign industries that have been denied entry into Japan are demanding that Japan begin to reciprocate by relaxing its rigid protectionism in imports and direct investment.

The Japanese are keenly sensitive, if not immediately responsive, to the new pressures and criticisms, and have in fact taken a first step through a partial relaxation of exchange controls. They are becoming increasingly worried about their image in Western nations. A comment in the *Economist* of London, which called Japan "an economic animal," caused an uproar in Tokyo.

As was the case in Europe in the early Sixties, the catalyst of the growth of public relations in Japan may well be provided by foreign companies. American concerns are now undertaking public relations activities for the first time, or are expanding their existing programs to take advantage of new opportunities, and to deal with problems that have become more acute.

Areas for Public Relations

With the trend toward liberalization of investment in Japan, the American partners in joint ventures will become comparatively larger, and more visible and more vulnerable to criticism. They will be obliged to do more for themselves than in the past, when the Japanese partner ran all interference. At the same time, competition is increasing. Products that are household words in the United States may be unknown in Japan. Much greater attention to product publicity and other public relations support to marketing will be required in the future.

The problem of recruiting well-qualified employees, which used to be merely acute, has now become infernal. Foreign companies simply do not offer the prestige that is conferred upon the young Japanese graduate when he joins one of the great Japanese banks or trading companies. As the foreign business community grows, competition for available personnel is becoming more and more intense. Obviously, the foreign company whose name is known and respected will fare best. This is one reason why many American companies are now embarking on corporate identity programs aimed at establishing their prestige.

With all the attention now being showered on Japan, particularly since the crescendo of publicity attending the opening of Expo '70, parent companies in the United States have been taking a new look at their Japanese subsidiaries. Japan is an important place to be, and therefore what a company does in Japan deserves more attention in house magazines and stockholder publications than it has received in the past.

Above all, the crucial area of government relations is going to become more difficult and complex—it is already far more difficult than in most Western nations. Under the Japanese system the government fully regulates every detail of every industry. To do so, its ministries must be fully informed about everything that is going on. The foreign company that ignores the rules, even through ignorance, does so at its peril. In view of some of the changes discussed earlier that now loom on Japan's socio-economic horizon, good public relations is going to require meticulous attention to good government relations.

Much the same applies to the press, in a country where there are five national newspapers, seven TV stations in Tokyo alone and scores of magazines. Historically, the daily newspapers have exerted enormous influence upon public and official attitudes. Consequently, the quality and effectiveness of any company's press relations in Japan have a direct bearing on the reputation it enjoys among Japanese leadership groups.

Achieving good press relations is easier said than done. The news-gathering process is organized in a complicated system of press clubs unlike anything known in the West. Each club is the exclusive preserve of its member reporters, who gather a particular segment of the news. For example, the Bank of Japan Press Club, located in the Bank of Japan Building, includes reporters for all major Japanese media who cover financial news.

There are about 30 such press clubs, many of which are attached to government ministries. Each has a chairman (Kanji), and the chairmanship rotates every three months among the journalists represented in the club. The chairman is the key contact within the club. He arranges members' attendance at press conferences, distributes press releases to members and is virtually all-powerful during his term. He can single-handedly boycott the news if he so wishes. To complicate matters, there is a strong and frequently bitter rivalry among the various clubs, and a number of gray areas develop when more than one club claims dominion over the news.

Learning to tread safely through these minefields is obviously difficult. Therefore, through insecurity or fear, most foreign companies have failed to cultivate the press, have missed opportunities to promote their good name or, conversely, have been sitting ducks for criticism. This is starting to change as companies realize that, in Japan as elsewhere, the press is responsive to newsworthy material and reasoned arguments.

For their part, Japanese companies have begun to pay close heed to the public relations efforts of American companies on their shores. They have good reason to do so. As Japan moves away from a purely export economy toward direct investment and equity financing abroad, she will have to look to her own public relations in other countries, particularly in view of the not-altogether-friendly reactions already prevalent in the West toward her existing export-import policies.

It would be wrong to conclude that a Golden Age of Public Relations, Western-style, is just around the corner in Japan. Things just don't happen that way in this very special country that has a personality, style and approach to problems uniquely its own. But it is true that most of the elements of public concern, controversy and debate that we have known in the West for several years are coming to the surface in Japan.

They are bound to have profound impact both on domestic and foreign business activities. Under these conditions, there is the strong likelihood, if not the certainty, that we may well be approaching the ''Japanese Decade'' in international public relations.

22

MNCs Under Attack

By Loet A. Velmans

Before the
International Operations Committee
Financial Executives Institute
New York City, May 7, 1975

SUMMARY: Two yardsticks to measure the seriousness of anti-MNC activity are proposed legislation and public opinion. Legislation, now being discussed in Western countries and in international organizations such as the United Nations, the OCED, the ILO, the European Economic Community, the Organization of American States and several others, is all aimed at further increasing government control. It covers taxation, financial disclosure and management-employee relations. Public opinion, as expressed through academics, trade union leaders, socialist thinkers, will have its effect. Mr. Velmans suggests a broad-based public relations program to combat these trends along with some changes in the MNCs themselves.

Loet A. Velmans, vice chairman of Hill and Knowlton, Inc., coordinates the international operations of the H&K group of companies in 18 countries throughout Europe. Australasia, Japan and Southeast Asia.

Let me try first to summarize the nature of the attacks on the multinational corporations. What do the critics say?

- First, MNCs allegedly export jobs—by diverting capital from the country of origin to foreign countries.
- Second, they rig prices, often overcharge the consumer and underpay labor. Also, by manufacturing in low labor-cost countries, they escape governmental controls.
- Third, they manipulate currencies and are responsible for monetary crises.
- Fourth, they cheat on taxes.
- Fifth, they generally help to increase the gap between the rich nations and the poor.
- Sixth, they use up available local credit, making scarce capital even scarcer for local enterprises.

Identifying the Critics

Who are the critics? You all know the most vocal advocates of the anti-MNC activity. They are modern-day pamphleteers. Many are academics at liberal schools of higher education. Some of them are journalists. Still others are ambitious trade union leaders and generally left-wing thinkers, particularly in Britain and in other European countries where some of them have reached ministerial rank.

Many of these spokesmen have active supporters in government circles and particularly among parliamentarians. Finally, there are the usual fringe groups, including Communist Party thinkers in Western Europe, radical youth leaders, and others.

How serious is the activity? This is hard to measure, but there are two broad yardsticks that could be applied. One would examine legislative measures introduced or contemplated; the other encompasses public opinion as expressed, or perhaps more importantly influenced, by the media both here and abroad.

The Legislative Outlook

With respect to legislative proposals, there are a number now being discussed in one form or another in Western countries and in international organizations such as the United Nations, the OECD, the ILO, the European Economic Community, the Organization of American States and several others.

Although it is obvious, perhaps it should be restated that all of the proposed measures further increase government control. They also stem from a basic philosophy that business which is big cannot be good for the welfare of a nation.

Legislators view taxation as generally the most effective way of exercising control. Once again in this country, remittance of profits has become a favorite subject in Washington, D. C. The current Tax Reduction Act (a somewhat ironic title) is aimed at oil companies. It fragments foreign-source income and limits the amount and the uses of tax credit on foreign income. This new legislation sets dangerous precedents for industries other than oil. In Europe, in the context of harmonizing taxation at the Common Market level and also in individual countries, legislators are considering tax measures regarding profit transfers from one country to another. The emphasis is on license payments and transfer pricing.

Another subject of interest to legislators is compulsory disclosure of more detailed financial information. The Labour Government in Britain is expected to introduce later this summer a bill requiring corporations to discuss in advance with government all investment plans and projects. Incidentally, the law is also expected to contain provisions giving the Ministry of Industry broad powers to block foreign takeovers of any British manufacturing companies, regardless of size and market share.

One of the Common Market's objectives in legislation concerning MNCs is, and I quote, "more information to be published in company accounts, irrespective of the legal form of the company and the presentation of consolidated balance sheets at world level."

Management-employee relations are also of concern to legislators. As you know, in some of the Scandinavian countries and in Germany, there already is worker representation on company boards. This trend is likely to continue. Common Market proposals, now under consideration, stipulate equal participation by three groups: stockholders, workers and so-called "neutrals." It may be assumed, however, that even the neutrals will include public figures, who, in their function as board members, will be influenced by their anti-free enterprise philosophy.

A recent Conference Board study also draws attention to the growing strength and activity of the multinational unions. One of these, the International Federation of Chemical and General Workers' Unions, has proclaimed a global program "to impose on companies' central management the obligation to discuss on a regular basis with ICF affiliates implementation of investments, mergers, acquisitions and commercial policies."

Another pro-labor concern is job security, which means protection against dismissal. Again, to quote from the Common Market objectives: ". . . from the social angle, it is particularly important to have a set of directives and international collective agreements to protect workers against the effects of decisions made abroad."

In several European countries it is now practically impossible to dismiss any employee. Perhaps the time will come soon when labor costs must be capitalized, as they become as immovable as a piece of equipment.

I would like to repeat that many of these legislative proposals are not exclusively aimed at MNCs. It just so happens that bigness often coincides with corporate interests across borders and that attention focuses on the MNC as a target.

Dealing with Public Opinion

To me it is unquestionable that many of the contemplated measures are framed by the antis. In the same way as the consumerist movement in this country has had its effect on legislation, one must assume that the Barnetts and Mullers (authors of Global Reach), trade union leaders like Levenson, the socialist thinkers like Britain's Minister of Industry, Antony Wedgewood Benn, will play their roles—and these are as significant as those played by Ralph Nader and others in like crusades.

I know I am surrounded here by people who, like me, are always analyzing problems and, more often than not, have to answer the question: What can we do about it? It is always easier to state the problem than to propose the solution. However, some 20 years of involvement with MNCs have convinced me that despite the excellent work performed by a few exceptional corporations, most businesses have dealt with the problem in a somewhat dilatory manner. This, I am afraid, is still true today. I experienced this during my 20 years in Europe and one of my first experiences in the U.S. seemed to confirm that things are not that much better over here.

I was asked by a writer of the *Chicago Daily News* whether I would comment on the position of the MNCs for a series of articles now appearing in that paper. The writer then told me that I was one of the very few who had agreed to collaborate with her, and that many of the corporation executives she was interviewing were not prepared to take a strong stand on any aspect of the role of the MNCs. Incidentally, the first articles in the series have appeared, and the MNCs do not come out as badly as might have been the case had we not cooperated. This brief personal experience leads me to the somewhat wider discussion of what might be done.

First of all, I favor more disclosure on a voluntary basis. Some companies are now breaking out European or other regional figures from their consolidated results. But the critics have a point when they say that companies are not disclosing enough. Unfortunately, MNCs have contributed to their own myth when they permit accountants and international tax lawyers to dictate policy decisions. Common Market staff hopes to have a formal directive ready by next year that would require consolidated accounts covering assets, liabilities, financial position and results for multinational companies based in Community countries.

Second, international management structures should be more broadly based. There is only a handful of American companies in which foreigners have been brought into top management. Also, there is still insufficient effort to internationalize shareholdings. Probably we will also need to continue to rethink the joint venture approach. Is it not better to go into a country even as a minority partner rather than not go in at all? Shouldn't joint venture partners be given more of a role either as board members or as members of special advisory committees to the CEO?

I know that some companies are cooperating with the proposed "Code of Good Conduct," which is one of the recommendations accepted by the United Nations from its investigation of the MNCs. The International Chamber of Commerce is active in this area—but is this enough? Current allegations that United Brands has been bribing government leaders in Honduras and officials in Italy will reflect on the MNC community as a whole. How would the proposed code deal with such problems? Some government officials (e.g. at the Common Market) consider the concept of "codes of good conduct" as hogwash. Yet, what if industry and business prepared a set of ground rules that were so intolerant of miscreants that no fair-minded person could fault it? Are we capable of such an objective approach?

Finally, when will the time come when governmental relations, including parliamentary relations, will be taken as seriously abroad as they are in Washington? Even in Washington, we have a long way to go before the cause of the MNCs will be understood by the new members of Congress. I recently heard an Undersecretary of Commerce say that in his contacts with the new members of Congress, he had been told that "the Russians are taking the MNCs for a ride." These same people hold the view that MNCs are making too much money—a clear contradiction.

Who is taking the time to spell out the facts of life, over and over again, to the unsophisticated men on the Hill? I can assure you that if this problem exists in Washington, it can be multiplied *ad infinitum* in other capitals of the industrialized world.

The Prospect for MNCs

To summarize, the public position of the MNCs continues to deteriorate; legislation will get more severe, and there is no effective counterforce in sight; companies will be forced to mount their own defensive actions and will have to continue to adjust to situations which will get more and more complex.

Saying all this does not mean that I believe the MNC is going down the drain. On the contrary, I think it will continue to exist and play a major role to the benefit of the economies of the industrialized world and perhaps also of the developing countries who need our know-how far more than, obviously, we need theirs.

Defensive and well-planned action, particularly in government relations, is more essential than ever before. But this is probably not enough. Basic, as in so many other problems today, is the need to convince the CEO that one of his top priorities should be the unfortunately not inconsiderable amount of time that he needs to spend on the MNC's short-term and long term public and government relations problems.

Role of the Critics

With respect to these problems, I have a point of view I'd like to share with you.

You remember, I started by outlining the attacks and identifying some of the critics of the multinational corporations. I should like now in closing to reiterate the role of some intellectuals and many of the trend-setting journals in the distorted picture of multinational power. I am not now questioning their motives; that would be an exercise in name-calling. What I want to underscore is the fashionable flavor that the attacks on the MNCs acquire by virtue of the fact that too many academicians, journalists and politicians have taken an adversary position.

Yet that position is not always easy to understand—especially when you consider the degree to which these same people have represented a liberal point of view. The fact is that the MNC is a force for international cooperation; it goes beyond the parochialism of national boundaries. It seems to me that in sounding the trumpet for national limits to economic enterprise, many intellectuals are taking an anti-liberal position.

Nonetheless, I would not want to give up on being able to get a coterie of disinterested, objective intellectuals on our side. I would hope, for example, they would come to realize that there is little a multinational company can do when operating in a foreign land that is not agreed to by the host country. Political power is stronger than economic. Or to quote from a study sponsored by the United Church of Christ: "As a sovereign nation, the host country is ultimately more powerful than the MNC, no matter how large the latter's world sales are. It follows that the government is increasingly sure to find ways to insure that transnational business will only invest in those industries that the rulers want. The rulers are now able, if they wish to do so, to direct the companies into channels that they think will help the country in the long run."

The study's point of view is clear. The authors write that "the basic developmental question is whether *people*, and not only national economies, are benefiting from the effects of transnational business . . ." That is also a point of view shared by many liberal intellectuals. Whether the study would influence them I can't say. I think we must have the patience to permit people from whom we might seek support to come to their conclusions by honest conviction. The day that a well-reasoned article by a disinterested academic or literary intellectual appears in *The New Yorker* or *Commentary* or the *New Republic* or *Harper's* or *Atlantic* is the day we can begin to hope that others, too, will reconsider their basically partisan position and judge the multinationals on an objective basis.

REPRISE:

THE CRITICAL ISSUE

23

Public Relations— A Magic Wall?

By William A. Durbin

Before the seminar on
Contemporary Communication Issues,
Graduate School of Corporate and Political Communication,
Fairfield University, Fairfield, Connecticut, March 26, 1975

SUMMARY: The single most critical problem facing many a professional communicator today is the problem of Lost Credibility. Unfortunately, many businessmen—including several who retain outside PR counsel or employ PR staffs—look on public relations as a magic wall that should shield them from public view, or as a cosmetic that improves their company's image.

William A. Durbin, formerly director of public relations of two multinational corporations. American Cyanamid Company and Burroughs Corporation, is vice chairman of Hill and Knowlton.

Understandably, my comments will be based largely on my own business experience in counseling Hill and Knowlton clients—who are, typically, leading executives in corporations and industrial associations. I'm hopeful that you will agree with this approach, since this is probably the area where I can make my best contribution to your discussions. I'll try to keep my remarks general enough to be applicable to your own fields of specific interest and to avoid any violation of client confidences.

I'd like to discuss some of the intertwined problems and opportunities confronting contemporary communications in American society, in connection with recent developments in communication techniques.

Perhaps the best place to begin is with the phenomenal evolution of communications technology in recent years. You are already familiar with the details of this phenomenon, so I'll move along and comment that this evolution has had a double effect on contemporary communicators. In many cases, this technological progress has presented journalists with new and serious problems, as well as unprecedented opportunities.

Today's media personnel have in their hands—and often literally at their fingertips—some of the most powerful and sophisticated communication machinery ever available to man. However, the financial investment which the media must make for the purchase, maintenance and operation of such machinery is also unprecedented. The burden of this investment in communications hardware has resulted in economic handicaps affecting the efficiency of journalists expected to produce the communications software, the actual messages which this machinery was designed to disseminate.

The Problem of News Coverage

The growing need for larger advertising revenues, to amortize this investment, demands greater and greater shares of media time and space, at the expense of the so-called "news hole" available for reporting and for editorial comment. This is especially true of the print media and radio, though television has also been affected. Recent expansion of TV news time has not met expectations that this innovation would permit more thorough coverage of complicated issues. Instead, much of the time made available by this expansion is filled with trivial or merely amusing items. This disappointment is partly a consequence of the broadcaster's need to hold the news audience till it can view all or most of the growing number of commericals. The result is news-as-entertainment, rather than vital information.

While communication machinery has grown more complex, so have the public issues on which all media must report and comment. As the news becomes less amenable to exposition and evaluation, competent personnel may not always be available or equal to these tasks, because of false economies imposed on media staffing. For example, much of the public confusion attending the onset of the energy crisis in the Fall of 1973 can be traced to some media's expedient creation of instant experts, some of these simply by a transfer from their regular and familiar assignments, to the new and baffling energy beat.

Quantitative and qualitative shortcomings of media staff can result in an unhealthy dependence, by underprepared and overworked communicators, on handouts from the very same factions on whose arguments and accusations the public wants to be guided or, at least, objectively informed. The harsh realities of communications *as a business* have come to place a premium on shallowness masquerading as succinctness and on glibness masquerading as expertise.

On the other hand, strenuous efforts by media staffers to give a semblance of order and clarity to an increasingly disordered and murky world have also encouraged the reading and viewing public to expect more of the same. The effect has been the pampering of a popular appetite that grows by what it feeds on: superficial statements and capsulized comments.

Reputation of American Business

Of course, I study these problems as they affect or could affect my clients. But I cannot be content with seeing their side of it only. Communication as a profession demands more than the prompt and courteous delivery of messages, whether for an employer or for a client institution. And here, again, I will touch on a subject with which you are already conversant. I refer to the well documented decline in the reputation of American institutions, most dramatically in the reputation of American business.

There are many studies available which trace this decline. The poll taken every two years since 1959 by Opinion Research Corporation provides an eloquent record. I'd like to cite it for that reason and because Dick Darrow, chairman of Hill and Knowlton, was associated with the announcement of the latest available results.*

Those results were presented and then discussed from many viewpoints at the Opinion Research Corporation Conference for Decision Makers, held in New York City on August 21, 1974. ORC's Executive Vice President Harry O'Neill was the first speaker to follow the welcoming address at that conference, and *his* welcome to the assembled rep-

*See pages 1-11.

resentatives of business and industry noted some discouraging changes in American public opinion between 1959—the first year of the biennial poll—and 1973—the latest year for which the poll has been completed.

For openers, the public's *agreement* with the following statement had *declined* from 60 percent to 46 percent: "Profits of large companies help make things better for everyone." Public agreement was *down* from almost two-thirds to less than half.

On the other hand, public agreement with the following statements had *increased:*

"In many of our largest industries, one or two companies have too much control of the industry." Public agreement was *up* from 57 percent to 76 percent.

"There's too much power concentrated in the hands of a few large companies." Agreement with *this* was up from 53 percent to 75 percent.

"As they grow bigger, companies usually get cold and impersonal in their relations with people." Agreement had gone up from 55 percent to 74 percent.

"For the good of the country, many of our largest companies ought to be broken up." Agreement here was up from 38 percent to 53 percent. This old and once rather radical idea was now held by a *majority* of the American people!

Public Attitude Toward Business

As for the public's overall attitude toward business, ORC had traced the following changes between 1959 and 1973:

"Little Approval" of business—The group that made this low evaluation of business had *grown* from 52 percent to 67 percent of the population.

"Moderate Approval"—This group had *declined* from 28 percent of the public to 25 percent.

"High Approval"—This group had been halved, from 16 percent to eight percent.

The final group, "Unclassifiable," which had included four percent of the American public in 1959, had totally *disappeared*. By 1973, *everybody* had an opinion of American business, and the approval trend was definitely *down*.

Harry O'Neill was not yet finished, however. Among his other findings were these facts: that the public rated Corporate Executives 13th on a list of 16 career groups evaluated according to Ethical and Moral Practices, and that Large Companies were rated last of all on a list of major American Institutions on the basis of deserving public trust and confidence, ranked behind two institutions with which business must regularly deal and sometimes contend—Labor Unions and Congress.

Perhaps this last finding was the most ominous of all. With its reputation in such decline, how could business re-establish its good name if it had also lost the public's trust and confidence? This is why the single most critical problem facing many a professional communicator today, the communicator who is employed or retained by business, is—in my opinion—this problem of Lost Credibility.

Now, I am well aware of the logical question which is already in your minds: with so much professional advice and assistance for so many years, how did American business suffer such a dramatic decline in reputation *and* in the credibility it now needs in order to regain its former approval by the public—*before* the public's representatives do irreparable harm to business and make irreversible changes in the social environment in which business must function?

I *could* reply by observing that the reputation and credibility of several other American institutions have also declined in recent years. That is a fact, and it is a fact of general interest to all communicators. But I shall stick to my last, enduring all the discomfort appropriate for any communicator who has counseled American business during the period covered by ORC's biennial polls.

Unfortunately, many businessmen—including several who retain outside PR counsel or employ PR staffs—look on public relations as a magic wall that should shield them from public view, or as a cosmetic that improves their company's image, or as a kind of deodorant spray that kills odors without disturbing germs. Or they look on communication as a means of telling *their* side of the story, rather than a way of hearing out their critics, of learning more about the other person's grievance or of getting a deeper understanding of the opposition's point of view. This is *also* communication, perhaps the more important half of the total process.

Without either half of the total, we do not perform communication fully deserving of the name. The fact that we even have to speak of "communication up *and* down" or "inward *and* outward communication" indicates that the word itself has come to mean *downward* communication or *outward* communication alone.

This is why I disagree with those who express their weariness with the term "dialogue." Unless and until communicators convince their clients and employers—and themselves—that communication denotes or, at least, connotes a two-way flow, I'm afraid we'll have to use the term "dialogue" to convey the whole of the idea.

And while I'm dotting both I's and crossing the T in communication, I ought to mention that communication, dialogue or what-have-you, this process of reaching—and being reached by—the human world around us relates not only to the public, but to the public's representatives, to its opinion leaders, to the people's delegates in government and even to those who style themselves "public advocates." Any program of communication with the public in general must include a simultaneous approach to those who do have the public's confidence, to any significant degree—and that can include militants.

Here, I'd like to state my belief that much of today's militancy is targeted at caricatures, that much criticism of business is based on ignorance of economic realities.

American business, of course, is partly to blame for a lot of this ignorance; it has failed to communicate the hard facts of economics by which business itself is constrained. This is no easy task, but it is essential to the survival of American business as it exists today.

Public Must Not Be Ignored

Many a businessman, as long as his business is prospering, fails to respect public attitudes unless and until they lead to legislative or administrative action. But by that time, the popular indignation has been so long frustrated that it is largely out of control. The public's anger is heightened by its suspicion that it has been despised and ignored. Then, when some official action is finally taken, that action can be almost vengeful. At that stage, governmental cures can prove worse than the original ailment. An example of this seems to be at hand now in the Environmental Protection Agency's tardy recognition that auto emission-control devices themselves pollute the air with sulphuric acid dangerous to the public the devices were supposed to protect, a public that demanded or approved the emission regulations because it had been persuaded by Detroit's critics that the auto industry was simply scornful of the people's health.

One basis for the scorn some businessmen feel is, I think, their belief that men and women are motivated chiefly by their selfishness, jealousy and envy. This belief cannot be generally true; we see too many evidences of human generosity and self-sacrifice. What these scornful businessmen forget, if they ever learn it, is the fact that people will fall back on simple self-interest if they have no better basis for a decision and yet must decide. If a controversy gets too complicated, the man in the street despairs of understanding it. If he must give either faction the benefit of his doubt, he can be counted on to give it to the faction that seems to favor *his* interests. This is the demagogue's ancient secret, and it is still very effective today.

Earning Popular Understanding

Now, what about honest businessmen, those who recognize that they operate under an unwritten public franchise, serving the community as stewards of its resources? Shouldn't such men be safe from popular misunderstanding, from misdirected indignation, from misguided militants? Not automatically. Though they deserve that protection, they must *earn* it, they must *work* toward it by communicating their stories to their publics. And public relations finds its highest justification in persuading and assisting them to do so.

It is essential that the honest businessman use words to publicize his good deeds and good intentions, just as cleverly and just as energetically as the dishonest businessman uses words to hide his crimes and criminal purposes.

In nature, one rotten apple can rot a barrelful. This is not literally true in human society, but a few rotten apples can make the whole barrel smell. To understand the impact of business scandals on the public mind, we must recall the power of self-interest as a decisive force in complex controversies. Even a handful of reports about high-level white-collar crime, the so-called "crime in the suites," tends to justify a common man's jealousy and envy toward business, emotions about which he would otherwise feel guilty.

Although communication is essentially an intellectual process, the communicator must always make allowance for emotions. As the Scholastics taught, "Whatever is received is received according to the disposition of the receiver." Whatever is read is read according to the emotional condition of the reader. Whatever is viewed is seen from the viewpoint of the viewer, through eyes focused according to his interests and personal feelings. Not only beauty, but ugliness and evil, are in the eye of the beholder.

This old axiom applies not only to outright crime. A community can be shown how some businessmen have offended the common good while remaining within the letter of the law. The resultant public indignation, anger and disgust then lead to changes in the law, to more restrictive legislation and administrative rulings, to the tightening of "loopholes." And the sweeping gestures of reform and retribution strike at *all* businessmen, honest or not.

Unfortunately, there have been many such offenses against the common welfare, and the critics of American business have energetically publicized them during the same years in which Opinion Research Corporation and other pollsters were busily documenting the decline in the reputation of American business.

Business' record is not entirely clean. That record has been zealously and effectively publicized by militant critics who accuse American businessmen of failing in their responsibilities to the public in a variety of ways. Most of those failures are linked to practices by which business formerly gained its own prosperity and even won a large measure of applause. Now that the side effects, consequences and external costs of those business practices are in the spotlight, the public assigns the blame for them where it formerly assigned the credit—to business.

The net effect of all this has been to drop the American businessman most of the way down to the bad reputation he had during the Thirties, when the Great Depression was blamed on his incompetence and greed. We sometimes forget that he was only rehabilitated by his civilian service during World War II. In the postwar prosperity, he managed to cling to his new height by turning a cornucopia of material goods and services on the delighted public. Today, the public has been presented with the total bill for all that prosperity, and it doesn't enjoy paying up.

Leveling with the Public

Of course, effective communication cannot make that payment an enjoyable experience. But the businessman must at least level with the public about all aspects of his business that affect the public welfare. He must reach toward the public, working as best he can through the appropriate opinion leaders: media people, educators, environmentalists, consumerists, even militant "public advocates" to the extent that they are reachable by frankness and the facts.

He must communicate with the public's appointed and elected representatives, in administrative agencies and in the legislatures, state as well as national; for the powers of state-level government have been vastly increased in recent years, through decentralization and revenue sharing.

Many businessmen are not yet aware of this growing power in state government, of the broadening of activities in the state houses and of the multiplication of state agencies. For example, the few hundred weak and uninfluential state agencies of the 1950s have grown to more than fifteen hundred and now wield great power over business and industry within their 50 jurisdictions.

What is most awkward about reaching the unhappy public, directly or indirectly, is the fact that the businessman—who once made it all look so easy—is now called upon to tell his audience exactly how difficult it was, and is.

This is exemplified in the plight of many executives who head multinational companies. They have long enjoyed a growing reputation as global managers, profitably scattering the blessings of modern technology across the face of the earth. Today, as they struggle amid critical complications in international trade and finance, they are simultaneously criticized as omnipotent masters of planetary commerce whose success and influence threaten the liberties and welfare of the nations in which they operate.

Some idea of what can happen to the multinationals in other countries can be calculated from the experience of large corporations in the United States. Today, as in the Thirties, there are angry calls for legislative and administrative action, for the imposition of new restrictions and for the retrenchment of old concessions. This mood is strong on all levels of government. Here, if I may use that tired word, is the interface between government and business, but here also is a meetingplace for sympathetic officials and the militant enemies of business—for critics not only of American business *practices* but also of the fundamental *theories* under which American business still functions.

Government Shapes the Future

And here, in legislative committee rooms and before administrative agencies, is where the future is being formed, where the new social environment is in the process of creation, an environment that can prosper the businessman or poison him. Here, in the halls of government, the businessman must get involved in the resolution of public issues. Here he must finally communicate—especially when he has neglected earlier opportunities to reach the public. Here, ultimately, he must tell his story, clearly and convincingly.

In order to do that, he cannot wait until the last moment, appearing under subpoena or seeking a hearing at the eleventh hour before some devastating bill is about to be voted out to the floor of the legislature, or some punitive edict is about to be imposed by a regulatory agency. He must keep informed of such threatening developments by constant surveillance of federal, state and even local governments, by foreknowledge of actions they are scheduled to consider. It will often fall to his communication specialists to provide him with such early warnings and to alert him to any growing dissatisfaction among those segments of the public affected by his policies. This inward and upward communication is as important as that which moves outward from the boardroom and the executive suite.

But communication alone will not be enough; the story that business tells must be admirable or at least respectable. It must be a record of honest performance, an accounting of good stewardship over the community's resources. It must be a description of beneficial deeds guided by benevolent policies. And the time for the businessman to prepare his story is not one frantic week before his testimony must be given.

His story must be prepared well in advance, by reappraisal of present policies, by improvement of present performance and, where necessary, by prompt reform. With his house in order, the doors of communication should be opened, and the public should be shown that business has nothing to hide and has good reason to be proud.

It is only on this double foundation of honest performance and honest communication that business can rebuild its credibility and its good name.

Index